HERE'S WHAT PEOPL

FLOUR

MW01027715

"What a fine book! Every foodie, every baker, everyone who values nutrition—why, every admirer of excellent bread, polenta, pasta, or gingerbread—will find it fun, fascinating and eye-opening...whether or not they think they need a home mill. If they do, it's indispensable."
Laurel Robertson, author of Laurel's Kitchen Bread Book *(Random House, NY, rev. 2003)*

"*Flour Power* is wonderful! I wanted information on using wholemeal flours and you certainly gave me just what I was looking for, FACTS, not a skimpy overview...wonderfully witty and entertaining as well."
Ruth A. Kohl, Port Townsend, WA

"Australians looking for good bread—very interesting...thorough research as well as nutritional info. Complete guide to the power of fiber and nutrients as well as how to find time, choose the right mill...complete info on mills...excellent scientific info on wheat, flours and breadmaking chemistry. Very good medical info on low fiber conditions, their causes and prevention. A great read!"
Joy Carr, Townsville, Australia

"Once I started reading, I just couldn't put it down. I read it from cover to cover in one night. I have to tell you that doesn't happen often. If you bake bread by hand, bread machine, mixer, or whatever you have to have this book."
Robert Barnett, Santa Rosa, CA
Amazon.com

"The author did a wonderful job of identifying a large variety of grain mills along with specific issues to consider about each, such as overheating which destroys the nutrients one tries to save by home grinding, grinding ranges–powder to chunks, dry versus oily–dust, weight, and noise...with appendices to find grain mills and grain sources."
An Amazon.com reader from St. Louis, MO

FLOUR POWER

A guide to modern home grain milling

Marleeta F. Basey

Jermar Press

JERMAR
PRESS

Albany, Oregon

ISBN Number 0-9705401-1-6
Library of Congress Card Number: 2004101671

Basey, Marleeta F.
Flour Power, A guide to modern home grain milling

Text design: MagicGraphix, West Fork, AR
Cover Design: Michael Fairchild, NDI Graphics, Albany, OR
Cover Photo: Effie M. Dorsey, Albany, OR

Jermar Press
1790 N. W. Grandview Drive
Albany, OR 97321-9695 USA

Dedication

This book is dedicated to my sister, Sherri, and my brother, Art, who never relented in their moral support and love;

to all the wonderful friends who bolstered me through one failure after another;

and, especially, to my husband, Gerald Peter Hansen, who supported me financially and loved me lavishly while I wrote this book.

Acknowledgments

Many, many people helped in my 20-year search for information about flour mills, wheat, fiber and wholemeal bread. Nearly all the American home flour mill manufacturers, distributors or dealers devoted time to my questionnaire and phone calls. Many offered mills for testing and promotion. The most active were Tom Dickson at K-Tec, manufacturer of the Kitchen Mill, Gabriele Russell at Best Mills, distributor for Fidibus, Christine Downs, at Cris Enterprises, distributor for the Family Grain Mill, Dick Righter of In-Tec, distributor for Diamant, Bill Beesley at Back to Basics and several people at Schnitzer Mills in Germany. I thank them all and hope that this book will stir up the flour mill market enough to keep them *all* in business.

Others who helped or encouraged me along the way include Dr. Warren Kronstad, Crop Scientist (retired), Oregon State University; the reference and circulation staff at the Oregon State University Library; Beehive Country Store in San Jose, California; Marcella of Marcella's Cooking School in Mountain View, California; the Lehman brothers at Lehman's in Kidron, Ohio, whose non-electric catalog has entertained me on many a dreary Oregon day; Mary Alice Chaney at First Alternative in Corvallis, Oregon; Matt Schrowe and Steve McDonnell at Montana's Best in Three Forks, Montana. I remain deeply indebted to the meticulous, detail-oriented proofreader of the first edition, Bodie Dickerson, and to Gerald Hansen for his invaluable technical advice and editorial contributions to this second edition. Finally, special thanks to three people who contributed to this book without reward: Rudy Schur, head of Square One Publishers, who told me how to transfer information from my brain into logical, sequential sentences; to Joanne Abrams, also with Square One Publishers, who showed me by example how to wield a sharp red editing pencil; and to Laurel Robertson, author of *Laurel's Kitchen Breadbook*, for her warm and generous encouragement.

Contents

Preface

There are three kinds of people in this world: those who like details; those who just want to get on with the task at hand; and those who fall somewhere in between. This book is intended for all of you.

First, for people who can swim for hours in technical details, I have filled the pool to the brim. Dive in and enjoy. For those who are truly frantic and just want to get started grinding flour and making bread, there is a *Quick-Pick Option* in Chapter 6 and a list of mills in the Appendix to help jump-start your home milling operation. For those people who have limited patience but can be persuaded to look more closely at an interesting topic, I hope to persuade you to stick through an entire chapter here and there, despite a nagging sense that it's not essential to the immediate task of buying a home flour mill. The information is fascinating. And whether you like the light, American-style breads that are emphasized in this book or hearty, earthy, European-type rye breads, you will learn how to buy the right wheat and the right grinder to make *any* loaf the best it can possibly be.

I wrote this book because I discovered an information gap. Well over a century ago, people in the industrialized world eagerly entrusted their home milling and baking jobs to professionals. As these jobs faded from the home, so did thousands of years of household knowledge about whole-grain flours. The knowledge that did survive in old books or was passed down in families, is not available to most people and, in any case, is of limited value because of changes in lifestyle, home appliances, and the very wheats we use for breadmaking.

And while scientific research flourished during the last century, it has not helped whole-grain bakers much either, because it focused almost exclusively on white flour and its products.

Despite periodic public displeasure with white flour and products made from it, the bulk of working Americans have consistently snorted at the suggestion that they re-adopt any labor-intensive kitchen jobs, no matter how incredible the nutritional and flavor rewards. Then the bread machine arrived from Japan and things began to change.

As the bread machine gained acceptance, people who recognized its possibilities began to discover that home milling devices had not, after all, totally disappeared. With renewed consumer interest, old mills were dusted off and painted new colors, new ones sailed over from Europe, and the Internet exploded into a modern, bustling bazaar for home flour mills and grains. I believe that bread machines and home flour mills make it entirely feasible for flour milling and breadmaking to return to every American home. After all, coffee milling, a common household task that died out about the time flour milling did, experienced a revival so vast that it penetrated even rural percolator strongholds. And home-milled coffee offers no more than improved flavor, whereas modern home milling provides both flavor and health benefits with no more work than that required by a coffee mill.

I could have presented far less information and still helped people buy a good flour mill. But when my research revealed the enormity of the loss in our knowledge base and the amount of misinformation swirling around the subjects of breadmaking, wholemeal, wheat and flour mills, I decided to include as much information about as many areas related to milling as I had time and space for. No doubt I have made my own grievous errors in piecing together facts and figures from different sources and attempting to extrapolate from white flour research. But I believe even an inadequate attempt to herd together the topics in this book is important because we are in the early stages of a technological revolution that may return an important source of nutrition and fiber to our homes. I hope some of you, too, will consider it important to restore this information base to our lives and will, therefore, read more details than you might ordinarily tolerate.

(*The poems and apparent quotes at chapter openings that are not attributed are my work.*)

Introduction

The Search for Delicious, Nutritious Bread

The Pig's Lament

Old Macdonald had a farm,
and a modern guy was he.
He had some pigs...
he loved those pigs...
so germ and bran fed he.
His modern wife in all good faith
served store-bought bread with tea.
And the porkers mourned
the master's death,
for the pigs ate better than he.

For five thousand years, Western man's favorite cereal food has been fresh, fragrant, nutritious, delicious bread. But have you noticed that bread isn't as good as it used to be? Even the stuff you make at home? You may have asked yourself, *"Where can I find that old-fashioned, good-tasting bread?"*

Well, if I blurt out the truth—that the only way to get nutritious, delicious bread is to grind flour at home—you'll be skeptical. After all, you should be able to buy the world's best-tasting, most nutritious bread or flour in any mom 'n pop store in this rich and bountiful country. Unfortunately, you can't. And that's why this book had to be written.

Now, the whole idea of home grain grinding may evoke images of bra-less, batik-skirted, long-haired earth muffins from the sixties. But this book isn't like that. No unrealistic pleas to stop and smell the roses. No admonitions about the soul-withering pace of your life. There are just the facts about a quick, easy, delicious way to get essential vitamins, minerals and fiber back into your diet, without more time in the kitchen.

Most people are surprised at the idea of grinding flour at home. They ask, *"Why bother?"* As you'll see, there are many reasons to mill at home, but let's start with the two most important ones–nutrition and flavor.

HOW NUTRITIOUS IS YOUR BREAD?

In 1999, the Food and Drug Administration (FDA) began to allow marketers to claim that their whole-grain products could reduce the risk of heart disease and cancer—as long as the product contained at least 51 percent whole grain. This slackening of the reins on the use of health claims in advertising resulted from a century's worth of scientific evidence linking diets high in whole grains, fruits and vegetables—but fairly low in fats—with lowered incidences of modern diseases like colorectal, breast and other cancers, diabetes, cardiovascular disease, diverticular disease, osteoporosis, arthritis and obesity. Americans have alarming rates of these and other diet-related health problems, so they are repeatedly urged by nutritionists, researchers, and doctors to cut down on saturated fats and eat more whole grains.

The recent revival of high protein and/or low-carbohydrate diets like Atkins, the Zone and others created a sense of dietary urgency within the medical community. Alarmed by the popularity of these diets, the Institute of Medicine included for the first time in its 2002 dietary guidelines a Recommended Daily Allowance (RDA) for carbohydrates: 130 grams per day, or 520 calories. By contrast, some low-carbohydrate diets recommend as few as 20 to 60 grams a day. (See the chapter entitled *Good Carbs, Bad Carbs* for more on this subject.)

All grains contain a rich supply of protein, fiber, vitamins, minerals, enzymes, and oils. Whole-grain wheat is similar to oats, rye, corn, brown rice, barley, millet and other grains, but is special in one respect—it alone has enough gluten to make light, flavorful loaves of leavened bread. Since bread is one of our favorite foods, we gladly eat lots of it. But if this is true, why are we constantly badgered by nutrition experts to eat more whole grains? The answer to this question lies in the fact that most prepared foods in the "grains" category on the United States Department of Agriculture's (USDA's) Food Pyramid are made from white flour, which does not contain the whole grain. In fact, only about one of our daily grain servings comes from whole-grain products. The others come from items like white bread, corn and tortilla chips, and other overprocessed products that use ingredients extracted from the whole grain.

To make white flour, as well as corn and rye flours, commercial millers start by breaking kernels into the following three parts:

- the *bran*, which contains most of the grain's fiber and minerals;

- the *germ*, which contains most of the vitamins and unsaturated fats;

- the *endosperm*, which contains most of the grain's protein.

Only one part of the grain, the endosperm, is ground up to make white flour. The nutritious bran and germ are discarded—and usually fed to animals—along with most of the fiber and minerals. Any vitamins not purposely discarded are frequently casualties of the long, destructive flour-milling process.

Of course, some of the nutritious elements that disappear in processing are added back through the government's mandatory enrichment program. But not all. The most significant loss is the insoluble fiber in the bran. This fiber is important because it has been found to help prevent and treat a throng of modern disorders, ranging from constipation to cardiovascular disease. The best way to restore this valuable fiber to the diet is to begin eating the whole grain again. And the quickest, most practical and delicious way to eat more whole grains is to grind them into flour and make bread at home.

But is it really necessary to mill flour at home? Couldn't you buy commercial whole wheat bread instead of white? Couldn't you order your deli sandwich on whole wheat, or—at most—make whole wheat bread at home using store-bought whole wheat flour? There's at least one problem with all of these plans: most commercial whole wheat flour has faced just as much processing as white flour. Even worse, many commercial whole wheat products are made primarily from white flour, with just enough bran peppered in to give them a healthful-looking brown tinge. (This is why the government limited the whole-grain health claim to those products that get at least 51 percent of the flour from wholemeal.)

Okay, but you can buy whole wheat flour from the health food store, right? Sure, it's there. But how old is it? The nutrients in flour begin to degrade the moment the protective shell is broken and the inner components are exposed to air. Heat and moisture can accelerate the chemical reactions that produce nutrient degradation. How many nutrients were destroyed by excessive heat during milling, or while sitting in the back of a hot van or next to a heater in the back room at the store? More important, was the wheat used to make the flour the best available for bread, or was it an inferior grain, with only enough gluten to produce harsh-tasting little bricks rather than tasty light loaves?

So, if you can't trust commercial whole wheat—and you'll be certain of that after you've read the first chapter of this book—there are really only two ways to get more whole grains in your diet. You can learn to prepare (and like) other whole grains, or find a quick, easy alternative to commercial wheat flour.

For most people, this is not a difficult decision. It's hard to launch an exotic new diet. It's easy to buy a home flour mill and a bag of wheat, and a bread machine if time is a factor. That's all it takes to eat more whole grains naturally. But will your bread be delicious? Read on!

 ## IS YOUR BREAD DELICIOUS?

Home-ground wholemeal makes incredibly delicious bread. You may be suspicious of this claim. In fact, lots of people *think* they don't like 100-percent whole wheat bread. They think it's heavy and earthy tasting. But if I grind up three and a half cups of fresh flour from my good grain and make a loaf out of it, everybody who tries it loves it. *Everybody.*

So why isn't whole wheat the hottest selling bread out there? Because store-bought whole wheat bread just doesn't taste good. Even bread made at home from most commercial whole wheat doesn't taste good. This is because the same overprocessing that destroys nutrients also destroys flavor. That's why the only way to make great bread is to start with great flour. And the only way to get great flour is to grind your own. In no time you'll be making fluffy, light, delicious loaves of wholemeal bread that will win the hearts of your friends and loved ones!

WHY IT DOESN'T STOP THERE

Many people are thrilled just to get nutrition and flavor back in their bread. They leave it at that. But others grip their grinders and dash into a bright new world of culinary possibilities. First, they start mixing wheats. Spring and winter wheats have individual personalities. A little durum or hard white wheat, or even fresh cornmeal, can add interesting flavor and texture to breads. Or for that hearty European flavor, freshly ground rye and wheat flours provide a slice of dark-bread heaven. Then, a delightful discovery for grain-grinding zealots is the incomparable flavor that soft white wheat gives to cookies, cakes, muffins and quick breads. Eventually, they move on to pizza dough, wholemeal noodles, buckwheat pancakes and polenta, then to bean or rice flours, and, finally, they even grind oily items like soybeans and nuts.

The right home grinder can turn a kitchen into a supermarket of exotic grains and flours—products that can be used not just for yeast breads, but many other delightful dishes, as well. Remember that gluten content pushed wheat to the top of the pop grain charts for *some* parts of the world, but rice, corn, rye, buckwheat, oats and millet have certainly had their centuries of fame, and are more popular than wheat in other cultures today. Many wonderful ethnic recipes that may be prepared only once or twice a year call for exotic flours. Small quantities of various grains can be stored for grinding when needed, so that the flour is always fresh and fragrant—as it should be. And there is *nothing* like fresh, fragrant, home-ground cornmeal!

But beyond nutrition, flavor and culinary exploration, some people like the idea of having a grain mill for food self-sufficiency. A store of grain—which keeps almost indefinitely under proper storage conditions—and a mill that converts from electrical to hand operation can provide a nearly endless food supply in the event of a natural disaster. The addition of powdered milk to dough turns bread into an excellent protein source.

Now you know how nutritious, delicious, and fun home flour grinding can be. All that remains for you to learn is how easy it is.

How Easy It Is

Nobody seems surprised to learn that white bread is so bereft of nutrients that laboratory rats died when placed on a diet of white bread and water. Yet people are astonished to learn that the whole operation of grinding flour and baking bread at home can be an easy daily task. True statement. Grinding grain is no more complicated than grinding coffee beans for breakfast. And bread machines have reduced the time we have to spend actually working at the breadmaking process from hours to minutes.

So now anyone—from a frantic working parent to a retiree who refuses to spend another minute in the kitchen—has time to make great bread. But how much time are we really talking about here? It depends. You don't need a bread machine, but it's the breadmaking—not grinding—that takes time, so many people do choose to buy one of these handy appliances. (At the very least, it does a superb job of kneading bread.) Then you need a grinder. Once you're set up with these two machines and some good, high-protein wheat, it will take about 10 minutes at night to grind the flour, throw ingredients into the bread machine, and clean up. If you're a coffee drinker, you can get that machine ready, too. Set both timers. Then, in the morning, the mingling aromas of fresh-baked bread and fresh-brewed coffee will lure you out of bed. When you get around to it, you can dump the bread out of the machine and fill the bread pan with soaking water. If you're retired, you can plop into a comfortable chair with your paper and toast. The rest of you can rip off a hunk of fresh-baked bread, grab your mug, and sprint for the car.

If It's So Easy, Why a Whole Book?

This is a good question, and it deserves a good answer. To begin with, although it's not our fault, most modern people are seriously ignorant in the areas of wheat, flour and breadmaking. Once we turned flour milling and breadmaking over to professionals, we no longer needed to know which wheat made the best bread or cake or bagels—or why. We didn't need to know how bran interfered with gluten and what adjustments were needed to compensate. We didn't need to know which flour mill would do the best and most healthful job of turning grain into flour.

Similarly, although modern machinery has made home grinding and breadmaking easy operations, most people don't know how to buy the right machines for the job. Most bread machines can produce great bread using home-ground wholemeal, but it's important to know why you might want to pay extra for options like a timer or a stronger motor. As to grain mills, the basic technical requirements are fairly simple: something that produces flour without overheating or overgrinding it. But the choice is complicated by the existence of dozens of grain mills offering many different styles and a surprising range of features. Which machine is best? Well, the real question is which machine is best for *you* and your lifestyle. If you buy the wrong one, you may be making a costly mistake.

The first problem you may encounter in picking the right machine out of this collection is finding the collection in the first place. Your local health food store may carry a couple of grain mills, but what about the many others that are sold through mail-order catalogs or the Internet? This book helps you find the entire collection.

What else will you find in this book? To begin at the beginning, Chapter 1 traces flour processing from crushing grains between rocks to the "microsurgery" performed by today's super-efficient roller mills, and explains why it is preferable to grind flour at home. Chapters 2 and 3 discuss the nutritional deficiencies of commercial flour and the disastrous impact flour milling losses have had on our national health. Chapter 4 discusses the importance of replacing refined or ""bad" carbohydrates with whole fruits, whole vegetables and whole grains, which are definitely "good" carbohydrates.

Chapter 5 moves beyond nutrition to other reasons why people choose to mill flour at home, such as achieving optimum flavor in bread, experimenting with grains such as corn and rye, adding whole grains to the diet of those with gluten allergies, ensuring food self-sufficiency and many more.

Chapter 6 explains how quick and easy home flour milling and breadmaking can be and how much it might cost. It also provides a "Quick Pick" option for truly harried bread lovers.

Chapter 7 gets into the technical aspects of flour mills, from basic milling mechanisms to the advantages and disadvantages of virtually every feature that will be encountered in the selection process. There is also an in-depth questionnaire that makes it easy to evaluate any flour mill.

Chapter 8 is a primer on wheat, with special emphasis on its breadmaking characteristics. You'll learn why not all wheat varieties make good bread and how to select the right wheat for a specific type of bread or any other baking project. Chapter 9 introduces other grains that can add variety and interest to the diet of a home miller. Chapter 10 gives tips on locating, ordering and storing grains. Chapter 11 discusses breadmaking and presents "secret ingredients" that make wholemeal bread light, airy and delicious, every time. Chapter 12 provides simple recipes for bread and related dishes and Chapter 13 tells you how to use wholemeal to make delicious desserts.

In addition, the Appendices contain a brief run-down on dozens of different mills and oat rollers/flakers, including addresses, telephone numbers and web sites where you can get more information. You will also find a list of those all-important sources for buying the best bread wheats, a list of sources for other grains and a list of books about wholemeal breadmaking.

There is no greater health and flavor bonanza than bread made from freshly ground grains. When modern flour mills and bread machines turned breadmaking into a minor kitchen task, even the busiest person gained the power to restore old-fashioned flavor and health to their diet. It is my hope that this book will encourage you to enjoy the power of flour every day for the rest of your life.

CHAPTER 1

Modern Flour Processing

If we processed meat
the way we process white flour,
we'd go to the meat counter
and pick out a big packet of fat.
The meat would be ground up
and fed to farm animals.
—G.P. Hansen, 1996

About 25,000 years ago, after the glaciers had done some permanent damage to the countryside, some of man's tasty game species started dying out. He needed a dependable food source to supplement the occasional gazelle rump. So he began munching on the seeds of wild grasses that grew about him. Later, the people around some river valley in the Fertile Crescent area of the Middle East got the bright idea of turning these grasses into a cultivated grain crop. But, as often happens, that solved only half their problem.

The other half of the food problem involved bran. As long as the protective layers of bran remained tightly wrapped around the grain, man's digestive juices couldn't get at the nutrients inside. As soon as man realized that extensive chewing of grains would be a disaster for his teeth, he set the inventors to work on alternatives. Over time, many different processes were found to remove, break up or soften the bran: man crushed the grain between rocks, soaked it, boiled it and brewed it to get at the nutrients. But by far his favorite process was to grind (and later, to mill) grain into flour and bake it into bread.

This chapter takes a look at the history of grain processing, from the earliest days in which small rocks were used to crush our grains, through the development of various flour mills, to our modern flour processing system, which puts grains through a mind-boggling series of operations from conditioning to milling to bleaching. The result of this advanced technology is an astounding range of flour products. So, for reference, you'll also learn about the commercial flours now available for baking and other uses. Most important, you'll come to understand how commercial processing has compromised the nutritional value of the grain products we use to make breads and other foods.

THE BASIC ELEMENTS OF FLOUR GRINDING

Although the processing of grains has changed greatly over the many centuries during which man has sought to turn them into a palatable foodstuff, certain elements have remained a necessary part of grain processing. One of these elements is, of course, grinding. Another is sifting. Before you learn about these processes, though, we need to clarify two terms—grinding and milling. For simplicity, this book uses the two terms interchangeably. But it is nevertheless important to understand that the terms are technically different. *Grinding* involves the crushing or pulverizing of a substance by any means that creates friction, but especially by rubbing the substance between two hard surfaces, like rocks. *Milling*, however, involves the crushing or pulverizing of a substance by the means of a mechanical device called a *mill*. With that said, let's look at the basics of flour grinding.

Grinding With Stones

Flour is created by feeding grains between two stones or some other mechanism that breaks, crushes or beats them into a meal or powder. Very early man looked around for a rock with a little dip in it, placed the grain in the dip, and crushed it with a smaller rock. As grain became more important, women pounded it in pot-sized mortars with stone pestles, while the men hunted. Women stayed with the job as the shape of grinding stones advanced but remained small. Eventually, though, the stones in large homes and temples got so big that men and animals had to take over the task.

When the wheel was invented, slaves and animals were harnessed to levers that pushed massive round stones in endless circles. These huge stone wheels produced more flour than the household or temple could use, so the family began to sell flour, and commercial milling was born. Commercial flour was wildly successful with any housewife who could afford it, because it saved hours of time and prevented her fingers from being literally ground to the bone.

At some point, the costs of buying, feeding, housing and whipping slaves and donkeys probably got too high for commercial millers. They overcame a natural resistance to newfangled contraptions and began to build water mills. Although this switch from manpower to water power required a huge outlay of cash and an inconvenient move to a waterway, it paid off in greatly increased production. And it started a long, slow transfer of the grain milling harness from men and animals to gravity, water, wind, steam and, eventually, electricity.

Sifting

Although many different grains, dried beans and seeds can be ground into a meal, the grain most favored in the Western world has been wheat. This is because we love bread and noodles and wheat is the only grain with enough gluten to make fluffy loaves of yeasted bread and many kinds of noodles.

Bread can be made from a meal containing all of the original wheat kernel. Or the bran and germ can be sifted out, leaving primarily the floury, white endosperm. To better understand this, we need to know more about a single kernel of grain.

An actual wheat kernel—also called a grain or a berry—consists of three basic parts: the endosperm, the germ, and the bran. The outer portion of the wheat kernel, called the *bran*, represents 13 to 15 percent of the kernel. Composed of several layers, the bran contains nearly all of the grain's minerals and insoluble fiber. The *germ*, the smallest part of the kernel, represents only two to three percent of the grain. Actually the embryo from which a new plant sprouts to life, the germ contains most of the grain's vitamins and unsaturated oils. The *endosperm*, which is the starchy inner portion of the kernel in a protein matrix, makes up the rest of the grain—up to 85 percent of the wheat kernel. It contains nearly all the grain's protein.

There has been a historical preference for flour with at least some of the bran sifted out. *Sifting* is a general term that has come to include several different processes used to separate grain particles. In its simplest form, sifting involves catching or pouring ground meal onto a basket, screen or tightened piece of fabric and agitating until all particles smaller than the mesh have passed through it. In commercial flour milling, this process came to be called *bolting* because of the bolts

SIFTING THROUGH HISTORY

Sifting goes about as far back as leavened bread itself. Egyptian tomb paintings show grain being broken up in mortars, sifted in baskets, ground again on saddle stones for a finer meal and then sifted again for flour. Pliny described the finest Roman flour, similago, as ". . .white, destitute of all flavor, and not oppressive to the stomach." In 1066 A.D., English flour was being sifted into fine flour (*smedma*) and coarse (*gryth*). Bakers in the Middle Ages used crude hand sieves (made from perforated skins, or woven pork or boar silk or horse hair) to sift meal.

From the beginning, many if not most people preferred the white flour that sifting produced. The whiter the flour, the more it cost, because more of the grain was lost in sifting and either fed to animals or reground for lower quality breads. The expense and scarcity of pure white flour made it a status symbol throughout most of history.

The closer the grain was to its origins as a wild grass, the more bran it contained and the lower the protein content. So even after sifting out some bran for animal food or medicinal purposes, ordinary Roman bread was so heavy it sank in water. Although there are many differences between "old" wheats and those we eat today, the most significant one for breadmaking purposes is protein content. Thanks to ancient and modern seed geneticists who developed wheats with higher protein content, modern bread wheats make an infinitely lighter and whiter bread than did earlier forms of this grain. This is one reason that modern wholemeal can make light, tasty breads even though the bran and germ have not been sifted out.

of cloth that were used to sift the meal. Strong consumer demand for white flour initially drove the milling industry to find better and better ways to separate the grain parts.

Commercial millers use the term *extraction rate* to measure their success at separating the endosperm of the grain—the portion used to make white flour—from the byproducts. Although the modern miller's dream would be to razor off *all* of the endosperm to grind up as pristine white flour, he can't do it, primarily because of the "crease" area of the grain kernel, where the germ, bran and endosperm are tightly rolled together. No matter how sophisticated the miller's machinery is, either bits of bran stick to the endosperm and "degrade" the whiteness of the flour or bits of endosperm stick to the bran or germ and are discarded. In what may be confusing at first to home millers, wholemeal has a 100 percent extraction rate, meaning that all of the grain remains in the extracted portion. The maximum practical extraction rate for white flour is about 75 percent without color from the byproducts tainting the whiteness.

Since stones tended to crush the grain into a relatively inseparable mass, the extraction rate for stone-ground white flour tended to be much higher than the 75 percent maximum that is generally achieved in white flour milling today. So years ago, even when people bought wheat flour from which the bran had been sifted, they ate more bran than people on a white-flour diet do now. During wartime shortages of wheat, millers stretched the supply of grain by increasing the extraction rate to 80 percent, which left more bran and germ in the diets of those eating the white flour.

Low Grinding vs. High Grinding

Until the 1890s, American flour was milled using huge round stones called *millstones*, most on waterways, and a process called *low grinding*. The goal of low grinding was to get the greatest percentage of flour from a single grind. It was a quantity rather than quality approach that had been used throughout most of history. The miller ground the grain only once, then sifted to separate one grade of fine flour from the byproducts. By modern standards this was an imprecise grind-and-sift operation, because all the byproducts could never be separated out. The flour was darker than today's flour and accepted more moisture, so it didn't keep as well, especially if the weather was moist or hot. Worse, the wheat itself was often still quite dirty, which affected taste and color. Finally, once-bolted leftovers were often reground with the next batch, further degrading the white flour with bits of dark bran.

Meanwhile, beginning in the 1850s, a process called *high grinding* began to gain popularity in Europe. The goal of high grinding was to produce several grades of flour. First, grain was ground into larger pieces called *middlings*, which were passed through various-sized screens, sieves or cloths to separate them by size. The largest particles then went back for a second finer grind. The bran and germ were then sifted out of this second meal, leaving a very high-quality—and very expensive!—white flour. Regrinding the various smaller sizes of middlings produced increasingly lower grades of flour, which were sold at lower prices. Although high grinding produced better quality flour than the American low-grinding system, Americans were slow to adopt the system because they could not spare the labor needed to move the grain parts through all the repetitive sifting and grinding processes.

 ## ADVANCED FLOUR GRINDING

By the mid-1850s when settlement of the Wild, Wild West got into full swing, there was a well-established eastern millstone-based flour industry. But as the influx of hungry immigrant workers, farmers, settlers, and adventurers began pushing westward, this industry faced a growing need to produce more flour without more labor. They also needed a way to mechanically eliminate the troublesome germ and the bran, which consumers didn't like. The germ not only appealed to weevils and other vermin, but its oils went rancid under the adverse conditions settlers encountered on long, hot cross-country trips.

Although the European system of high grinding could meet their needs, Americans basically ignored the system until the 1880s, when they made a relatively sudden and profound change. In a mere ten years they adopted, adapted and perfected machinery that separated grain parts to a degree never before achieved in the history of flour milling. Four elements that merged to make this phenomenon possible were the American automated factory, the European roller mill, a machine called the purifier and a change in the wheat growing patterns of the American farmer.

The Automated Factory

An omnipresent image in flour-grinding history was a labor force that was underpaid or even unpaid, and poorly if not brutally treated. Young girls in temples grinding on saddle stones until their knees and fingers were raw and the whip-scarred backs of Roman slaves or animals pushing huge mills in nonstop circles are just two examples. That's why it is a shame that every school child has heard of Eli Whitney and the cotton gin and Henry Ford and the Model A, but virtually no one has heard of Oliver Evans and the first automated flour mill.

This key figure in American milling history was born in Newport, Delaware, in 1755. At the age of 16, he was apprenticed to a wheelwright, and in the following years turned a critical eye on the stone gristmills of the day. Grain mills, he found, were dirty, noisy, sweaty places that wasted both product and labor and failed to produce a consistently high-quality flour. These were important issues in a country with a labor shortage and an exploding demand for high-quality flour.

Evans identified seven tasks—normally done by seven different men to avoid work stoppages—that could be accomplished by machines. He then combined existing technologies into the first American "factory," where machines, instead of men, performed these seven tasks. It took several decades for these factories to mature, and even the highly advanced descendants of Oliver Evans's mechanized mills were a clanking, clattering maze of elevators, conveyors, and spouts that had flour dust explosions on a regular basis. These millstone-based factories were capable of producing huge quantities of a single grade of flour because they removed bottlenecks and because they ground and sifted only once.

But as important an innovation as Evans's automated factory was, it could not by itself change flour milling into the mega-industry it was destined to become in America. During the first half of the nineteenth century, as Evans's automated factories limped toward acceptance in America, two key technological innovations, the roller mill and the purifier, were beginning to take hold in Europe.

The Miraculous Roller Mill

The Hungarians had been instrumental in popularizing the process of high grinding, which produced several grades of flour. But in the 1850s they advanced milling to a new level by replacing traditional millstones with cylindrical porcelain rollers. The significance of this change was that rollers could "break" the grains into discrete pieces that could be separated from each other, whereas stones tended to crush grain pieces into an inseparable mass. But the labor-starved Americans didn't adopt the superior roller mill system until another super machine, the purifier, solved the labor problem by separating grain parts mechanically.

The Miraculous Purifier

In the late 1890s, American milling was changed forever by the purifier, which started a revolution in the process of sifting. Primitive attempts to develop a purifier can be traced back to France in 1807 but many improvements were necessary before an acceptable version satisfied the labor-hungry Americans. The purifier used air streams to blow lighter bran fragments off the middlings, which were then dropped down through a stack of vibrating cloth screens in order to separate the grain particles by size. After decades of delay, it took little more than a decade for virtually the entire American flour industry to abandon stone gristmills and incorporate the roller mill, purifier and repetitive grinding system into American factories. And a whole category of related machines—bolters, sifters, sieves, classifiers, and more—turned sifting into a complex, repetitive, microscopic separation of grains parts that transcended anything that preceded it.

A Shift in Grain-Growing Patterns

A final force that pushed American millers to change from stone mills to the modern roller system was a shift in grain-growing patterns by American farmers. Until 1860, farmers had grown primarily soft wheats. Consumers preferred soft wheats over hard wheats, and stone mills did a better job of grinding them. But demand for wheat was beginning to exceed production, so farmers gradually switched to hard wheats because of their significantly greater yield per acre. By 1878, 80 percent of Kansas's farmers had switched from soft to hard winter wheat. The demand for flour was also exceeding production. The fact that roller mills were more efficient than stone mills at refining the hard wheats that farmers were now growing made the adoption of the roller mill virtually inevitable. Once the purifier could efficiently and mechanically clean, size, and separate broken grain fragments, it and the roller mill were quickly incorporated into a descendent of Oliver Evans's automated factory and the most efficient milling system in the history of the world was born.

 ## MODERN FLOUR PROCESSING

When the roller mill, purifier, hard wheats and the mechanized factory all came together at the end of the nineteenth century, American millers found themselves at the beginning, not the end, of a battle to increase production. They were sandwiched between improved grain yields that resulted from agricultural mechanization and constant growth in demand for flour. During the next half century, a myriad of innovations—of which you will see a mere glimpse in this chapter—led to an ultraefficient system of cleaning, conditioning and milling grain. The different processes involved in modern flour milling are so numerous and so complex that an entire book could be devoted to describing them. The following descriptions do, however, give a hint of the extensive processing that produces the flour you now have on your kitchen shelf.

Cleaning the Grain

Before grain is milled, sifted, or otherwise processed, it is cleaned, usually at the granary. Yet even this step is anything but simple.

Typically, the grain starts by passing through a vibrating screen that removes straw and other coarse materials. It then goes through a second screen that removes smaller items like seeds. Air is used to blow off lighter particles like chaff, rodent hair and dust as the grain moves in a stream across screens. The grain then hits discs that are revolving on a horizontal axis. The discs have indentations that catch the grains while larger or smaller materials are rejected. The discs then discharge the wheat into a hopper or into the continuing stream. Next, beaters attached to a central shaft throw the wheat violently against a surrounding drum, which buffs each kernel and breaks off the beard (grassy hairs at the tip of some wheats, which trap dirt). Air currents lift off the dust and particles of bran. The wheat then passes over a magnetic separator that pulls out iron and steel articles like nuts, bolts, rivets or other metal fragments broken off of machinery or elevators.

Then the wheat enters a washer-stoner, where high-speed rotors spin the wheat in a water bath. Centrifugal force is used to throw off the water and the stones drop to the bottom and are removed, while lighter materials float off with the water, leaving only the cleaned wheat. Some mills use a dry stoner as well. Finally, the wheat passes over an inclined, vibrating table that has a kicking action to push stones and other heavy material up and away from the lighter wheat that is now ready for milling.

The Break System

In modern flour processing plants whole grains are fed between two corrugated steel "break" rollers. The flutes along the rollers "shear" open each grain, frequently along the crease, and roll out layers of bran with a thick covering of endosperm. This is called the "break stock." Essentially, the break stock fragments are various-sized chunks of endosperm with bran and germ attached to them. These broken particles are fed into a box-like sifter and shaken into a series of bolting cloths or screens for *sizing*, or separating by size. There may be as many as 27 horizontal frames in each sifter, with increasingly finer meshes from top to bottom. The larger particles are shaken off from the top—or *scalped*—and the finer endosperm fragments sift toward the bottom. The scalped fractions and various-sized particles of endosperm are then carried to their own separate purifiers.

In a purifier, a stream of air lifts flecks of bran from the endosperm and bolting cloth separates the remaining particles by size and quality. The fragments of break stock that still have bran and germ in them have now been separated by size, cleaned of loose bran and endosperm and are ready to return to a second set of break rollers that have been set slightly closer together. The break stock produced by this run through the rollers then goes through a new sifter and new purifiers and the large fragments are sent back to yet another set of break rollers. This process of successively breaking and separating grain parts is usually repeated four to five times. At each stage along the way the almost-pure endosperm fractions are separated out and sent to the "reduction" section for grinding.

Reduction

The reduction system of the mill actually *reduces* the endosperm into flour, using anywhere from 8 to 16 different grinding stages.

The reduction process is similar to that of the break system, but this time the rollers have a flat, textured surface so the grain fractions are crushed, rather than broken. Once crushed, the fragments are divided by size and purified by air currents and gravity to separate bran from endosperm particles, which are then sent back for regrinding. As with the break system, the entire process of crushing, sizing and separating is repeated until as much bran and germ have been eliminated as possible and the pure endosperm has been milled into a silky white flour.

Conditioning

Wheat conditioning is a process that uses heat to adjust the moisture content of either whole grains or flour. Conditioning is very important in commercial milling because it improves the milling quality of grain and, sometimes, the baking quality of the flour. Whole grains may be conditioned to adjust the distribution of moisture within the kernels. Flour may be dried or dampened as necessary to attain an ideal or consistent amount of moisture. Conditioning is one of the reasons that commercially milled flour produces consistent bread under a wide range of baking conditions.

Flour conditioning can be accomplished by *warm conditioning*—heating the flour up to 115 degrees—and then cooling it; or by *hot conditioning*—heating the flour above 140 degrees. Hot conditioning is faster, and thus more economical, than warm conditioning. But severe heating of wheat makes gluten harsher, tougher, and less elastic, so high-protein bread wheats are generally not conditioned above 110 degrees, to avoid degrading baking quality. But because hot conditioning is faster and cheaper, we cannot be certain that non-bread wheat flours have been conditioned at equally low temperatures.

"Aging" and "Improving"

It is generally accepted that the breadmaking quality of flour improves when the flour is "aged" for a month or two after grinding. But storing tons of flour would be prohibitively expensive for commercial millers, so chemical "improvers" are added to flour and dough to improve elasticity. These improvers range from potassium bromate to ascorbic acid.

Bleaching

The endosperm of wheat contains a yellow pigment that disappears naturally when flour is exposed to air. For cosmetic reasons, millers speed up this whitening process with bleaching agents. Chemicals used to bleach the flour include chlorine dioxide, nitrogen peroxide, chlorine, benzoyl peroxide, and acetone peroxide.

Enriching

Indications of widespread nutritional deficiencies in the American population became prominent in the 1920s and 1930s. While the government lumbered along, as bureaucracies do, considering what to do about the problem, the milling and baking industries began to enrich bread products on their own. Finally in May of 1941, as a wartime health measure, the government mandated addition of the following nutrients to flour: thiamin, riboflavin, niacin, iron and, optionally, calcium. (The enrichment program also mandated fortification of other foods, such as the addition of vitamin A to butter and vitamin D to milk.) Since that time, few changes have been made to the enrichment list for cereal grains, beyond certain quantity boosts and a single addition to the list in 1998: folacin (folic acid).

 ## MODERN MIRACLE OR DISASTER?

We owe a debt to the farmer, the miller, the baker, and all the brilliant men who invented better and better machines to feed more and more of us. They gave us what all successful social groups must have to progress: more food than we can eat. And that is the miracle of modern white flour. But we can appreciate the energy and intelligence that delivered us from the threat of starvation without being blind to some consequences that ultimately accompanied that miracle.

As you've learned, modern milling produces flour in the same basic way as two rocks with some grain between them. The difference is that rocks crushed the grains and the modern roller mill performs microsurgery on them. It practically peels back the bran, scrapes out the germ and leaves pure endosperm particles to be ground into flour.

Modern flour milling also sifts the endosperm from the byproducts in the same basic way as an Egyptian with a basket. The difference is that modern machinery is vastly more successful at separating the grain parts. Today's multi-storied flour mills use gravity, conveyor belts and air streams to transport grain parts through hundreds of screens that agitate or circulate or tip or dump in every conceivable direction. It's a dizzying mechanical repetition of sifting, cleaning and separating grain specks by size, shape and weight, all to gradually extract every particle of white endosperm so that it can be milled into a pristine white flour that is cheap and plentiful by historical standards.

But the continuing push for higher production, better extraction rates and better baking predictability has led modern commercial millers far beyond just grinding and sifting. They have added processes that made extraction faster or easier or more thorough. They have added processes that improved the appearance of the flour or kept machinery heat from destroying the product. And, in the process, they have turned the miracle of flour into a nutritional disaster. How? Here are some specific ways in which the modern commercial milling process may harm the very product it produces.

Losing the Bran and the Germ

Without a doubt, the most serious damage done by modern white flour milling is the efficient removal of the nutritious bran and germ. A nutrient comparison of whole-grain spring wheat, *un*enriched white flour and enriched flour (See Table 1.1.) reveals extensive milling losses of fiber, minerals, vitamins and unsaturated fats. But even this does not tell the whole story. Roller-milled flours have also lost many enzymes and other poorly measured or as yet unknown nutritional components that undoubtedly play chemically complex roles in body metabolism.

Turning Up the Heat

As you've already learned, about 115 degrees of heat is the high limit in conditioning bread flour to improve its baking quality. In addition, we know that any milling process that involves friction generates heat. In fact, a small electric grinder with metal or stone burrs can push flour temperatures up to 110 degrees and above if too much grain is ground in one stretch. It is easy to imagine the heat buildup that occurs as millions of wheat kernels run through banks of metal rollers that operate for hours on end.

Unfortunately, heat is, was and always will be a potential enemy of nutrients. Any process involving excessive heat may destroy thiamin (vitamin B1) and vitamin E. Excessive heat may push lipids (fats) toward rancidity. Plus heat can inactivate or destroy the hundreds or thousands of enzymes in wheat, many of which play chemically complex roles in our bodies.

At what temperature does heat begin to damage nutrients? Vitamins begin to degrade at temperatures above 115 degrees. Some enzymes may become inactive or unstable above 122 degrees. And baking quality begins to degrade at temperatures above 140 degrees because of changes in the water-absorbing capacity of the gluten.

And while we're discussing heat, let's talk about oven heat. Won't those vitamins be destroyed anyway in a 400-degree oven? Although this is rarely discussed in the scientific literature, it has been claimed that the fermentation process in breadmaking involves enzymes that protect vitamins during baking. In the case of the B-vitamin thiamin, only 5 to 35 percent is lost in baking, because starch provides some protection. Recently discovered powerful antioxidants in the orthophenols of wheat survive the baking process.

Bleaching Out Vitamin E

Earlier, you learned that bleaches like chlorine dioxide are used to treat refined flour so that the natural yellow pigment of the endosperm is removed, leaving the flour a pristine white. Although the yellow pigment being removed is said to have no nutritional significance, chemical bleaching agents can make no such claim. They have long been known to destroy virtually all the vitamin E that survives the milling process.

Doesn't It All Get Put Back?

Under the U.S. government's enrichment program, certain vitamins and minerals that are deemed potentially deficient in the American diet are added to flour and related products. In fact, white flour contains more of these added nutrients than were present in the original grain. But does this enrichment actually restore all the nutrients removed or destroyed during milling? Take another look at Table 1.1. When compared with the whole grain, enriched white flour shows significant losses in 15 of the 22 nutrients listed in the table.

TABLE 1.1 NUTRIENT COMPARISON
Hard Red Spring Wheat Berries, Unenriched and Enriched White Flours *(per 100 grams)*

Nutrient	Wheat Berries	Unenriched White	Enriched White
Total Dietary Fiber	12.2 gr	2.7 gr	2.7 gr
Calcium	25 mg	15 mg	15 mg
Iron	3.6 mg	1.17 mg	4.64 mg*
Magnesium	124 mg	22 mg	22 mg
Phosphorus	332 mg	108 mg	108 mg
Potassium	340 mg	107 mg	107 mg
Sodium	2 mg	2 mg	2 mg
Zinc	2.78 mg	0.7 mg	0.7 m
Copper	0.41mg	0.144 mg	0.144 mg
Manganese	4.06 mg	0.682 mg	0.682 mg
Selenium	70.7 mcg	33.9 mcg	33.9 mcg
Thiamin	0.504 mg	0.12 mg	0.785 mg*
Riboflavin	.110 mg	0.04 mg	0.494 mg*
Niacin	5.71 mg	1.25 mg	5.904 mg*
Pantothenic Acid	0.935 mg	0.438 mg	0.438 mg
Vitamin B6	.336 mg	0.044 mg	0.044 mg
Folate, Total	43 mcg	26 mcg	183 mcg*
Vitamin E (alpha)+	1.01 mg	0.06 mg	0.06 mg
Total Fats	1.92 gr	0.98 gr	0.98 gr
Saturated	0.314 gr	0.155 gr	0.155 gr
Monounsat.	0.303 gr	0.087 gr	0.087 gr
Polyunsat.	0.765 gr	0.413 gr	0.413 gr

Source: *USDA Nutrient Database for Standard Reference*, Release 16 (July, 2003)
*Increased under the U. S. government's mandatory enrichment program
+Unbleached white flour (not shown) contains 1.62 mg. of Vitamin E (alpha-tocopherol per 100 grams)

Modern Flour Processing **15**

And no attempt is made to replace the most significant component that is lost in milling—insoluble fiber. In any case, adding synthesized nutrients to food has never been the ideal way to eradicate dietary deficiencies. Here's how the Food and Drug Administration started out when it issued its 1943 policy on the enrichment of cereal products: *"Even though adequate nutrition could be better assured through the choice of natural foods than through reliance on enrichment…"*

I couldn't agree more.

 ## MODERN COMMERCIAL WHEAT PRODUCTS

American farmers grow many different varieties of wheat and each variety has a set of characteristics that makes it ideal for a specific type of product. Some wheats are best for bread, for instance, while others are perfect for cakes, for pasta, or for another use. Commercial mills can and do combine different flours or different grain components to produce "mixed" flours both for commercial food producers and for home use.

Standardization

The characteristics shared by a single variety of wheat—characteristics such as moisture content, protein, or nutrients—can vary widely with soil, weather, fertilization practices, and even the corner of the field in which the grain was grown. This means that the flour made from a single variety of wheat can also vary widely. Variations in moisture or protein content can pose problems for commercial bakeries, which process dough in huge batches with minimal human oversight. Serious losses can result if flour doesn't perform as expected in a recipe for 400 loaves.

In a constant effort to meet the commercial baker's need for consistency, millers began using the new roller-milled flour in innovative ways. For instance, a "stream" of flour from one wheat could be mixed with a "stream" of flour from another wheat. The resultant mixture would have an ideal amount of protein for certain baked goods. Producing flours that always performed in the same way had tremendous advantages for millers, commercial bakers, and consumers alike. This is one reason that consumers so quickly embraced the new white flour

GRAHAM FLOUR

During the 1830s and 1840s, Dr. Sylvester Graham (1794-1851) of Connecticut lectured and wrote about the benefits of eating coarse unbolted wheat meal instead of "superfine flour." His ideas were so popular, so widely publicized in newspapers and so timeless that they experienced numerous revivals as subsequent generations rediscovered the shortcomings of white flour.

The term "graham flour" has for many years been used interchangeably with "whole wheat flour." But the original "Definitions and Standards for Food Products" published by the Department of Agriculture specified Graham flour as "unbolted wheat meal" and further described meal as "the clean sound product made by grinding grain." To reiterate, this means nothing added and nothing taken away. This definition would exclude the reconstituted whole wheat flour produced by modern roller mill factories. Perhaps it is time for yet another revival of Dr. Graham's ideas.

produced by the roller mill in the 1890s.

As scientific research exploded during the first half of the twentieth century, millers benefitted. They became ever more efficient and thorough at separating the grain parts. Inevitably, they came to view a kernel of grain much as a scientist did, as a collection of atomic particles that could be taken apart then recombined into a new product altogether. This led them to combine components from different wheats into new flours that met specific baking needs and performed consistently with every batch. They began to standardize moisture content, protein content, starch, and much, much more.

As the miller created more and more new products from the basic raw material of wheat, the term "flour" ceased to describe a single product. As a result, we, as consumers, are sometimes confused or even misled about what we're eating, and we need a better understanding of the differences between wholemeal milled at home and the various flours that are produced commercially.

Wholemeal

Wholemeal is a floury meal containing all the bran, all the germ, and all the starchy endosperm from the grain. Nothing has been added and nothing taken away. Other names used historically for this product are graham flour, entire wheat, and unbolted wheat meal. All home flour mills create wholemeal. Although it is technically possible for commercial millers to produce wholemeal using the modern roller mill, this is rarely done. Virtually the only true wholemeal sold commercially today is unbolted wholemeal ground by old-fashioned stone mills. All wholemeal contains the perishable germ, and should only be purchased if milling date is known and proper storage conditions have been assured.

Commercial Flours

At the opposite end of the flour spectrum from wholemeal is white flour, which is pure endosperm that has been extracted from the whole grain via the complicated milling process previously described. Many flours exist that look alike but are designed for specific purposes. While some are available only to commercial bakers, others can be bought in any grocery store. It is helpful for the home baker and the home miller to understand the differences among these flours.

All-purpose flour is a medium-gluten flour that offers home bakers one general-purpose option for the creation of many products such as quickbreads, cookies, muffins and some breads. Usually milled from hard red winter or soft winter wheat, protein levels are 9 to 11 percent.

Self-rising flour is all-purpose flour blended with salt and leavening intended for scratch biscuits, pancakes and cookies. Usually milled from hard red winter or soft red winter wheat, protein content ranges from 9.5 to 11.5 percent so that baked products will not be tough or "relax" during baking or cooking.

Bread flour is milled from hard, high-protein wheat that contains enough breadmaking gluten to produce good loaves. Other products include pizza crusts and specialty baked goods. In the past, this flour was available only to commercial bakers but became prominent on grocery store shelves after the bread machine generated a revival in home breadmaking. (Since then, most all-purpose flours contain too little gluten to make good bread.) Protein levels vary from 10.5 to 12 percent and the flour is usually malted.

Cake flour is a finely textured, silky flour with a low gluten content because gluten makes cakes tough. Cake flour blends easily and absorbs moisture readily. It has virtually disappeared from American grocery store shelves and is marketed only to commercial bakers. It is milled from soft winter wheat with protein content typically at 8.5 to 10 percent.

Vital wheat gluten contains a combination of flour components, has up to 45 percent protein and low starch content. Small quantities of gluten flour can be added to lower-protein flours to improve dough structure and baking quality in yeasted bread products. It is a highly processed product, however, and unless it is labeled "vital," the gluten may be too damaged by heat in processing to have any beneficial effect on the bread. It is derived by washing the wheat flour to remove the starch. The gluten that remains is dried and ground into a powder.

Pastry flour contains more gluten than cake flour, as gluten prevents crumbling that may occur due to the large quantity of fats used in pies and pastries. Pastry flour is sold principally to commercial bakers. Milled from soft winter wheat, this flour is very starchy and has a protein content of 8.5 to 10 percent. (Something called "pastry flour" is also sold at health food stores but is generally intended for cakes, which require low gluten content.)

Semolina is a coarse, granular yellow flour milled from the endosperm of extra-hard, high-protein durum wheat. It is processed like white flour, with the bran and germ removed, and is used in couscous and fine pasta products like spaghetti, vermicelli, macaroni and lasagna noodles. Other grains can also be milled to the size of semolina, but the term has become associated with durum wheat. Durum flour, a byproduct of semolina production, is used in some noodles and can be a fine addition to bread for both flavor and performance.

Wheat flour. Any commercial white flour that is ground from wheat can be called "wheat flour" or even "100 percent wheat flour." Products made from it can be similarly labeled. But this labeling is misleading, as it usually appears on products that are all or in large part white flour, with just enough of the bran and germ added back to give it a healthful-looking brown tinge. Wheat flour is usually milled from hard red or hard white wheats and protein levels range from 11.5 to 14 percent, higher than white bread because of the presence of more wheat components.

100 percent whole wheat flour. Despite the label, much commercial whole wheat isn't whole at all, at least in the sense that it contains the whole grain, with nothing added or removed. In fact, this flour has been processed like white flour, with the bran and germ separated from the endosperm. Then bran, germ and white flour are recombined according to some standard formula that may or may not be the same as Mother Nature's. It is milled from hard red or hard white wheat with protein content from 11.5 to 14 percent. This product is perishable due to the fat in the germ, which becomes rancid under adverse conditions.

Not All Grain Becomes Flour

Commercially processed grains are used for much more than just flour, bread, noodles, cookies, and cakes. For instance, grains like wheat and barley are a significant part of the malting, brewing and distilling industries. And wheat bran and germ, the byproducts of flour milling, are certainly not discarded. The ingredients list on a package of dried cat or dog food provides a glimpse at the most common destination for grain byproducts. Not just wheat, but also corn, rice, and other grains are used by the millfeeds industry, which provides food both for pet dogs, cats, hamsters, and pot-bellied pigs, and for farm animals like chickens, pigs, horses, laying hens, and dairy cows.

Smaller quantities of bran and germ are used in products intended for the health-conscious consumer—products such as bran cereals, wheat germ, and "whole-grain" crackers. A constant array of "healthful" products is also being created by a relatively new branch of the food industry called "nutraceuticals," which creates products for consumers who want to eat a more healthful diet. Close scrutiny of labels is advised with these products, as the advertising can be misleading. Many contain huge amounts of white flour and sugars such as dextrose, sucrose, fructose, or corn syrup, with only minuscule amounts of the healthful ingredient they advertise. Other supposedly healthful ingredients, such as fruit juice, sometimes experience such a high degree of processing that they lack the original food's full complement of nutrients.

THE PIGS EAT BETTER THAN WE DO

Americans have more food than almost any group of people in the history of the world. Yet scientific studies have revealed that many of us may be deficient in some basic, and commonly available, vitamins and minerals. This means that we are eating more and benefitting less. We also walk less, sit more and are rapidly replacing real foods like fruits, vegetables, and whole grains with overprocessed, nutrient-poor snack foods. In fact, snack foods now provide an amazing 20 percent of our calories. Although snack foods may appear healthful— and the occasional one may even be healthful—our heavy reliance on them has contributed to high rates of diet-related disorders like cancer, heart disease, high blood pressure and diabetes. If we want improved health, we must reduce our intake of these high-calorie, low-nutrient foods. And we must find quick, easy ways to eat real food instead. We can begin this ambitious program by eating at least as well as our pigs do. And the simplest and most healthful move in that direction is to start eating the grain, the whole grain and nothing but the grain.

CHAPTER 2

Fiber Power

*The value of insoluble fiber
in human diet is undisputed.
Yet we as a nation have failed to provide
a quick, easy, inexpensive supply to our citizens.
This is a national travesty.*

Early in the twentieth century, Dr. Harvey Wiley, the first head of what is now the Food and Drug Administration (FDA) tried to make white flour illegal. His intent was actually to use the newly enacted Pure Food and Drug Law of 1906 to classify refined and bleached flour products as "adulterated" foods, thus preventing their shipment between states. In the end, his efforts were thwarted by powerful supporters of the flour processing industry, but he wasn't the first, nor the last, to rail against the deficiencies of white flour.

In the late 1920s an epidemic of heart attacks surfaced in America and science discovered the existence of several vitamins and other nutrients. It wasn't long before a ruckus broke out between devotees of wholemeal bread and the white flour industry. Like Dr. Wiley nearly a decade before, wholemeal "food faddists" (or "fakirs" as the white flour industry called them) believed that white flour was unhealthful because the bran and germ had been removed. Millers and bakers believed just as fervently that white flour was superior to wholemeal because it had more digestible protein, and that nutritional losses from milling were negligible as long as plenty of vegetables were consumed.

Beware The Food Fakirs!

During the 1920s, when mechanized factories were facilitating a shift in the national diet from natural to processed foods, a public battle erupted over the nutritional inferiority of processed foods. The loudest voices in the melee came from wholemeal advocates—many of them women—who attacked white flour. Their claims, which were based on suspicions not yet—and some never to be—supported by scientific evidence, spurred an industry-wide defense of white flour products that eventually degenerated to name-calling, as can be seen from the following examples:

"When we began the scientific study of food, we opened up a field for the crank, for the faker, the quack, the fanatic and the plain ordinary nut—and these gentry invaded it from all sides...The country is all cluttered up with food faddists, each shouting that his scheme is the only way to digestive salvation."

> *The Journal of the American Bakers' Association,*
> November 1927, quoting Samuel Blythe

"[the food faddists and fakirs] are spouting out theories on how to be healthful and blaming bread for being the cause of most ills with which mankind is afflicted...the malicious statements of the food fakirs which appear in newspapers...the first shot in a campaign by the American Bakers' Association to silence the food faddists and fakirs..."

> *Bakers Review,* October 1927

"If the deductions of many food faddists, accepted as facts, were really operative, it would be difficult to explain how the human race has survived."

> *Time,* August 15, 1927

Although consumer demand for white flour prevailed, since those initial debates a virtual river of scientific research has confirmed and reconfirmed the benefits of eating whole grains. And while more and more benefits are being attributed to vitamins and minerals, strong evidence continues to attribute many health benefits to the wealth of fiber found in whole foods. How important is dietary fiber? Evidence has repeatedly linked a shortage of dietary fiber in industrialized nations to constipation, irritable bowel syndrome, high serum cholesterol levels, colorectal cancer, coronary heart disease, diverticular disease, obesity, diabetes, hemorrhoids and many other health problems.

This chapter begins by telling you exactly what fiber is, then presents some of the benefits provided by this important component of plant foods. Then, after a brief look at some of the common health disorders that have been linked to a shortage of plant fiber, you will learn how much of it is needed in your daily diet to promote optimum health.

 ## WHAT IS FIBER?

Fiber is a collective term used to describe the structural portion of plants that the human body can digest only partially or not at all. Only plant foods, such as cereal grains, fruits, vegetables, nuts, and seeds, contain fiber. (Although animal-based foods contain indigestible components, they are not currently included in discussions of fiber.) As you will see in the next section, there are many different forms of fiber. Each one acts differently in the body and is important to health in its own way, but for nutritional purposes, they can be separated into two general categories—soluble and insoluble fibers.* Many health benefits attributed to one type of fiber may in fact be due to a mixed-fiber diet. Examples are psyllium seed husks, oats and oat bran which contain different fibers but all increase stool weight and improve laxation (stool passing) and lower blood cholesterol levels. Still, it is valuable to look at the differences between these two types of fiber.

---

*The *Dietary Reference Intakes: Proposed Definition of Dietary Fiber* (National Academies Press, 2001) suggests that eventually these two categories will be phased out and replaced by a single term that reflects the health benefits attributable to a mixed-fiber diet.

Insoluble fiber

Insoluble fibers (*cellulose, lignin and some hemicelluloses*) pass through the digestive system basically unchanged (undigested). This type of fiber has long been seen as particularly important to the body because it swells up and expands the weight of the stool, thus eliminating constipation and the many disorders related to it. Some insoluble fibers have additional benefits related to the binding of bile acids which, among other things, keeps them from being stored as fat. Examples of foods high in insoluble fiber are whole grains, mature fruits and vegetables (such as broccoli, green beans, Brussels sprouts, turnips, cauliflower, beets and cabbage), psyllium seeds and nuts.

Soluble fiber

These viscous fibers (*pectins, gums, mucilages, and some hemicelluloses*) are softer than insoluble fiber and can be fermented by microbes in the bowel, which break them into smaller molecules that can be partially digested by our systems. Soluble fiber appears to be particularly valuable in binding bile acids, and is thus important in lowering serum cholesterol. When soluble fibers are present, the rate at which glucose appears in the blood is slowed and insulin secretion is subsequently reduced, effects most noticeable in diabetics. Indications are that fiber may protect against duodenal ulcers and cancer in the gastric cardia region. Examples of foods high in soluble fiber are oats, beans, peas, brown rice, barley, citrus fruits and strawberries.

 ## FORMS OF FIBER

Accepted definitions of fiber are limited to plant fibers. There are several forms of fiber, each with a distinct molecular structure and distinctive beneficial roles in body metabolism. Because different types of fiber are found in different foods, only by eating a wide variety of whole foods can you enjoy all of the benefits that fiber has to offer. Below, you'll learn more about the different types of fiber that should be supplied by diet for optimum health.

Cellulose

Cellulose, which consists of long, thin threads, is the largest component of plant cell walls and the most prevalent form of fiber. Cellulose is insoluble in water—in other words, it doesn't fall apart—and can absorb and hold up to seven times its own weight in water. Food-grade powdered cellulose, primarily from wood, is added to a vast array of commercial foods, from bakery goods to soft drinks to instant puddings. Dietary sources include whole grains, legumes, fruits and vegetables with skins, nuts and seeds. Bran is an excellent source of cellulose.

Gums and Mucilages

These two similar forms of fiber are generally not digestible by humans, but are widely used in food processing as thickeners and stabilizers. Familiar names of gums found in various plants include gum arabic and gum tragacanth (from trees), agar and carrageenan (plant extracts) and guar gum and locust bean gum (from beans). One recognizable mucilage is found in okra, which forms a viscous, sticky gel used to thicken gumbo. Psyllium, from the psyllium plant, is used in commercial laxatives and in some breakfast cereals.

Hemicelluloses

Also called pentosans, hemicelluloses, along with pectin, form the matrix of the plant's cell walls in which cellulose resides. These fibers can be only partially digested. Because of their water-holding capacity and ability to bind bile acids, they have many important functions in body metabolism. The hemicelluloses in some foods appear to have superior binding capacity and thus more beneficial effect on health. These fibers are found in all plant foods, but the primary dietary sources are whole grains, nuts and seeds. Bran is an excellent source of hemicelluloses.

Lignin

Lignin is the least digestible form of fiber but its limited role as "cement" in the cell walls means it is also less plentiful. Because lignin is generally discarded with the tough or woody portions of plants before we consume them, wheat bran is the major source of lignin in the human diet. Indications are that lignin has important antioxidant properties.

Pectins

Pectins are gelatinous, rather than thread-like, in consistency. They are generally water soluble and hold large quantities of water. Most commercial pectin comes from the white layer of citrus peel and dried apples, but pectins are present in smaller quantities in sunflower, mustard, sugar beets, onions and soybeans. The excellent binding sites in pectin make it valuable for human health. This type of fiber is found mostly in fruits and vegetables.

 ## THE FIBER HYPOTHESIS

Adequate intake of both soluble and insoluble fibers is essential if we are to enjoy all the benefits associated with the general term fiber. Sadly, the elimination of bran from white flour has resulted in a national deficiency of *insoluble* fiber. And our failure to eat adequate amounts of fruits and vegetables has resulted in a national deficiency of *soluble* fiber. Inevitably, the cost of these fiber losses from diet has been near-epidemic proportions of many serious diseases. Unfortunately, this is not *new* news. The *food faddists* railed about it during the Roaring Twenties. Then, as scientific research got a firmer foothold in American culture, Dr. Denis Burkitt revived the issue in the 1960s when he presented his Fiber Hypothesis.

Awareness of the harmful effects of eliminating bran and germ from our daily bread started to sink into public consciousness in the 1960s, when Dr. Denis Burkitt, a British doctor who had lived among African bush populations for 20 years, presented what he called his Fiber Hypothesis.

Dr. Burkitt's observations had convinced him that a diet high in the fibers of unrefined whole grains, fruits, and vegetables and low in fat would prevent modern diseases such as colorectal cancer, hemorrhoids, and diverticular disease, as well as disorders such as hiatal hernia, varicose veins, appendicitis and atherosclerosis. Since then, scientific research has been so supportive of the Fiber Hypothesis that many other health disorders have been added to Dr. Burkitt's list, and virtually every health entity in this country recommends eating more fruits, vegetables, and whole grains, and reducing dietary fat.

If nutritionists are so adamant about our need to eat more of the fiber provided by fruits, vegetables and whole grains, does this mean fiber is more valuable than the food components found in meat, eggs and dairy products? Decidedly not. But researchers who study modern diseases to determine their causes continue to reaffirm Dr. Burkitt's observations. If researchers were instead uncovering protein deficiencies, as was the case throughout most of history, we would be encouraged to eat high-protein foods.

 ## DISORDERS LINKED TO FIBER-POOR DIETS

Although actual deaths from diseases linked to low-fiber diets may be declining because of advances in medical science, fiber-related disorders themselves remain pervasive and on the increase. To better understand the link between fiber and disease, let's start by looking at health problems such as constipation, diverticular disease and hemorrhoids, which are associated primarily with shortages of insoluble fiber. Then we'll look at diseases like colorectal cancer, cardiovascular disease, diabetes and obesity, which have been linked to a lack of soluble fiber or dietary fiber in general. Let's begin with a very common problem related to low fiber intake, constipation.

Constipation

One health benefit attributed to dietary fiber that has endured long scrutiny is its ability to normalize the bowels so that fecal matter is passed on a daily basis, sweeping waste materials and impurities out of the body with it. But because the diet in industrialized nations is so low in fiber, a large number of Americans are plagued by constipation, a condition that is defined as the passage of hard stool less than three times a week. Without the fiber needed to regulate bowel function, dry, segmented stool languishes in the intestinal tract, forcing the intestinal walls to exert pressure to move it along and sometimes resulting in painful elimination.

Fiber encourages healthy bowel function in several ways. It contributes to the formation of large, soft stool that moves through the system quickly and is eliminated without straining. As an added benefit, bran has sharp edges that sweep impurities out of the intestinal tract as it passes. Fiber also promotes healthy bowel function by nourishing the microorganisms in the large intestine. As these good bacteria multiply, some die and become part of the stool, adding bulk and water that further enhance transit time and ease of elimination.

Much of the $250 million spent each year on laxatives in the United States and Britain is used to purchase "bulking agents," which are designed to enlarge the stool. Many people believe that these laxatives, which may be made from natural or cultured fibers, are preferable to harsh chemicals, but there are hidden costs to replacing natural sources of dietary fiber with commercial bulking agents. First, whereas natural fiber from whole foods relieves constipation in a pleasant, regular way, commercial bulking agents may not duplicate this natural process exactly and can lead to unpleasant side effects, such as bloating. Remember, too, that sufficient water must be consumed with these products or they become clay-like and may exacerbate constipation. Commercial products also fail to supply the body with the valuable food components like vitamins, minerals, antioxidants and enzymes present in whole grains and other fiber-rich foods. Finally, bulking agents may actually provide too much fiber, leading to mineral deficiencies. This possibility, related to the bioavailability of minerals, will be discussed in more detail in the next chapter.

Clearly, a high-fiber diet is an important part of bowel health because of increased stool bulk. The insoluble fiber in whole grains is particularly helpful in this regard if the grains are coarsely ground. In fact, while fine wheat bran has been found to increase fecal bulk by about 25 percent, coarse bran has been found to increase it by 100 percent. Naturally, bran size can be controlled only by grinding flour at home.

Diverticular Disease

Diverticular disease is a recent disorder. It appeared at the beginning of the last century, a couple of decades after we became capable of removing virtually all the bran from flour. It is now the most common colon disease in the industrialized world, occurring in 50 percent of Americans by age 60 and nearly all by age 80.

Diverticular disease develops as a result of constipation. When the body produces small, hard stool instead of large, soft matter, extra pressure is placed on the intestinal walls to move the stool through the intestines. This pressure causes weak spots (around blood vessels) in the wall of the large intestine to pop out into balloon-like pouches called *diverticula*. Although diverticular disease usually causes no symptoms, it can lead to *diverticulitis*, an inflammation or infection of the diverticula. Fortunately, this is generally a benign condition, which does not appear to be linked to cancer, but it can be painful. Research has shown that a high-fiber diet is the best means of reducing any symptoms of diverticular disease. Coarse bran, rather than highly processed bran, is preferable, as it absorbs more water and produces larger stool. Small seeds or husks are discouraged as a precaution against having these small items lodge in a diverticulum. Although fiber cannot remove existing pockets, it can prevent development of new ones.

Hemorrhoids

Hemorrhoids are enlarged veins in the lower rectum or anus. These veins can protrude, can cause surrounding tissues to swell and become painful, or can bleed. Like diverticular disease, hemorrhoids can be caused by constipation and repeated straining during bowel movements. By preventing constipation, fiber can prevent hemorrhoids. And by contributing to the formation of large, soft stool that is easily eliminated, it can also alleviate the pain that accompanies hemorrhoids.

Colorectal Cancer

Cancer of the large intestine and rectum, called *colorectal cancer*, is the third most common form of cancer, excluding skin cancers. It is expected to be responsible for about 10 percent of all cancer deaths in 2004. Mortality rates are higher for African Americans than for any racial or ethnic group in the nation. Although heredity has been found to influence the risk of developing this disorder, diet is also believed to play a role. This is important, as in the absence of a real cure for cancer, environmental factors take on great significance.

Research continues to link diets high in fats and refined carbohydrates to colorectal cancer. While controversy remains about whether or not high-fiber diets reduce risk of colorectal cancer, studies continue to suggest such a link. For example, a study that appeared in the May 3, 2003, issue of *The Lancet* compared fiber intake of 33,971 subjects without colon polyps to 3,591 subjects with at least one adenoma in the large bowel. The study found that dietary fiber, particularly from grains, cereals and fruits, decreased the risk of colon cancer, but *not* bowel cancer. Similar results came from another study reported in the same issue of that publication. This time 519,978 people aged 25 to 75 from 10 European countries were studied for a possible relationship between fiber intake and incidence of colorectal cancer. After an average follow-up of 4.5 years, the cancer risk was 25 percent lower in those consuming 35 grams of fiber a day compared with those at 15 grams per day. In populations with low intake of dietary fiber, the authors wrote, "...an approximate doubling of total fiber intake from foods could reduce the risk of colorectal cancer by 40%."

To put a finer point on this, a study of 38,451 women with colorectal cancer published in the February 4, 2004, issue of the *Journal of the National Cancer Institute* concluded that a diet with high glycemic load may promote colorectal cancer. (See the chapter entitled *Good Carbs, Bad Carbs* for more on glycemic load.) This means that refined carbohydrates like white bread, white rice, and white sugar may create a metabolic environment conducive to tumor growth.

A number of theories have been offered for mechanisms by which fiber may reduce risk for colon, and perhaps rectal, cancer:

- Insoluble fibers, such as those in bran, bulk the stool and dilute the contents, thus reducing contact between colon walls and potential carcinogens or tumor promoters.
- A bulky stool sweeps quickly through the colon, taking many potential carcinogens with it.
- Faster transit time leaves less time for bacteria to produce carcinogens or promoters, and less opportunity for carcinogens to make contact with colon walls.
- Fiber changes the intestinal environment, making bacteria less likely to produce carcinogens or promoters.
- Some bacteria that feed on fiber may generate byproducts that fight the development of cancer.
- Some soluble fibers may surround carcinogens and carry them off in the feces.
- Some soluble fibers may act as antioxidants that break up the carcinogens.
- Fiber may bind to mutagens (materials that turn healthy cells to cancerous ones) and remove them from the intestinal tract.

Or, it may be that a high-fiber diet includes less fat, less insulin-producing carbohydrates and more of the vitamins, minerals, phytochemicals and other healthful components that Mother Nature designed as the perfect fuel for our bodies. After all, studies have variously suggested that increased intake of calcium, or vitamin D or folic acid (folate) may lower colorectal cancer risk. Another factor may be yet-unknown components in high-fiber foods that are cancer fighters. For example, researchers at Kansas State University discovered powerful antioxidants in wheat's orthophenols. According to Kansas State biochemist Dolores Takemoto, "In the past, we thought the fiber in wheat prevented cancer...This discovery shows that there are antioxidants, in addition to fiber, which are responsible for preventing cancer."

In April of 2000, the American Health Foundation issued a "scientific consensus statement on the prevention of colon cancer." This statement was authored by 11 global diet and cancer experts after evaluating more than 100 scientific studies conducted during the past 25 years. These experts agreed that colon cancer was largely preventable if people would add more fiber to their diets and get regular screenings after age 50. According to one of the experts, Joanne R. Lupton, Ph.D., professor of nutrition at Texas A&M University, "Experimental studies show that of all the fibers tested, wheat bran is the most protective against colon tumor development."

Cardiovascular Disease

Over 65 million Americans have some type of cardiovascular disease, which includes coronary heart disease, stroke, high blood pressure, congestive heart failure, and congenital defects. The most common type of heart disease, affecting 7 million people in the United States, is coronary artery disease (CAD), which results from a thickening of arterial walls through a process called *atherosclerosis*. Also known as hardening of the arteries, this process involves the slow buildup on artery walls of *plaques* from fat, cholesterol, calcium and other cellular refuse from blood. These plaques narrow and harden arteries throughout the body, potentially blocking blood flow to the heart muscle, which can result in a heart attack, or to the brain, which can result in a stroke.

Cholesterol, a factor in atherosclerosis, is a fat-like substance that performs many valuable functions in our bodies and is, in fact, essential to life. The liver can produce about 1,500 milligrams of cholesterol each day, but many people add another 400 to 500 milligrams daily through diet. Cholesterol circulates in the bloodstream in particles called lipoproteins: low-density lipoproteins (LDL), high-density lipoproteins (HDL), and smaller very low-density lipoproteins (LDL).* *Dyslipidemia*, the term for imbalances in these blood fats, indicates increased risk for cardiovascular trouble.

Concern about imbalances in blood lipids is rooted in the different jobs they do. LDL carries cholesterol to cells throughout the body where it is needed. It is referred to as "bad" cholesterol because *if* it delivers more cholesterol than the cells can use, it may deposit the excess on artery walls in the form of plaques. High blood levels of LDL indicate an increased risk for atherosclerosis. HDL, on the other hand, is referred to as "good" cholesterol because it picks up cholesterol and carries it back to the liver for recycling or disposal. High blood levels of HDL indicate a reduced risk of atherosclerosis.**

Now let's look at the primary mechanism by which increased intake of both soluble and insoluble fibers lowers risk for this deadly disease. Fiber lowers levels of LDL by binding bile acids (see inset) and excreting them in the feces, thereby reducing the amount of fat absorbed by the body. The stars of scientific research in this regard have been the soluble fiber in rolled oats, which reduces cholesterol by nearly 73 percent, and psyllium. But research indicates that the insoluble fiber in wheat is also extremely valuable in this regard as bran can bind large amounts of four bile acids and lesser amounts of several others.

---

*Triglycerides are another blood fat that, when present in higher-than-normal levels, can indicate increased risk for coronary artery disease in some people. Triglyceride levels are: normal (under 150 mg/dl), borderline-high (150 to 199 mg/dl), high (200 to 499 mg/dl or above), and very high (500 mg/dl or above).

**Risk levels in dyslipidemia are: HDL below 47 mg/dl; LDL above 130 mg/dl for most people or 100 for those with other cardiovascular risk factors; increased triglycerides, and increased quantities of LDL particles that may be more easily deposited on artery walls. The ratio of HDL to LDL, known as the Framingham Risk Score, is also of concern, so cardiovascular risk can be reduced by either a decrease in LDL or an increase in HDL

BINDING BILE ACIDS

After a fatty meal is eaten, the gallbladder excretes bile acids into the digestive system for use in fat metabolism. One benefit of eating a diet that includes fiber-rich foods is related to fiber's ability to "bind," or attach to, bile acids and carry them out of the body through the feces, so they cannot be stored as fat. Bile acid excretion is the primary vehicle for eliminating internally produced cholesterol. The fibers most effective in this process are found in foods like oats, string beans, legumes, apples, celery, lettuce, potatoes and whole grains. But different fibers bind with different bile acids, so it is important to eat a well-balanced diet that supplies the full range of fibers. A meal containing more than one vegetable, a whole-grain product and fruit for dessert would do the job.

According to a study published in the July 23/30, 2003, issue of *The Journal of the American Medical Association*(JAMA), adding soy protein, fiber like that from psyllium husks, and almonds to a low-fat diet can be as effective as statin drugs in lowering cholesterol. This is significant in view of the staggering estimated cost of $368.4 billion to manage and treat cardiovascular disease and stroke in 2004.

An earlier report in the February 14, 1996, issue of the *Journal of the American Medical Association* (JAMA), a study of male health professionals showed that men who eat more than 25 grams of fiber per day have a 36 percent lower risk of developing heart disease than those who consume fewer than 15 grams daily. It also appears that risks continue to fall by 29 percent for every 10-gram increase in daily intake of cereal fiber. A 2003 study in this same publication analyzing participants in the Cardiovascular Health Study showed that elderly people should also increase consumption of cereal fiber, which was associated with lower-risk of cardiovascular disease. More recently, the results of a pooled analysis in the February 23, 2004, issue of the *Archives of Internal Medicine* suggest that fiber from fruits and cereals, *but not from vegetables*, can reduce risk of coronary heart disease. Risk was 10 percent to 30 percent lower for each 10-gram-per-day increment of cereal or fruit fiber. (In my opinion, the vegetable issue may be revisited...)

GETTING THE TERMS RIGHT

Until recently, the term "crude fiber" was used in most food tables to designate the fiber content in foods. But the process used to estimate crude fiber (treating plant material with a fat solvent, hot acid and alkali) destroyed some cellulose, hemicellulose and lignin and, therefore, understated the total fiber in the food tested. In 1984, the more accurate method of measuring total dietary fiber (TDF) became internationally accepted. Fiber values may still be stated as either crude fiber or TDF but TDF gives a more accurate measurement.

To complicate matters, definitions for "dietary fiber" have varied over time and across nations. In 2000, the American Association of Cereal Chemists included health benefits promoted by fiber in their definition. A new definition (in three parts) proposed by the Institute of Medicine in 2001 differentiates fibers that occur naturally in plants from other fibers such as those from animals and those that are synthesized or manufactured. If adopted for use in food regulations, this definition might affect which fiber-like food additives get counted as *fiber* on nutrition facts labels. Anyway, future definitions for fiber may look something like the following:

"Dietary Fiber" consists of nondigestible carbohydrates and lignin that are intrinsic and intact in plants;

"Added Fiber" consists of isolated, nondigestible carbohydrates that have beneficial physiological effects in humans; and

"Total Fiber" is the sum of Dietary Fiber and Added Fiber.

Foods with fibers that lower blood cholesterol include apples, barley, beans and other legumes, fruits and vegetables, oatmeal, oat bran and rice hulls and psyllium seed husks. Two of these foods, oats and psyllium husk, have received authorization from the FDA to bear claims that they "reduce the risk of heart disease," as long as they contain at least 0.75 and 1.79 grams, respectively, of fiber per serving. Many other studies have identified other components in plant foods as risk reducers in cardiovascular disease. These include folate, soy protein, garlic, coenzyme Q-10, fish oils, vitamins B6, B12, C and E and many more.

Unfortunately, good cardiovascular health cannot be achieved by eating one particular food component or type of food. An entire range of risk factors like tobacco use, excess weight, hypertension, and diabetes must also be addressed. Fortunately, adopting a high-fiber, low-fat diet can reduce *all* these risk factors except the tobacco problem, which does seem to depend totally on determination.

Diabetes

Diabetes is now the sixth leading cause of death and the leading cause of kidney failure and new blindness in adults. More than 60 percent of leg and foot amputations unrelated to injury are among people with diabetes. This metabolic disorder is characterized by elevated blood sugar (glucose) and is grouped into two types. Type 1 diabetes, which generally strikes at a younger age, is caused by *insulin deficiency*. Type 2, which doesn't hit until an average age of 40, is caused by *insulin resistance*. The term *insulin sensitivity* is a measurement of how sensitive any individual is to the presence of insulin.

Type 1 diabetes accounts for only about 10 percent of the diabetics in the United States. At the heart of this metabolic abnormality is an *insulin deficiency* that results from a malfunction in insulin-producing cells that prevents the pancreas from producing enough insulin. Treatment of type 1 diabetes involves daily insulin injections, although diet and exercise are important in controlling symptoms.

Type 2 diabetes accounts for the remaining 90 percent of diabetics. The *insulin resistance* associated with this type of diabetes occurs when the pancreas is able to produce normal amounts of insulin but body cells are "resistant" to its action. In an effort to overcome this resistance at the cell level, the pancreas produces more insulin. If the point is reached where the pancreas cannot keep up with production, both glucose and insulin levels in the blood remain high long after eating. Over time, insulin-making cells in the pancreas wear out and insulin production slows then stops. Most type 2 diabetics are insulin resistant. Treatment of type 2 diabetes focuses on diet and exercise because obesity and sedentary lifestyle (as well as smoking) aggravate insulin resistance.

In the February 5, 2004, issue of *Annals of Internal Medicine*, Harvard School of Public Health researchers linked the common Western diet–which is high in red meat, processed meats, high-fat dairy products and refined grains–with a high risk for type 2 diabetes in men.

Research also shows that replacing refined carbohydrates with high-fiber foods can reduce risk of contracting type 2 diabetes and help control diabetic symptoms. A group of studies from various issues of the *American Journal of Clinical Nutrition* show a consensus in scientific opinion that fiber helps protect against diabetes. A 2003 comparative study of 20 postmenopausal women measured the effects of either a high-fiber rye or white-wheat bread diet on glucose and insulin metabolism. Researchers concluded that fiber and whole-cereal intakes may protect against type 2 diabetes by increasing insulin response. Men are similarly protected according to a Health Professionals Follow-up Study in the September, 2002, issue. In a third study, published in the March, 2003, issue, Finnish researchers reported that consumption of whole-grain foods such as fiber-rich breakfast cereals, brown rice, barley and oatmeal can be protective against risk of type 2 diabetes and proposed two possible mechanisms for this benefit. First, fiber-rich carbohydrates are digested and absorbed slowly, reducing insulin demand. Insoluble fibers, found heavily in bran, pass through the intestines more rapidly, leaving less time for carbohydrates to be absorbed.

Although studies have attributed benefits to either soluble or insoluble fibers, and in some cases suggested roles for other components, protection from diabetes results from the combined synergistic action of known and unknown components in whole foods. With so much evidence linking fiber-rich plant foods to reduced risk of contracting type 2 diabetes, eating more whole fruits, vegetables and grains should be a first line of defense. But other issues that must also be addressed include an overall cut in calories, cessation of smoking and a plan that includes at least 30 minutes a day of aerobic exercise. Maintaining healthy weight is a central objective in the treatment of diabetes because weight loss alone can reduce risk factors for diabetes, as well as other diet-related diseases in our modern, industrialized society.

Excess Weight

The problem of excess weight, particularly in children, has reached epidemic proportions in the United States. The government estimates that over half of all Americans are overweight. The solution to this growing problem is complex and encompasses a number of measures, including a reduction in dietary fats and sugars and commitment to regular exercise. But a well-balanced diet that features fruits, vegetables, and whole grains can do a great deal to help lose weight and keep it off. Here are some ways that fiber helps shed extra pounds:

- High-fiber foods eaten during a meal can keep some of the fat eaten at the same meal from being completely absorbed, by binding bile acids so they are excreted rather than stored as fat.

- High-fiber foods such as whole grains, vegetables and fruits generally provide fewer calories than comparable amounts of high-fat or high-protein foods.

- High-fiber foods require extra chewing, so they take longer to eat. (Since about 20 minutes elapse between the time food is ingested and the time the brain signals that enough has been eaten, eating slowly reduces the risk of overeating.)

- High-fiber foods make you feel full on less food because fiber absorbs water.

- High-fiber foods slow down digestion so that blood sugar levels remain steady. This eliminates repeated surges and plunges in blood sugar that lead to overeating.

- A recently identified factor in carbohydrates called "resistant starch" passes through the digestive system undigested without contributing to calories.*

---

*Up to 35 percent of the resistant starch in legumes escapes digestion. Small amounts of resistant starch are also produced in the milling and baking of cereal and grain products, and the resistant-starch content of a potato doubles if it is cooled before eating.

As will become clearer in the next two chapters, the moderating effect of fiber on blood sugar levels may be its most significant role in weight loss. In fact, easy-to-digest refined carbohydrates like the *four whites* (white flour, white pasta, white rice, and white sugar) are so detrimental to health and weight that low-carbohydrate diets, which are nutrient-deficient in the long run, have actually provided a service to this country by removing *all* carbohydrates from so many diets. Once carbohydrates are gone and the sugar roller coaster is derailed, it is a minor step to add back only the "good" carbohydrates in whole fruits, whole vegetables and whole grains that actually help stabilize blood sugar levels. Not only will this single change cause you to lose weight, but you will reduce your risk of contracting one or more of the diseases that are debilitating and killing us in extraordinary numbers. Of course, reducing calories is the key to losing pounds, so slathering butter on high-fiber foods is not part of the weight solution.

 ## HOW MUCH FIBER?

You now know many health reasons to increase consumption of high-fiber foods. Fiber can keep your digestive system in good working order, help prevent heart disease, diabetes and cancer, and even help you lose weight. But how much is enough? There is some quibbling among experts regarding exactly how much fiber we need daily. No minimum daily requirement has been set by the Food and Drug Administration. The Food and Nutrition Board of the Institute of Medicine recommends total daily intake in grams at 38 and 25, respectively, for men and women 50 years and younger. For the over-50 group, men need 30 and women need 21 grams, due to decreased calorie consumption in this age group. Many fiber advocates recommend a minimum of 40 grams a day. Strict vegetarians get up to 60 grams per day. Yet most Americans consume only 14 to 15 grams of fiber a day, an insufficient amount by most standards. Certainly, it would be wise to double or even triple daily fiber intake, aiming for 30 to 40 grams a day. As always, water is an important component in fiber's health benefits. Although fruits and vegetables contribute water to diet, additional liquids remain necessary and healthful.

Table 2.1 TOTAL DIETARY FIBER IN SELECTED FOODS

Food Item	Serving Size	Total Dietary Fiber (gr)
All-Bran cereal	½ cup	9.6
Apple, unpared	1 medium	3.3
Banana	1 large	3.5
Bread, white	1 slice (30 g)	.7
Bread, wholemeal*	1 slice (30 g)	2.4
Carrot, raw	1 medium	1.8
Cornmeal, bolted	100 gr	7.4
Corn, whole grain	100 gr	15.7
Quaker Oats, instant, dry	100 gr	9.4
Oats, whole grain	100 gr	10.6
Orange	1 medium	3.1
Peas, raw	½ cup	3.7
Pinto beans, canned	½ cup	5.0
Prunes, pitted	½ cup	5.6
Raisins	½ cup	3.3
Rice, brown, cooked	½ cup	1.6
Rice, white, cooked	½ cup	0.3
Spinach, cooked	½ cup	0.6
Wheat, wholemeal	100 gr	12.2

Source: USDA Nutrient Database for Standard Reference, Release 16 (July, 2003)
*Extrapolated: One pound (454 gr) of wholemeal has 54.9 gr of fiber. A 30 gr morsel (smaller than the average 45 gr slice that provides 3.66 gr of fiber) of the resultant 1.5 pound loaf of wholemeal bread contains 2.39 gr of fiber.

How can you boost your daily consumption of fiber? The first step should be to eat more *whole* foods, like fresh fruits, vegetables, cereals, legumes and, of course, wholemeal bread. Are you actually eating the recommended three to five servings of fresh fruit every day? Are you including six to eleven servings of bread, cereal, and pasta, with *several* from whole-grain products? (In a later chapter you will see how feasible it is to make *all* your carbohydrate selections from *whole* foods.)

In order to increase fiber intake, it is helpful to have a general idea of the fiber content of certain foods. For instance, two large slices of wholemeal bread from a bread machine provide about 7.5 grams of fiber, while two slices of commercial white bread provide less than 2 grams of fiber. Table 2.1 presents the fiber content of some common foods to help estimate how much you are currently eating and what foods can help you eat more.

 ## STARTING OUT SLOWLY

Some people can increase dietary fiber without any unpleasant physical consequences. Others experience gurgling, bloating, cramping, socially embarrassing gas and even loose—and possibly urgent—bowel movements. This is common when people switch suddenly from a low-fiber diet to a more healthful high-fiber diet. *Don't panic.* This is a temporary phenomenon. But do resist the temptation to solve all your fiber problems in one day. In other words, don't start your new, improved diet with a big pot of pinto beans, corn polenta made from coarsely ground meal, and bread pudding. Instead, take it easy for two to three weeks, and slowly, gradually, and steadily increase your fiber intake. Remember that your ultimate goal is a diet that provides 30 to 40 grams of total dietary fiber daily. Remember, too, that you need both soluble and insoluble fibers to keep your body in optimum working order. This means adding not just more whole grains to your diet, but also more fruits, vegetables, and legumes as well.

SUMMARY

As repeated throughout this book, much clinical energy has been devoted to tracing health benefits to individual components in a high-fiber diet. But there is so much general evidence that fruits, vegetables and grains contribute to good health and freedom from disease that a pleasantly rational trend seems to be developing in this country: blanket recommendations from many different sources to eat more *whole* fruits, *whole* vegetables and *whole* grains. This is because so often clinical trials can trace improved health to increased intake of these foods but can't explain exactly which components are doing the good work. But even if we could scrutinize every clinical detail until we discovered how each and every plant component helped us, we would not know anything more important than what we know now: the more fiber we eat from whole foods, the healthier we get. Period.

The best approach to switching from refined to high-fiber foods is to take it in small, manageable steps. Step one would be to eat more *whole* fruits, *whole* vegetables, *brown* rice and legumes (beans and split peas) because they are readily available and easy to prepare. Before you can cut out many refined grain products, though, you'll need to take the inevitable next step of buying a grain mill and/or oat roller and begin replacing those white flour and pasta products with delicious, easy-to-prepare whole-grain foods like bread, pancakes, bread stuffing, cookies and muffins.

Why do I say this step is inevitable? Because different types of fiber do different things in the body, so a practical, feasible daily source must be found for *all* of them. And the most under-consumed and hard-to-find type of dietary fiber—*insoluble fiber*—is supplied primarily by the bran of whole grains. And given what we learned in the last chapter about the incompleteness of commercial flour products, home milling is the only way for the average person to eat *the grain, the whole grain and nothing but the grain.*

Of course, if fiber were the only reason to eat whole grains, you might not need a home mill. You could simply buy ground-up trees, add flavoring, and sprinkle the result on your sundaes and pizzas. So, now that we've talked about how increasing fiber improves health and wards off disease, let's learn about the many *other* health benefits available to those who mill grains at home.

Chapter 3

Nutrient Power

A home flour mill may not change the world,
but it will change the quality of your life.

Chances are good that your great-grandmother or great-great-grandmother lived on a farm. She never saw a Department of Agriculture food pyramid yet she served a variety of nutritious foods. A typical dinner included meat, potatoes, a green and yellow vegetable, bread or biscuits, apple pie and a glass or two of milk. The vegetables dripped butter, the potatoes swam in gravy, the pie crust included lard and the milk was full-fat. These calorie-packed meals were beneficial—even necessary—as long as people performed hard physical labor. They contained so many nutrients that people could afford to waste some, by cooking vegetables to mush, pouring vitamin-rich boiling water down the drain, and eating white flour products.

In the last century, however, particularly during the 1930s and 1940s, Americans migrated from farms to cities, initiating a progressive decline in the quality of our national diet. As we traded the hard work of ploughing, chopping wood and kneading bread for lighter activities like sitting, driving, and shopping, and as America's wealth and technology produced machines that lightened our daily workload while producing more food, we faced the difficult choice of eating less or getting fat. Unfortunately, those who cut down on food also ate fewer of the vitamins, minerals, and other nutrients that had been plentiful in large, country meals. Unfortunately (again), they did not always eat fewer calories. Why? Because at the same time, the food industry was responding to a growing market of women working outside the home who were eager to buy new preprocessed foods that reduced kitchen time. These foods also contained more calories and fewer nutrients than meals fixed at home from whole foods. During the last 30 years, we made matters very bad indeed with a steady move away from regular, well-balanced meals in favor of "grazing," or continually snacking on high-calorie, nutrient-poor quick foods. As a consequence, diseases linked at least partly to lifestyle began to skyrocket and the fight against excess weight became a national obsession

Heart disease, stroke, high blood pressure, diabetes and some cancers are among the most prevalent, costly and preventable of all health problems. The extended pain and suffering of prolonged diseases like diabetes, arthritis and osteoporosis decrease quality of life for millions of Americans. And the two most significant factors beyond genetics that contribute to our extraordinary rates of disease and disability are excess weight and poor food choices. The most important message in our health statistics is that we must improve the nutrient-to-calorie ratio in the foods we consume.

Perhaps at this point, you are wondering exactly what a nutrient is. Simply put, nutrients are components of food that fuel, rebuild and replenish our bodies. The main nutrient groups are proteins, carbohydrates, fats, vitamins and minerals. Water and fiber are also essential to the body, but are generally not included in nutrient lists. Although nutrients play diverse and important roles in body metabolism, the idea that they can be isolated and lumped into simple groups is misleading. This compartmentalized view of nutrients has encouraged too many of us to attempt to boost health or solve suspected nutritional deficiencies by eating synthesized or extracted food components. In truth, a nutrient group actually consists of hundreds of chemical compounds, chains, isomers, derivatives, molecules and other sub-components that participate in endless, interactive, interdependent chains of chemical events within the body. Popping supplements of selenium or magnesium which are plentiful in whole grains, for example, does not guarantee the health benefits that have been linked to a diet rich in whole grains. Good health ultimately depends on eating more of the high-nutrient foods that tend to be underconsumed in our modern diet—whole fruits, whole vegetables and whole grains.

It is valuable to be aware of how individual food components contribute to good health. Not so we can buy supplements to make up for a lousy diet, but so we understand why whole grains are so widely recommended—almost like medicines—for preventing and curing diseases. Let's start by looking at proteins, carbohydrates and fats. As the components of food that supply energy (i.e., calories), they are important in our ongoing struggle to be healthy while maintaining normal weight. Then we'll look at vitamins and minerals and then three increasingly prominent categories of nutrients: phytochemicals, antioxidants and enzymes.

ENERGY-PRODUCING NUTRIENTS

Proteins, carbohydrates, and fats are components of food that the body can burn (metabolize) to produce energy. Nutritionists measure this energy in calories. Technically, one kilocalorie, or 1,000 calories, is the amount of energy required to raise the temperature of a kilogram of water one degree Celsius. In terms of calories, the energy-producing nutrients are not equal. Fat, a concentrated source of energy, provides nine calories of energy per gram of food. Carbohydrates (sugars and starches) and proteins provide only four calories per gram. Food from each of these three calorie groups is essential to different body functions. Good health depends on eating a basic minimum from each group, but once we have satisfied this minimum, we have great latitude in deciding which sources we tap for our other calorie needs. And that's where we get into trouble.

At one time Americans got 40 percent of their energy from the starches in cereal grains. During the last century, however, grain consumption dropped by almost half, in favor of animal proteins, sugars and fats. Because the last century also saw skyrocketing incidences of diet-related diseases, virtually all governmental and health organizations that make dietary recommendations suggest that we reduce our intake of high-fat meats and other sources of saturated fat, and eliminate trans fats whenever possible. They also recommend replacing refined carbohydrates with complex carbohydrates like those in whole grains. To better understand the consequences of our food choices, let us look separately at proteins, carbohydrates and fats.

Proteins

Protein supplies energy to rebuild cells, tissues, muscles and bones. It is also the basic constituent of such important body materials as blood, lymph fluids, hormones and enzymes and plays many other important roles, such as carrying oxygen, boosting chemical activity and fighting infection. But how much protein does the body actually need every day?

During the last century, the amount of protein thought to be required for good health fell steadily. In 1902, adult Americans were advised to eat 125 grams of protein per day, because that is the amount the average working man consumed. By 1941, recommendations had dropped to 70 grams for men and 60 for women. Since then, recommendations have seesawed between 65 and 30 grams per day. Current recommendations have moved away from specific quantities to emphasizing a well-balanced selection from all of the food groups shown on the Department of Agriculture's (USDA's) food pyramid, with some experts suggesting that only 10 percent of daily calories should be supplied by protein. Remember, though, that individual protein needs vary with such factors as age, gender, physique, activity level, stress, illness and pregnancy. And it is still possible for people who are ill, inactive, older or who make poor food choices to eat too little protein. In the next chapter, we're going to talk about the high protein content of popular low-carbohydrate diets currently being followed by 32 million Americans. Be aware for now that differences of opinion remain about what constitutes an appropriate amount of protein in diet and also that it remains possible to cut back on higher fat proteins without sacrificing total protein intake.

Protein is available from both animal and plant sources. Meat, fish, poultry, dairy products and eggs are the primary sources of animal protein. Grains, beans and vegetables are the best sources of plant proteins. Protein is made up of compounds called amino acids. The body can manufacture some of these amino acids, but eight (*methionine, tryptophan, threonine, valine, isoleucine, leucine, phenylalanine* and *lysine*) must be supplied by animal or plant food and are, thus, referred to as essential amino acids.

Because animal proteins are complete, that is, they contain all eight essential amino acids in an ideal balance, they have been traditionally viewed as superior to plant proteins, which in most cases are deficient in one or more essential amino acids. Fortunately, foods with incomplete protein become complete when combined with foods that are rich in the missing amino acid(s). For example, dairy products or eggs can be added to bread to "improve" its protein value by ensuring that all the essential amino acids are present in the proper proportions at the same time. Beans and rice can also be eaten together for complete protein. Combining foods in this way is called *complementing*.

Most active people eating a balanced diet can meet their body's need for complete protein, even if they are vegetarians. But pregnant women and older, sick or inactive people with peckish appetites may need to consciously complement if they want to depend on plant sources for all of their protein.

As more and more research has linked serious problems like cardiovascular disease and cancer with eating too much saturated fat, most health organizations recommend replacing some high-fat animal proteins with plant-based proteins. This does not mean that plant proteins are a better source of energy than animal proteins, but that in making difficult choices amongst calories, favorite foods and nutrients, this option has many benefits and must be considered.

Carbohydrates

Carbohydrates are plant components produced by photosynthesis. As nature's most common organic compounds, carbohydrates are an important source of energy for humans. Although some populations, such as natives in Alaska and Greenland and the Inuits in Canada, appear to suffer no adverse effects from diets with minimal quantities of carbohydrates, research suggests that low carbohydrate consumption results in long-term health problems for populations that are not genetically or traditionally adapted to such a diet.

Carbohydrates can be separated into two groups according to molecular structure and individual characteristics. If the molecules are small and simply configured, a carbohydrate is referred to as *simple* because the body can break it down easily. Examples of simple carbohydrates are glucose, sucrose, lactose, maltose and fructose (found in foods like fruits, honey, maple syrup, many vegetables and sugar cane). If the sugar molecules are in long, complicated chains, the carbohydrate is called *complex*. Examples of complex carbohydrates are starch and cellulose (found in whole grains, beans, peas and potatoes).

Although all carbohydrates satisfy energy needs, complex carbohydrates are more beneficial than simple carbohydrates for at least two important reasons. The fiber in complex carbohydrates provides many health benefits described in the last chapter and *unrefined* complex carbohydrates contain a rich supply of nutrients.

Adults should get 45 to 65 percent of daily calories from carbohydrates. Recently, the basement for carbohydrate consumption was set at 130 grams per day by the Institute of Medicine. This may seem reasonable considering the median daily intake of 200 to 330 grams by men and 180 to 230 grams by women. But recommendations on some low-carbohydrate diets can be as low as 20 to 40 grams per day, substantially below any minimum requirement. Worse yet, these numbers do not reflect whether the carbohydrates are supplied by refined or whole foods, which have vastly different consequences for health and weight. But do remember that any carbohydrate, whether empty and simple or nutritious and complex, consumed in excess of energy needs will be stored as glycogen or fat! (More about this in the next chapter...)

And since we've broached the subject of fat, let's look more closely at this seriously maligned food component.

Fats

Fat is our most concentrated source of energy, providing nine calories per gram compared with four calories per gram for carbohydrates and protein. Fat aids in vitamin absorption and tissue development. Because it does not dissolve in water, fat can store or transport throughout the body such substances as the fat-soluble vitamins A, D, E, and K. Fat also helps produce several hormone-like compounds called prostaglandins that help regulate blood pressure, heart rate, blood vessel constriction, blood clotting and the nervous system. It acts as insulation to keep us warm or cool, cushions our internal organs and makes us feel full after a meal so we don't keep eating. Unfortunately, too much fat can increase risk of heart disease, high blood cholesterol, diabetes and some kinds of cancer. It can also lead to obesity, which is a risk factor for diabetes, cancer, gallstones, liver disease and osteoarthritis.

Fats are made up of basic components called fatty acids. The liver can manufacture certain of these fatty acids from any food that supplies calories, but others (*linoleic* and *linolenic*) are referred to as essential fatty acids because they must be supplied by food. Fortunately, we need only 10 grams a day of these essential fatty acids, which are readily available in vegetables, grains, fruits, nuts and fish.

In recent years, scientific research has suggested that certain consumed fats may carry greater health risks than others. It is important to understand that no natural form of fat is really "bad." Each performs important functions in the body, but when eaten in excess, a particular kind of fat may exceed its role and create problems. To understand how and why this happens, we need to know something about three kinds of dietary fats: *saturated*, *unsaturated* and *trans* or *hydrogenated* fats.

The chemical form in which most fat exists in food as well as in the body is *triglycerides*. The triglycerides in our bodies are derived from fats eaten in foods or made from other energy sources like carbohydrates. The fats and oils that we consume are also made up of triglycerides, which contain three molecules of fatty acids and one of glycerol. If the chemical bonds between the fatty acid molecules have all the hydrogen atoms they can hold, the fat is *saturated*. If the bonds can still hold more hydrogen atoms, the fat is *unsaturated*. Although the fats we eat are classified as predominantly saturated or unsaturated, any fat actually contains varying quantities of both kinds of fat.

Saturated fats, which are generally solid at room temperature, are plentiful in animal-based foods like beef, lard, butter and cheese, but are also present in plant foods like cocoa, and coconut and palm oils. The primary sources of saturated fatty acids in the American diet are meats, bakery items and full-fat dairy products

Unsaturated fats, which are generally liquid at room temperature, are plentiful in plant foods like avocados, olives, some nuts and many vegetable oils. Unsaturated fats are viewed as more healthful than saturated fats because they appear to reduce levels of total cholesterol and low-density lipoprotein (LDL) in the blood and increase levels of high-density lipoprotein (HDL). Two types of unsaturated fat appear to be exceptionally valuable in diet—*monounsaturated* fats which are plentiful in olive, peanut and canola oils, and *polyunsaturated* fats which are plentiful in sunflower, corn, soybean and safflower oils. Essential fatty acids in these fats, alpha-linolenic acid (an omega-3 fatty acid common in fatty fish) and linoleic acid (an omega-6 fatty acid common in vegetable oils) protect against cardiovascular disease. These beneficial fatty acids, which must be supplied by food, are available from milk, nuts, avocados, olives, flax seeds, and soybeans.

Trans fatty acids (also called *trans fats*) are saturated fats that have been created synthetically through a process called *hydrogenation*. This process, which employs high heat, a metal catalyst and hydrogen gas, changes the molecular shape of liquid unsaturated fats into trans fats, which are semi-solid or solid at room temperature. Partial hydrogenation, a process used with such products as soybean oils destined for use in commercial salad dressings, extends shelf life by destroying volatile fats that would otherwise become rancid. Full hydrogenation, a process used to make margarine or other products that are solid at room temperature, converts all of the unsaturated fats in liquid oils to solid trans fats.

Several health problems are associated with the synthetic saturated fats created by hydrogenation. These fats interfere with nutrient absorption, are difficult to purge from the body, and increase risk of heart disease by increasing LDL and decreasing HDL. In fact, trans fats have shown *double* the effect of saturated fatty acids on the ratio of bad to good cholesterol.

Where else do we find these commercially generated trans fats? In addition to salad dressings, shortening and margarines, trans fatty acids are found in oils used to cook French fries, donuts and other fast foods and are added to baked goods such as cookies, crackers and cakes to protect against spoilage. Candy and many other processed snack foods include partially hydrogenated vegetable oils. No doubt trans fats are more prevalent in our diets than most of us are aware because they are not yet present on food nutrition labels. Despite delays, as this edition is being written, mandatory listing of trans fats on nutrition labels looks imminent.

Health and nutrition experts generally recommend getting 20 to 35 percent of daily calories from fat, while limiting saturated fat to 10 percent. Significantly, whole grains are relatively low in both unsaturated and saturated fats, and, of course, they contain no trans fats. The catch is that valuable unsaturated fatty acids are lost when the germ is removed from commercial white flour products–leaving half the entire grain's fats but only one-third of its monounsaturated fats.

WHERE'S THE FAT?

The average American diet contains 14 to 18 percent saturated fat. Here are the proporations of saturated fat in some common foods:

Coconut oil (86%)

Palm kernel oil (81%)

Butter (62%)

Beef fat (50%)

Lard (40%)

Vegetable shortening (31%)

Chicken fat (30%)

The average daily intake of trans fatty acids is 2.6 percent of calories. Because of early advertising claims, many people mistakenly believe that margarine (hydrogenated vegetable oil) helps prevent heart attacks, so it remains a significant source of these unhealthful fats. Here is a snapshot of the products that supply trans fats.

Cakes, cookies, crackers, pies, breads, etc. (40%)

Animal Products (21%)

Margarine (17%)

Fried Potatoes (8%)

Potato chips, corn chips, popcorn (5%)

Household shortening (4%)

Salad Dressing (3%)

Breakfast cereal and candy (1% each)

MINERALS, VITAMINS...AND MORE

Food substances needed in small amounts for human growth, vitality and freedom from disease are referred to as *micronutrients*. Vitamins and minerals are micronutrients that support critical functions in the body, initiating or participating in sometimes long chains of chemical activities. According to a study that appeared in the July 16, 1999, issue of *Science* magazine, people in highly industrialized nations like the United States frequently eat less than the recommended daily minimums of vitamins and minerals, in spite of their calorie-packed diets. This is due in part to our irrational food choices and in part to a food industry that removes or destroys vitamins and minerals during processing.

Increasingly, scientists are studying other compounds in plants called *phytochemicals* that also play important roles in human health. These components, and possibly many more yet to be discovered, perform their beneficial activities in our bodies whether we know about them or not. This is one important reason why eating more whole foods is a far better way to improve health than taking supplements. Let's look more closely at minerals and vitamins, then move on to some of the other valuable components packed into whole grains.

Minerals

Minerals are minute specs of metallic material that are essential to the body for strong teeth and bones, making hemoglobin in red blood cells and assisting in the transfer of nerve impulses. Minerals also interact with vitamins and enzymes in regulating body functions and are vital to many other chemical reactions in the body. The human

MISSING MINERALS

Most grain minerals are located in the bran. Discarding wheat bran results in significant losses of calcium, iron, magnesium, phosphorous, potassium, zinc, copper, manganese, selenium, and all of the trace minerals located only in the bran. The government's enrichment program adds back only one of these minerals, iron.

body needs at least 15 different minerals, which must be supplied entirely through diet, since the body cannot manufacture them.

The bran and germ of cereal grains are excellent sources of *potassium*, *magnesium*, and *calcium* and provide significant amounts of *iron*, *manganese*, *zinc*, and *copper*. They also provide trace amounts of many other elements, such as *iodine*, *molybdenum*, *chromium*, and *selenium*, and very tiny amounts of minerals like *silicon*, *tin*, *nickel*, *arsenic*, and *fluorine*. Hard wheats, used to make bread and pastas, generally supply more minerals than soft wheats, but in reality the quantity of minerals in any plant can vary widely with the farmer's soil and fertilization practices. For example, selenium is usually high in American cereals.

Any discussion of the rich supply of minerals in whole grains would be incomplete without considering a controversy involving a grain component called *phytic acid* and a phenomenon known as *bioavailability*. Wheat, rice and oat brans are high in minerals. But they also contain a lot of phytic acid. The scientific observation, supported by a great deal of research, is that when phytic acid is present, the bioavailability of minerals is reduced, which means that the body absorbs fewer of the minerals present. The chemical reason for this is that if a mineral is "bound" (at the atomic level) to insoluble material like bran, it cannot be broken loose by the digestive system, so it scoots out in the feces or urine. Phytic acid appears to be the culprit in this process because it has excellent binding sites for the minerals and because the phenomenon is not present with white flour.

At first glance, the phytic acid problem looks like bad news for whole-grain fans, since it could produce mineral deficiencies in those eating large quantities of bran. But deeper digging into the research reveals interesting additional information. For example, research also shows that a normal, healthy person eating a well-balanced diet does not develop trace mineral deficiencies from the reduced availability of minerals in the presence of phytic acid. But food faddists who shovel oat bran on everything and constipation sufferers who rely heavily on fiber bulking agents may want to consider these other findings:

- The fermentation process in breadmaking produces enzymes that release bound minerals so they can be used by the body.

- Certain microorganisms in the large intestine produce enzymes that release these minerals.

- Studies have shown that adding 10 to 20 grams of wheat bran to a well-balanced diet creates no imbalances in iron, zinc or calcium.

- Adding meat or mineral supplements to the diet seems to reverse mineral binding.

Finally, while studies have implicated phytic acid in the reduced availability of minerals when bran is present, some believe the case has not been proven that this necessarily presents a health risk. Inasmuch as science has been right about so many things, however, the wisest nutritional course would be to eat more whole grains, not just the fiber, and to integrate them into a well-balanced diet.

Vitamins

The body needs very small quantities of vitamins in order to grow, reproduce and remain in good health. Vitamins play important roles in body chemistry, most notably in the body's use of proteins, carbohydrates and fats. They are also important in forming blood cells, neurotransmitters, DNA and hormones. Beyond these basic body-building functions, though, vitamins are active in virtually every aspect of health and disease prevention.

The body can manufacture many vitamins, but often not in sufficient quantities to meet demand. The deficiencies, plus 13 essential vitamins the body cannot make, must be obtained though diet. These 13 essential vitamins are categorized as either *fat soluble* or *water soluble*. The fat-soluble vitamins, A, D, E, and K, can be stored in the body for varying lengths of time—up to six months for A and D, less time for E and just a few days for K. The water-soluble vitamins, C and the B-vitamin complex, remain in the body a relatively short time and must be supplied on virtually a daily basis.

Some foods are better sources of specific vitamins than other foods. Vitamins supplied in significant quantities by cereal grains are *thiamin* (B1), *riboflavin* (B2), *niacin* (B3), *pyridoxine* (B6), *folate*, *pantothenic acid* and *vitamin E*. These vitamins are highly concentrated in either the germ or bran of grain, so commercial milling routinely reduces their presence. The progressive decline in our consumption of leafy green vegetables and legumes since we left the farm has exacerbated the B-vitamin losses caused by white flour refining. These losses are further compounded by stress, coffee and alcohol, which increase the body's need for some B vitamins. Additionally, the need for B vitamins may be greater for women on oral contraceptives, people who rely heavily on snack and processed foods, alcoholics, pregnant or lactating women, the ill and the elderly. The government's enrichment program, which became law in 1941, attempts to restore some of these nutrients to the national diet. But as you can see by referring back to Table 1.1, the selective addition of synthesized vitamins and minerals to refined flour (usually in greater quantities than existed in the original grain), does not make these products equal to those we mill at home from whole grains.

Vitamin content does not vary drastically from one grain to another except in the case of *niacin*, which is higher in barley, wheat, sorghum and rice than in most other grains. We can cause nutritional losses through cooking. Some B vitamins, for example, are heat sensitive and may be lost in processing, storage or cooking. All are water soluble and may be lost if cooking water is discarded.

Here is some information about the individual vitamins that are plentiful in whole grains.

Thiamin (B1)

Thiamin was the first B vitamin discovered. It is water soluble, so little can be stored in the body and constant intake is required. It is easily destroyed by cooking in water. The heat generated in baking bread also leads to thiamin losses of from 5 to 35 percent (because the presence of starch provides some protection). Thiamin's vulnerability to heat can be exacerbated by anything (such as soda) that changes the pH environment to seven or above, which renders thiamin unstable and can lead to large cooking losses.

Thiamin is essential for carbohydrate metabolism. Any condition that increases metabolism (rapid growth, fever, hyperthyroidism, pregnancy or lactation) increases the need for thiamin. Inadequate intake or inability to assimilate thiamin leads to beriberi, a disease known throughout history that is characterized by inflammation or degradation of the nerves, digestive system, and heart. Because thiamin is one of four nutrients included in the enrichment of white flour, rice and pasta products, deficiencies are not widespread in industrialized nations. But it has been suggested that unidentified thiamin deficiencies may be more widespread even in Western industrialized nations than previously thought. Early deficiency symptoms that may be missed include anorexia, weight loss, apathy, decreased short-term memory, confusion, irritability or muscle weakness. People at particular risk are the elderly and others who base their diets on snacks and highly refined and processed foods or who have digestive or health problems that interfere with thiamin absorption or utilization. Whole grains are an incomparable source of this vitamin, and other good sources include pork, legumes and sunflower seeds. Recommended daily intake is 1.2 mg for men and 1.1 mg for women.

Riboflavin (B2)

Like other B vitamins, riboflavin is an essential part of the extensive enzyme activity that goes on in the body and is important to the eyes and skin. Overt symptoms of riboflavin deficiency are rare in the developed world, but sore throat, magenta tongue, cracks at the corners of the mouth and oily, scaly skin inflammations may indicate a deficiency. Diseases such as cancer and diabetes can precipitate or exacerbate deficiencies, which often appear in conjunction with other nutrient deficiencies. Severe deficiency may impair vitamin B6 metabolism and conversion of tryptophan to useable niacin (see niacin, below). Riboflavin is present in at least small quantities in most foods, but a primary source is milk products. If milk is stored in clear glass under light, however, losses occur. Whole grains contain generous amounts of this important vitamin. Recommended daily intake is about 2 mg for men and 1.5 mg for women.

Niacin (nicotinic acid or nicotinamide)

This vitamin is important to health of the skin, nerves and digestive system and in proper metabolism of fats, proteins and carbohydrates. Niacin comes from foods containing nicotinic acid and nicotinamide and from the body's conversion of the amino acid tryptophan to niacin. Pellegra, the classic disease resulting from severe niacin deficiency, is characterized by a symmetrical pigmented rash resulting from sun exposure, vomiting, constipation or diarrhea, and bright-red tongue. Although niacin is widely available in nature, deficiencies occurred with corn-based diets of the past, because corn is low in both niacin and tryptophan. Processes using alkalis (such as lime-soaking of corn) helped reduce prevalence of this disease by releasing otherwise unavailable niacin in corn. Pellegra still appears in

India, Africa and parts of China. Niacin deficiencies are also common in alcoholics eating a low-nutrient diet.

Niacin is stable to heat but water-soluble, so there are leaching losses if cooking water is discarded. The niacin in mature cereal grains is only about 30 percent available to the body because it is chemically bound. Niacin added through mandatory enrichment of cereal grain products is of a type that is "free" so about 85 percent is available to the body. Other foods that contain free niacin are beans and liver, but most foods have not been evaluated for niacin availability.

Recommended daily intake, which allows for some conversion of the amino acid tryptophan to niacin, is 16 mg for men and 14 mg for women.

Vitamin B6

This vitamin has three basic forms. Two (*pyridoxine* and *pyridoxamine*) occur primarily in plant foods and one (*pyridoxal*) occurs mainly in animal foods. Among its many functions, B6 enhances the immune system, maintains glucose supply during calorie deficit, helps convert tryptophan to niacin, is involved in red cell formation and metabolism and the formation of neurotransmitters. It also appears to play a role in lipid metabolism. B6, along with B12, is important in reducing plasma homocysteine concentration, an independent risk factor for premature atherosclerosis. Early studies hold hope for a B6 contribution to improved cognitive function in the elderly. The classic symptom of B6 deficiency is seborrheic dermatitis, characterized by greasy-looking, scaly, itching areas along the sides, or above the bridge, of the nose or behind the ears. Persistent, itchy dandruff is also a symptom.

This vitamin is heat stable but water soluble so losses result from discarding cooking water. Some studies indicate that women may have lower intake than recommended amounts; however, caution should be used with supplements, as the upper intake level recommended for this vitamin is 100 mg per day.

Although ready-to-eat cereals provide almost 11 percent of men's and 14 percent of women's daily intake of this vitamin, B6 enrichment of cereal products is not mandated and not usually provided. For reference, whole grains contain .336 mg of B6 as compared with 0.044 mg in enriched or unenriched white flour per 100 grams. Recommended daily intake for adults under 50 is 1.3 mg. Adults 51 and older need 1.7 mg for men and 1.5 for women. Only about 75 percent of the B6 in a mixed diet is absorbed.

Folate (folic acid)

Folate is a generic term for this water-soluble B vitamin, which exists in many forms. *Folic acid*, the most stable form, occurs rarely in food but is the form used in supplements and enriched foods. Those forms occurring naturally in food are called *food folates*. Folate is essential to DNA and protein conversions and the formation and growth of red and white blood cells. It can prevent changes to DNA that may lead to cancer and reduces risks of heart disease and stroke. It works with B12 and can substitute for it partially. Beginning in 1998, the FDA mandated the addition of folic acid to white flour and related products under the government's enrichment program because about one third of all pregnant women in the world were thought to be deficient in folic acid. Since then, world-wide incidences of neural tube birth defects in women have dropped by 20 percent.

Lengthy cooking, holding at high temperatures, and long storage can destroy from 50 to 90 percent of the folate in a food. Deficiencies can result from gut disorders such as sprue, Crohn's disease and ulcerative colitis. Folic acid is valuable in treating pernicious anemia. Oral contraceptives reduce body stores of the vitamin; requirements increase with pregnancy, lactation, infancy and inadequate diets.

Good food sources of folate include leafy greens such as spinach, dry beans and peas, grain products and fortified cereals. Although wheat bran may reduce availability of this vitamin under some circumstances, many forms of bran appear to have no effect at all.

Pregnant or lactating women need 500 or 600 mcg daily from enrichment and supplementation combined, in addition to folate consumed through a varied diet. Other adult women and men need 400 mcg daily. Upper limits of folates from enrichment or supplements is pegged at 1,000 mcg a day. Care should be taken with supplementation because excessive intake of folate may mask the symptoms of B12 deficiencies, *which may become permanent if not recognized and treated.*

Pantothenic Acid

Pantothenic acid is sometimes lumped in with the complex of B vitamins. It plays an important role as part of a major metabolic agent, coenzyme A. This vitamin is widely distributed in foods but intake seems to have decreased since 1960. Diets high in fat or low in protein may affect pantothenic acid levels, and pantothenic acid has a wide range of interactions with other vitamins and minerals. People who might get too little pantothenic acid include alcoholics, diabetics, women taking oral contraceptives, and people suffering from colitis or ulcers.

This vitamin is fairly stable during ordinary cooking and storage. If the pH environment is above seven or below five, however, pantothenic acid becomes unstable at high temperatures so losses could result from high-heat cooking. Since this vitamin is water soluble, discarding cooking water could also cause losses. Good food sources are chicken, beef, potatoes, oat cereals, tomato, liver, kidney, yeast, egg yolk, broccoli, and whole grains. Adults need 5 mg of pantothenic acid per day.

VITAMIN E
Whole Grains vs. Commercial Products (mg per 100g)

Rye

Home-ground meal	1.28
Rye flour, dark	1.41
Rye flour, medium	0.79
Rye flour, light	0.43

Wheat

Home-ground meal	1.01
Bleached all-purpose	0.06

Corn

Home-ground meal	0.49
Whole-grain cornmeal	0.42
Cornmeal, degermed, enriched	0.15

Source: USDA Nutrient Database for Standard Reference, Release 16 (July, 2003)

Vitamin E

This fat-soluble vitamin, discovered in the 1920s but not considered essential to humans until 1966, takes eight forms, each with its own level of biological activity in the body. The most active form is alpha-tocopherol. Laboratory versions of alpha-tocopherol are not identical and not as active as the naturally occurring form and supplements often contain high quantities of less active forms as well. Studies indicate that vitamin E has a wide range of health benefits, the most accepted being its ability to prevent neuropathy and its role as a powerful antioxidant. It apparently protects vitamin A in the body from oxidation, appears to be important in maintaining a healthy immune system, and may play important roles in preventing cancer, cataracts, and cardiovascular disease.

Rich supplies of vitamin E are found in unrefined vegetable and nut oils, nuts, leafy green vegetables and the germ of whole grains. One important reason to use whole grains as a source of vitamin E is that the mineral selenium, located in the bran, enhances the antioxidant effects of vitamin E. As evident in the inset, all-purpose white flour lacks most of the vitamin E present in wheat, although manufacturers are voluntarily enriching some products with vitamin E. Heat-processing considerably reduces vitamin E in oils so it is important to buy oils that have been minimally processed without the use of solvents. These may be labeled cold-pressed, expeller-pressed or unrefined. Exposure of vitamin E to light and oxygen is also detrimental.

Individual needs for vitamin E are difficult to determine because they increase as intakes of polyunsaturated fats increase but required daily amounts are set at 22 IU for both men and women and 28 IU for lactating women.

 ## PHYTOCHEMICALS

We have all been told that foods like oranges, garlic, onions, tomatoes and carrots are good for us. We are now beginning to learn why. Scientists have recently focused their microscopes on a category of compounds that occur naturally in plant foods but have no known nutritional value. In addition to fiber, these natural plant compounds, called *phytochemicals*, include, for example, *allyl sulfides* in onions, garlic, leeks, and chives, *isoflavones* in soybeans, and *phenolic acids* in tomatoes, citrus fruits, carrots, whole grains, and nuts. The growing list of known phytochemicals also includes *oligosaccharides, inositol, lignans, phenolics, phytates, phytoestrogens, protease inhibitors* and *saponins*.

Indications are that phytochemicals may be responsible for many of the health benefits previously attributed to the vitamins, minerals and fiber also present in fruits, vegetables and grains. For example, certain phytochemicals appear to be important antioxidants (see below) and have been linked to lower blood pressure, reduced cholesterol, cancer prevention, and a wide range of other beneficial effects in human health. This area of research will no doubt provide specific evidence that all the admonitions to eat more fruits, vegetables and whole grains are dead right. But more importantly, it seems to be confirming that the use of supplements to make up for an inadequate diet is not only costly but may be largely ineffective as well.

 ## ANTIOXIDANTS

It is hard to pick up a magazine or turn on the TV these days without seeing something about the dangers of free radicals and the miraculous health benefits of antioxidants.

In metabolism, body cells use oxygen to break proteins, fats and carbohydrates into smaller components that fuel the cells. This process is called *oxidation*. During the oxidation process, *free radicals* are released. The release of free radicals enhances the effect of oxidation, much like pouring salt water on rusting iron or gasoline on a campfire (both of which are oxidation processes). The presence of too many free radicals can cause damage to cell walls, genetic material and so on. Antioxidants are chemicals that tend to attract free radicals, combine with them and reduce the quantity available to cause damage.

As the body ages, it may produce fewer antioxidants, and thus become susceptible to the negative health effects of excessive oxidation. Ever since scientific evidence first revealed that eating foods high in antioxidants like fruits, vegetables and whole grains could reduce the negative health effects of free radicals, research has been prolific in this area.

The most extensively studied antioxidants are vitamins C and E, beta-carotene and selenium. This does not mean, however, that they are the *only* antioxidants nor that all antioxidants are equal. In fact, an overemphasis on individual antioxidants has encouraged people to use pills as a substitute for fruits, vegetables and whole grains. It cannot be overstated that scientists know that a balanced diet containing moderate amounts of fat and ample servings of fresh fruits, vegetables and whole grains offers extensive health benefits. But it remains to be proven whether any individual component in a food is so much more valuable than the other components that it can replace the food itself. For example, future research may find that the *lycopene* in tomatoes, or the *lutein* and *zeaxanthin* in spinach have even stronger antioxidant benefits than vitamins E, C or selenium. The question is, *Why not eat the whole vegetable, the whole fruit and the whole grain, just in case?*

ENZYMES

Enzymes are catalysts that initiate or speed up specific biochemical reactions, both inside and outside the cells, without undergoing any change themselves. Enzymes are required for all cell metabolism, including *making enzymes*. For example, they aid in digestion by helping break food into simple components that can be easily absorbed. One enzyme generally specializes in just one type of chemical reaction, but it plays its role repeatedly, always with a team of other highly specialized components such as *substrates* and *coenzymes*. The entire team must be present before the enzyme is activated. So, for example, a vitamin that functions as a coenzyme must be present before the enzyme that works with it can do its job.

Roughly 4,000 enzymes have been identified in human cells. The body can manufacture the enzymes it needs, but they are also plentiful in plants. The activity of enzymes is affected by the pH, or acid-alkaline environment, in which they are working. For example, pancreatic enzymes are active at a neutral pH but inactive in an acidic environment. Improved digestion and colon health result when plant enzymes are present, because they remain active in a broader pH range than those produced by the body. The enzymes that occur in plants usually have an *ase* on the end of their names and are divided into different categories depending on what they do. For example, the *hydrolases* work with water, the *lyases* work alone, the *transferases* transfer chemical groups between different molecules, etc. Unfortunately, enzymes are heat sensitive so cooked or processed foods may have experienced enough heat to render them inactive (although science may yet uncover unknown mechanisms that protect them).

A kernel of grain contains hundreds or thousands of enzymes, making it difficult-to-impossible to know what they all do, let alone how they interact with other enzymes or micronutrients in the complex chemical laboratory of the human body. If certain enzymes prove to be more heavily concentrated in the germ and bran of grain (as vitamins and minerals are), the discarding of these important grain parts by commercial millers must certainly result in similar losses of enzymes. Finally, since many enzymes become inactive or unstable above 122 degrees (and some say this process starts at 109 degrees), milling temperatures should be kept as low as possible and some raw foods should be eaten each day.

CHOOSING HIGH-OCTANE FOODS

Remember that your body, like a high-powered engine, gives its best performance and gets its best mileage with the high-octane fuel it was designed to run on. The optimum fuel is a well-balanced diet that includes six to eleven servings each day of a food that has fueled us for over 25,000 years—cereal grains. Minimum octane is *three servings from whole grains*. Maximum octane is *all servings from whole grains*. Most governmental and health organizations suggest replacing refined carbohydrates with complex carbohydrates whenever possible. Whole grains, particularly, supply not only the energy we need but the many other nutritional components described in this chapter. Clearly, the easiest way to improve diet is to find ways to break the unhealthful snack-food habit, at least some of the time. Remember that once the body receives its minimum requirements of protein, carbohydrates and fat, we can choose which foods we eat to satisfy our remaining energy needs. And since being overweight is a significant factor in many diseases, and detrimental to the body's overall health as well, our food choices must be low in calories and high in nutrients.

While it is relatively simple to add fruits and vegetables to the diet because they can be eaten raw, many people find them an unsatisfactory replacement for quick-energy snack foods. Whole grains, particularly those milled at home, on the other hand, supply lots of energy and satisfy appetite while providing none of the simple sugars, hydrogenated fats and salt that dominate processed foods. Fortunately, home-milled wholemeal can restore a daily supply of fiber and nutrients to the diet in wonderfully delicious foods that can be prepared in advance and used as snack foods, with a very reasonable commitment of time.

But before we get to time and the mechanics of becoming a home miller, let's look at a special and very important area of nutrition regarding whole grains that we've touched on before—the importance of "good" and "bad" carbohydrates in our struggle to maintain healthy weight.

CHAPTER *4*

Good Carbs, Bad Carbs

Reality

The wife gave me a scoop of ice cream with bits of fruit.
I ate it in three bites and pushed it back...
...Can I have more?
...The ice cream is gone and I'm not buying any more.
...Why!?
...From now on, all you get for dessert is fruit.
...Why!?
...Fruit has fiber and antioxidants...what has ice cream got?
...Antidepressants?

Ever since the 4,000-calorie-a-day diet that took this country from sagebrush to skyscraper became excessive, Americans have struggled to maintain normal weight. With 34 percent of us currently overweight and another 30 percent obese, governmental agencies and nutrition experts are in a frenzy to derail the calorie express taking disease and chronic health problems to every American home. But their pleas for a well-balanced diet are barely audible anymore in the clatter of "miraculous" weight loss schemes that populate advertising and the Internet—everything from herbs and drugs that burn fat, speed metabolism or alter body chemistry to exercise equipment, stomach stapling, jaw wiring and a plethora of good, bad and disastrous diets.

The traditional well-balanced diet (the one that discourages fat and encourages carbohydrates) has had a good run. After all, a giant body of scientific evidence has *proven* that this approach should work. Yet almost two-thirds of us remain overweight and 32 million have swerved over to the newly re-vived low-carbohydrate diet. This "diet revolution" as Dr. Atkins aptly named it when he kicked it off *this time* eventually garnered a sufficient following for clinical studies to begin appearing in scientific literature.

We'll take a look at those studies, which—not to spoil the sus-pense—have concluded that low-carbohydrate diets *do* work. But we also need to understand why the traditional low-fat, high-carbohy-drate diet has not worked for so many. And whether there are long-term health risks associated with low-carbohydrate diets, as has been sug-gested. Before that, though, we will start with the goods and bads of the proteins, fats, and carbohydrates from which we cut calories when we want to lose weight. And because low-carbohydrate diets are based on the premise that carbohydrates are metabolically *bad*, we'll glance over some terms that pop up in arguments about which diet is best and why. These terms include insulin problems, glycemic index and glyce-mic load, metabolic syndrome and ketosis. Finally, we'll see what the research tells us about selecting an appropriate weight loss program and implementing it in a healthful way.

Oh, yes...and I'll be telling you—yet again—how to make any diet plan nutritious by milling grains at home.

 ## PROTEINS, FATS AND CARBOHYDRATES

Proteins, fats and carbohydrates are *macronutrients* that our bod-ies metabolize for energy, which we measure in calories. Each of these food components plays important roles in different body functions and is essential to survival. Official dietary recommendations are an at-tempt to establish what quantities of these nutrients are necessary to maintain good health and prevent disease.* Standard recommenda-tions fall into the range of 45 to 65 percent of total calories from carbohydrates, 20 to 35 percent from fat, and 10 to 35 percent from protein. Without repeating the technical details presented in the last chapter, let's look at how we can select the *goods* over the *bads* within the options of proteins, fats and carbohydrates.

---

*Recommendations reflect averages and throughout this discussion it is ex-ceedingly important to remember that individual needs may vary by age, ge-netics, gender, physique, activity and stress levels, illness and pregnancy.

Good Proteins, Bad Proteins

Proteins are available from both animal and plant sources. Meat, fish, poultry, dairy products and eggs are the primary sources of animal protein. Grains, beans and vegetables are the best sources of plant protein. Controversy exists about which proteins are good and which are bad. Vegetarians oppose animal proteins based on poor treatment and unnecessary death of helpless animals. Some also oppose animal flesh because of residual hormones, antibiotics and environmental pollutants that may be present. Carnivores, on the other hand, see animal proteins as superior to plant proteins because they are "complete," meaning that they contain all the essential amino acids in proper balance. Animal proteins are the linchpin of low-carbohydrate and caveman-type diets because they are nutrition powerhouses that slow down digestion of sugars and starches, which we'll get to shortly. Many on all sides recommend restrictions in animal proteins that are high in saturated fat. Most recommendations for protein intake range from 30 to 65 grams per day (about eight grams a day for every 20 pounds of body weight), although low-carbohydrate diets typically place few, if any, limits on protein. Ultimately, it seems to me that choosing the goods and bads in this particular category is more a matter of personal choice and individual need than clinical research, as long as more calories are burned than taken in each day.

Good Fats, Bad Fats

Fats (also known as lipids) are our most concentrated source of energy, providing nine calories per gram compared with four calories per gram for carbohydrates and proteins. Fats are categorized as unsaturated (mono or poly), and saturated. Although controversial views linger in some circles, there is wide agreement about which fats are good and which are bad.

Staunchly in the good category are unsaturated fats, two of which appear to be exceptionally valuable in diet–*monounsaturated* fats, which are plentiful in olive, peanut and canola oils, and *polyunsaturated* fats, which are plentiful in sunflower, corn, soybean and safflower oils. The fatty acids within these mono- and polyunsaturated fats, which are alpha-linolenic acid (an omega-3 fatty acid common in fatty fish) and linoleic acid (an omega-6 fatty acid common in vegetable oils) protect against cardiovascular disease.

Saturated fats, on the other hand, are frowned upon because of their potential for increasing LDL, or bad cholesterol, in a high-fat diet. There are two types of saturated fat, those that occur naturally and those that are created mechanically. In the recent past, saturated fats that occur naturally in both plant and animal sources (lard, butter, palm and coconut oils as well as fats in beef and pork) have been universally discouraged. There are rumblings from the technical health-food crowd, though, that plant-based saturated fats are so beneficial that they should be taken out of the bad-fat doghouse and restored to diet.*

The most universally condemned type of saturated fats (with few defenders outside the manufacturing community that is responsible for their existence) are trans fatty acids. These fats are created when commercial food processors change liquid oils to semi-liquid or solid form using a process called hydrogenation. Trans fats, as they are also called, interfere with nutrient absorption, are difficult to purge from the body, and increase risk of heart disease by increasing LDL and decreasing HDL. As noted earlier, trans fats have shown *double* the effect of natural saturated fats on the ratio of bad to good cholesterol.

Although foods are viewed as predominantly saturated or unsaturated, a given fat source actually contains varying quantities of both types of fat. For example, coconut oil is 86 percent saturated, lard is only 40 percent saturated and chicken fat is a low 30 percent saturated. Recommendations for total fat intake vary from 20 to 35 percent of daily calories (or 44 to 77 grams for a 2,000-calorie-a-day diet) and saturated fat is generally limited to no more than 10 percent (or 22 grams for a 2,000-calorie-a-day diet). High-protein diets have generally not restricted any particular fat, although recently the Atkins Diet appears to suggest that only 20 percent of dietary fat should be saturated.**

Know Your Fats, by Mary G. Enig, Ph.D. (Bethesda Press, 2000), is a treatise on fats and oils that provides minute technical detail and alternative opinions about what are good and bad fats in diet.

**According to the Institute of Medicine, saturated fats, trans fats (which are saturated) and cholesterol have no known beneficial role in preventing chronic disease and are thus not required at any minimum level in diet.

Good Carbs, Bad Carbs

Carbohydrates are a rich source of vitamins, minerals, fiber, enzymes and a growing list of phytochemicals. All carbohydrates can be separated structurally into two groups, *sugars* and *starches*. Sugars, referred to as simple carbohydrates because they consist of short chains of sugar molecules that are easily digested, are found in foods like fruits, honey, maple syrup, many vegetables and sugar cane. Starches, referred to as complex carbohydrates because they consist of longer chains of sugar molecules that are absorbed more slowly, are found in foods such as cereal grains, beans, peas and potatoes.

Although all carbohydrates satisfy energy needs (i.e., provide calories), complex carbohydrates are good because their fiber slows down the rate of absorption in the gut and regulates the sites at which nutrients are absorbed. Simple carbohydrates are bad because they can cause blood sugar levels to zoom and plunge in a way that creates metabolic problems that we will discuss shortly. When a complex carbohydrate is refined and the fiber is removed, there is no longer anything preventing it from being absorbed quickly, so it *acts* like a simple carbohydrate. Whether a simple carbohydrate or a complex carbohydrate that has been refined, if it can be absorbed very quickly, it is viewed as bad from a metabolic standpoint. Examples of bad carbohydrates are white sugar, white flour, white rice, white pasta and fruit juices. Examples of good carbohydrates are whole grains, legumes, and whole fruits, vegetables and nuts. (The term *empty* has also been applied to refined carbohydrates because many essential nutrients including fiber have been manufactured out, rendering the carbohydrate a nutritional shell of its former self.)

Official organizations have not generally recommended daily minimums for carbohydrates under the assumption that bodily needs would be easily exceeded because people liked grains, fruits, vegetables, nuts and legumes. Alarmed by the popularity of diets that recommended as few as 20 to 40 grams of carbohydrates per day, however, the Institute of Medicine for the first time in 2002 established a recommended daily allowance (RDA) of at least 130 grams, or 520 calories. Median carbohydrate intake appears to be between 200 to 330 grams per day for men and 180 to 230 grams per day for women. But these figures do not differentiate refined from unrefined carbohydrate intake. Considering availability, refined carbohydrates obviously account for most of total consumption.

METABOLIC FACTORS

We know that eating and sitting too much are at the root of our national epidemic of excess weight and obesity. But scientists have diligently attempted to determine the impact of various aspects of body chemistry on weight and susceptibility to disease. Unfortunately, their investigations are complicated by the fact that our bodies are exquisitely complex machines, with backup systems, pinch-hitting capabilities, and an unending maze of interactions. Ultimately, scientists may never fully comprehend the vast diversity within the body's metabolism.

Our own efforts to make sense out of claims about how a particular diet works metabolically can be ill-fated if we are confused by clinical terms that underlie claims about the superiority of one diet over another. The following will help in understanding why so many diets reduce, or virtually eliminate, carbohydrates.

Insulin Problems

Carbohydrates are consumed then broken down by the digestive system into sugars that arrive in the blood as glucose. The presence of glucose stimulates the pancreas to release enough insulin to transport the glucose to the cells of the brain, muscles and other organs where it is used for energy or stored as glycogen. If this delivery is successful, the insulin level drops back to normal and a sensation of hunger signals a need for more food.

This system works best with a moderate and steady supply of glucose. If the glucose level spikes, as happens when a large quantity of simple carbohydrates is consumed at one time, extra insulin is released, which rushes in to carry off the glucose. When the blood glucose level then plunges, a more urgent hunger signal is sent out and people respond by eating or suffering the miseries of hunger. Repeated spiking and plunging of blood glucose, which has names like *reactive hypoglycemia* and the sugar roller coaster, is a significant factor in our epidemic of excess weight because it leads to overeating and, thus, to excess glucose to be disposed of.

Glucose (as well as fructose and galactose, two other byproducts of carbohydrate metabolism) that is not used immediately is stored in the liver and muscles as glycogen, which can be converted back into glucose as a quick source of energy. Any glucose not used in body processes or stored as glycogen is converted into fat and stored in the fat cells. Once it has been stored as fat, however, it cannot be converted back into glucose but must be burned just like any fat in order to provide energy.

Because refined carbohydrates contribute to the sugar roller coaster and the weight gain that results, they are seen as bad actors, metabolically speaking. In fact, low-carbohydrate diets slash *all* carbohydrates from diet in order to jerk the sugar roller coaster to a stop. Unfortunately, although this approach works, it is an oversimplification that ends up eliminating *both* good and bad carbohydrates.

Now let's look at some terms involved in how well or poorly insulin does its job of removing glucose from the bloodstream.

Insulin sensitivity is a measurement of how sensitive a particular individual is to the presence of insulin. According to Dr. Gerald M. Reaven of the Stanford University School of Medicine, about half of the difference in insulin sensitivity among individuals can be accounted for by genetics with the other half attributable equally to weight and status of physical fitness. Research suggests that replacing refined grains with whole grains can improve insulin sensitivity.

Insulin resistance is the diminished receptivity of cells to the glucose that insulin is trying to deliver. In an effort to overcome this "resistance" at the cell level, the pancreas produces more insulin. If the point is reached where the pancreas cannot keep up with production, both glucose and insulin levels in the blood remain high long after eating. Over time, insulin-making cells in the pancreas wear out and insulin production slows then stops. Most type 2 diabetics are insulin resistant and an estimated 25 percent of people with normal glucose tolerance are thought to be severely insulin resistant but still secreting enough extra insulin to overcome the resistance.

Impaired glucose tolerance (IGT) occurs when the level of glucose in the blood remains higher than normal but is not yet in the diabetic range. This abnormality is also referred to as prediabetes because it is a transition phase between normal glucose tolerance and diabetes and sufferers risk developing type 2 diabetes in the future. Weight loss and exercise may help return glucose levels to normal. Reduced fat intake is generally recommended for weight loss, although some believe that emphasis should be placed on a high intake of monounsaturated fats.

Glycemic Index (GI)

The glycemic index is an attempt to predict how fast a given carbohydrate will get sugar into the blood stream. This is particularly important for diabetics who need to maintain a constant blood sugar level. Some diets rely on the glycemic index to direct dieters away from foods that shoot blood sugar levels high and produce the kind of intense hunger that can derail even the most devoted dieter. This list ranks individual carbohydrates by the rate at which they raise blood sugar in comparison to the same quantity of white bread, which is set at 100. Foods with low numbers raise blood sugar more slowly than foods with high numbers. Thus, pumpernickel bread at 69 raises blood sugar more slowly than white bread at the baseline of 100. At 150, maltose, the sugar present in beer, increases blood sugar at a substantially higher rate than white bread. A glycemic index of 70 or more is high, 56 to 69 is medium, and 55 or less is low.

Glycemic Load (GL)

Glycemic load* is a relatively new and more comprehensive attempt to assess the impact of carbohydrates on blood sugar. It indicates not only how rapidly a particular carbohydrate turns into sugar, but how much carbohydrate there is in a serving of a particular food. For example, the carbohydrate in watermelon has a high glycemic index, but since there isn't much carbohydrate in the fruit, the glycemic load is actually much lower. Glycemic load is calculated by multiplying the glycemic index in percent by the grams of carbohydrate in a serving of the food. A glycemic load of 20 or more is high, 11 to 19 is medium, and 10 or less is low. The typical diet contains about 100 glycemic load units, although amounts may vary from 60 to 180 units.

Glycemic index and glycemic load are valuable tools, but do not present a total picture of the speed at which blood sugar rises in response to carbohydrates. This is because other factors influence how quickly food is broken down, such as food preparation or the simultaneous presence of components that slow down digestion. For example,

---

*The University of Sydney website (http://www.glycemicindex.com) has a searchable list of foods by both glycemic index and glycemic load. A list also appeared in the July 2002 issue of the *American Journal of Clinical Research*.

if boiled potatoes are mashed, the glycemic index rises by 25 percent. And an extra day or two of ripening can almost double the glycemic index of a banana. Absorption is also slower when a high-numbered food is consumed with fiber, fat, protein, or anything acidic, all of which interfere with the digestive process. According to an article in the September 1, 2002, issue of the *Journal of Nutrition*, for example, a (commercial) cereal's glycemic peak can be cut in half if the cereal contains 10 percent beta-glucan, the soluble fiber in oat bran. Also, a phenomenon called "resistant starch," which passes through the body undigested, is unaccounted for in this system. Finally, judging the value of a food by the glycemic index alone could lead one to believe that a candy bar is preferable to a slice of whole wheat bread.

Metabolic Syndrome

The metabolic syndrome* is a cluster of five metabolic abnormalities that occur together in an individual more often than might be expected by chance and that increase the likelihood of developing diabetes, heart disease or stroke. The five risk factors vary but there is agreement on the essential components: glucose intolerance, insulin resistance, central obesity, hypertension and dyslipidemia (abnormal blood fats). The more components present, the greater the risk to health. Blood lipid characteristics of concern in metabolic syndrome are increased triglycerides, low HDL or "good" cholesterol, high LDL or "bad" cholesterol, and increased small, dense LDL particles. It has been suggested that insulin resistance is at the heart of all these metabolic abnormalities, but there remains disagreement on this. Forty-seven million American adults, and approximately 910,000 adolescents have metabolic syndrome, including 10 to 15 million adults with type 2 diabetes. Diets should include lots of whole grains, beans, fruits and vegetables to provide plenty of dietary fiber, which can lower insulin levels.

---

*Older names for this cluster of risk factors may still be encountered, from deadly quartet and plurimetabolic syndrome to syndrome X, and the more recent moniker, insulin resistance syndrome. In 1998, the World Health Organization (WHO) suggested replacing older terms with the single, unifying term metabolic syndrome.

Ketosis and Protein

Ketosis is a metabolic state induced by drastically restricting carbohydrates until the body switches from its normal burning of glucose to burning its own fat for fuel. During ketosis, which is encouraged by some low-carbohydrate diets, small carbon fragments called ketones created by the breakdown of fat provide energy and reduce sensations of hunger. There is some indication that short-term benefits of a ketotic diet may exist, including weight loss, reduction in serious seizures in epileptic children, and improved brain function in adults. Researchers note, however, that these potential benefits may be related more to a reduction in calories than the chemistry of ketosis.

Although not yet clinically demonstrated, possible long-term risks of high-protein diets and ketosis have been postulated on the basis of known health risks. The decrease in fluid volume and possible dehydration associated with ketosis, for example, may put people with kidney disorders or those on hypertensive medications at risk. High-protein diets result in a higher-than-normal excretion of calcium in urine which may, over time, increase the risks of osteoporosis and kidney stones. For example, an article by Uriel Barzel and Linda Massey in the *Journal of Nutrition* points out that "a 50-milligram increase in calcium excretion per day works out at 18.3 grams per year. Over a period of 20 years, this represents a 30-50 percent reduction in bone mineral density." While not strictly related to ketosis, the most vocal criticism against high protein intake involves compensatory reductions in nutrient-rich carbohydrates.

So, while there is a biochemical basis, similar to that of starvation, for the weight loss experienced through ketotic diets, before intentionally inducing change in a system as complex and carefully balanced as body metabolism, unintended consequences should be considered.

 ## OPTIMIM WEIGHT LOSS

Now that we've had an overview of metabolic issues involved in the best-diet debate, we can look at clinical studies that have attempted to determine how successful low-carbohydrate and other diets are for weight loss and, more importantly, for long-term health and reduced incidences of diet-related diseases.

First, I admit to a growing crankiness as it dawned on me that diet-related conditions like obesity, heart disease, stroke, diabetes and cancer went on a statistical rampage during the reign of the established well-balanced diet. But I rankled at clinical suggestions that hacking nutritious carbohydrates from a diet could result in weight loss and improved blood chemistry. But I was persuaded by the preponderance of clinical evidence that low-carbohydrate diets *work*, and I grudging conceded that they might not be all that bad, at least for short-term weight loss.

To see how I got there, let's look at representative studies on the effectiveness of low-carbohydrate, usually high-fat diets. A sweeping literature search for all studies of low-carbohydrate diets published between 1966 and February, 2003, appeared in the April 9, 2003, issue of the *Journal of the American Medical Association*. Stanford University Medical Center researchers and Yale collaborators found 107 articles reporting data on 3,268 subjects, 663 of whom received diets with 60 grams of carbohydrates per day or less and 71 of whom received 20 grams per day or less. The conclusions were as follows:

- Low-carbohydrate diets result in weight loss.

- When weight loss takes place, it is more likely related to longer dieting and restriction of calories than to lowered carbohydrate content.

- No significant short-term adverse effects were found on serum lipid level, fasting serum glucose level, serum insulin level or blood pressure.

- Evidence is lacking on long-term effects since only five of these studies lasted longer than 90 days.

- Insufficient evidence was found to determine impact on older adults, since none of these studies included people over 53.

Studies conducted after the study's search period have continued to confirm these rosy results, even on occasion showing greater weight losses on low-carbohydrate diets than either low- or moderate-fat diets. One longer-duration example is a six-month study of 53 healthy obese women published in the April, 2003, issue of the *Journal of Clinical Endocrinology and Metabolism*. Researchers concluded that dieters on a very-low-carbohydrate plan lost more weight than those on a low-fat diet, with no deleterious effects on cardiovascular risk factors. For a slightly different take on the low-fat recommendation of most traditional diets, we can look at another study of 53 overweight or obese healthy men and women during a 10-week period, which appeared in the February, 2004, issue of the *American Journal of Clinical Nutrition*. Authors concluded that a moderate-fat diet following current guidelines for saturated fat was more effective at improving lipid profiles than a low-fat diet, although weight loss was similar. Finally, a couple of year-long studies that appeared in the *New England Journal of Medicine* in 2003 suggested that benefits of a low-carbohydrate diet present at the six-month level had disappeared by the end of the study.

In sum, the flavor of current research is that low-carbohydrate diets are effective for weight loss and, *at least in the short term*, show no significant increases in the risk factors for cardiovascular disease despite fat and protein levels above what are currently considered healthful.

Then I encountered a study released later that year that gave me a new perspective on the whole issue of diets. On November 10, 2003, Dr. Michael L. Dansinger, assistant professor of medicine at Tufts-New England Medical Center in Boston, presented results from a study that compared the Atkins, Ornish, Weight Watchers and The Zone diets for effectiveness in decreasing both body weight and cardiovascular disease risk factors. (See Table 6.1, which summarizes these findings.)

I found it interesting that only half the subjects finished their diets (65 percent in the case of Weight Watchers and The Zone and 50 percent with Atkins and Ornish). This calls into question claims that low-carbohydrate dieters adhere longer than other dieters because the increased intake of protein and fat is more satisfying. No doubt it is...for awhile. Then, apparently, adhering to *any* diet becomes a matter of determination.

Even more interesting, participants on the Ornish Diet, an extremely low-fat, high-carbohydrate vegetarian plan, produced the best results in every measurement except one, a desirable rise in the very important HDL cholesterol that transports excess cholesterol back to the liver for recycling or disposal so that it cannot be deposited on arterial walls. Ornish's weak showing in HDL severely lowered its Framingham Risk Score, which is the ratio of HDL to LDL. This ratio between good and bad cholesterol is increasingly believed to be a signifi-

TABLE 6.1. COMPARISON OF FOUR DIETS FOR DECREASES IN WEIGHT AND CARDIOVASCULAR DISEASE RISKS

Diet Name Food Type (Completion Rate)	Reduction in Weight	Reduction in Insulin	Reduction in Low Density Lipoprotein (LDL)	Reduction in Framingham Risk Score (HDL/LDL Ratio)
Atkins Low carbohydrate (52%)	3.9%	7.7%	8.6%	12.3%
Ornish Low-fat vegetarian (50%)	6.2%	19.9%	16.7%	6.6%
Weight Watchers Moderate fat (65%)	4.5%	8.8%	7.7%	14.7%
The Zone Moderate carbohydrate (65%)	4.6%	16.5%	6.7%	10.5%

Source: Michael L. Dansinger et al, *One Year Effectiveness of the Atkins, Ornish, Weight Watchers, and Zone Diets in Decreasing Body Weight and Heart Disease Risk.* Abstract 3535, American Heart Association annual meeting, November, 2003.

cant factor in cardiovascular disease. Dr. Ornish argues that this ratio is only in play when there is excess blood cholesterol to be eliminated by HDL. Ornish's high scoring on the other measurements is a blow to claims that low-carbohydrate diets result in more weight being lost and faster than on low-fat diets.

Since all dieters in this comparative study lost weight, and all had some improvement in the disease-related metabolic measurements, we can infer that any diet can work and when it does, weight loss itself is a significant factor in improved health. To restate this, any plan that persuades the dieter to eat fewer calories than the body burns each day results in weight loss. The longer this input/output imbalance persists, the more pounds disappear. This equation is so absolute that eating just rice or just chocolate ice cream or just meat will drop pounds, as long as fewer calories are consumed than burned. Obviously, a diet based just on chocolate ice cream would be suicidal. It supplies *energy*, which is important, but it fails to provide many of the nutrients found in other foods that are clearly essential to good health and even survival. That's why we need to select a diet that not only slims us down but also gives us the best shot at long-term health and freedom from disease. And although vitamin-mineral supplements are often suggested as replacements for lost nutrients, supplementation is inferior to getting the nutrients from food itself.

 ## OPTIMUM HEALTH

Before we get too far, I want to address the unique role that exercise plays in weight loss and weight maintenance. It slims us down without sacrificing nutrients and builds muscle so that we look more shapely in the process. It also makes us more energetic, fires up our brains, and makes possible an occasional dip into the forbidden foods areas of our cornucopia. In fact, new food pyramid dietary guidelines to be finalized in January of 2005 will address our epidemic of excess weight with the new dieting message that *increasing exercise is as important as reducing food intake*.

But because the only exercise many of us get is swimming in a pool of tempting food choices, many people will be forced to reduce calories as well. And that brings us back to the issue of what foods we can and *should* cut back on to lose weight. This may shock some, but I agree wholeheartedly that carbohydrates are the most logical target for the first cuts. After all, carbohydrates *can* trigger overeating if the sugar roller coaster is running rampant in the blood stream or insulin starts to malfunction. Obesity is caused by (then exacerbated by) insulin problems; diabetes is a consequence of insulin problems; and cardiovascular disease involves insulin problems.

I certainly don't advocate cutting out *all* carbohydrates, just the *bad* ones–like processed sugars, white flour products, white rice and fruit juices. By replacing these fragmented carbohydrate foods with *whole* fruits, *whole* vegetables and *whole* grains, enough calories will still be needed to allow for more protein and the good fats in olive oil, peanut oil, nuts and fish. I frame it this way because it remains unclear that one diet can work for everyone in a country that is as genetically and physiologically diverse as this one. After all, daily recommended quantities for proteins, fats and carbohydrates are presented in ranges, not absolutes. And weight loss is a result of reduced calorie intake. There is room for individual preferences, providing that calories are reduced and a healthful balance in food choices is maintained. But in this regard, I think that the two-week induction period in many low-carbohydrate diets wherein few or no carbohydrates are eaten can be a valuable tool for any healthy person. It breaks the refined-carbohydrate habit and initiates substantial weight loss without consequences to health. After that, however, whole fruits, vegetables and grains must be integrated into any weight reduction plan that aims to be healthful.

 ## THE EDITORIAL

Now to that nagging question about why the well-balanced diet hasn't kept us thin. First, of course, there's that pool of tempting food. Then there are the excess fats and refined carbohydrates in virtually any prepared food we can buy. But that still leaves a two-headed problem that has plagued and debilitated the well-balanced diet for years: a fuzzy message and poor logistics.

First, the message. Although governmental agencies, health professionals and nutritionists have slogged away at the well-balanced diet message to *eat more fruits, vegetables and grains*, that's only part of the message. It has been a stupendous mistake to tell people to eat more grains without making clear that they should be *whole* grains. Suggestions to eat *only* three servings of *whole* grains out of the 6-11 daily grain servings misleads people into believing they can improve health by eating more refined grain products like pasta, rice and white bread. We know now that refined carbohydrates contribute to weight *gain*, not to weight *loss*.

Now for the logistical problem. The idea of eating more whole grains is entrenched in dieting dogma. Even low-carbohydrate diets are now conceding that *if you must eat bread, make it whole wheat.* But the second chapter of this book is devoted to the nutritional deficiencies of the commercial products on which the average person must rely for all daily grain servings, whole or otherwise. There's no fiber left, no flavor left, and very few of the nutrients are left, even in what is advertised as "whole wheat." Worse yet, unless these allegedly whole wheat products are infused with sugar, salt or fat, they don't even taste good, which is why most people won't buy them and why few people are even eating *three* servings a day.

So, even if we did convince people to eat more whole grains, where would they buy them? Nowhere...and, as I've said elsewhere, that's why this book was written. It does what everyone touting a well-balanced diet needs to do. It helps Americans realize that there is a feasible way to eat delicious and nutritious whole-grain foods made from fresh, non-rancid wholemeal. And that thanks to a well-established and growing supply of modern home flour mills and the help of a bread machine, even the busiest person can get *all* their daily grain servings from whole grains, just by flipping a switch on the mill and pressing a button on the bread machine.

Remember, grains are a beautiful creation of nature, full of nourishing elements that are vital to health and freedom from disease. Finding a way to reintroduce into our national diet the nutritious grain parts that we have been throwing away or feeding to our pigs is as important as the post-Great-Depression goal of producing and distributing enough food to ensure that every man, woman and child in this country could eat a balanced diet.

(It is unfortunate that we are still working on the last part of *that* problem...)

CHAPTER 5

More Reasons to Mill

The Miller Was an Evil Man

In the Middle Ages—when famines were incessant, deaths black, and cities built like fortresses—the miller was an evil man. He rented his water mill from a land Lord who also rented plots of land to tenant farmers, called serfs. The Lord forbade the use of any flour mill—including those stashed in the farmers' homes—other than the one rented to the miller. The miller, who needed to protect his paltry profits to pay rent, spied on home grinding miscreants, and tattled to the Lord, who ordered his thugs to break in and destroy any offending home mill. Worse yet, the miller was a thief. His fee was one-third of the grain the serfs brought for milling. But he reputedly stole whatever more he could, then mixed sand in the flour to hide his deed. During this period, millers were low-life swindlers, the most loathed of all creatures. In times of famine they risked being killed by gangs of starving citizens.

Throughout all of history, people have persisted in grinding flour at home, no matter how dire the consequences.

Fortunately, no one will burst through the door and confiscate your mill if you defy Archer-Daniels-Midland and grind flour at home. But why would you do something so apparently drastic? For most people, the most powerful reason to mill at home has already been discussed: the health bonanza that fresh wholemeal provides. But you may be surprised to learn that people buy home grain mills for many other reasons as well.

In this chapter you will learn that a grain mill is a versatile and important kitchen appliance that grinds not just wheat for bread but other grains as well. This versatility means that people who cannot tolerate the gluten in wheat can still enjoy a wide variety of whole grains, from low-gluten rye and spelt to non-gluten staples like corn, barley, millet, or brown rice. The ability to grind unusual grains, seeds or beans also opens the door to an exciting world of exotic dishes for gourmet cooks. In addition, beer makers can crack wheat or barley to make mash for home-brewed beer, even using gluten-free grains. More interesting family needs can be met with a grain mill that is capable of grinding healthful nut butters and/or rolling oats and seeds.

But grain mill versatility goes beyond just the kinds of items that can be run through them. For example, the availability of so many *different* grain mills means that those who travel or live in recreational vehicles can enjoy whole-grain health every day, despite space limitations or lack of electricity. And, finally, there is one reason to own a flour mill that many may consider as important as all the others combined: it provides a secure food source in case of natural disaster or civil unrest.

Many will be surprised and delighted by the different milling possibilities touched on in this chapter. But everyone will be thrilled with a basic benefit that is enjoyed by each and every home miller, no matter how simple or sophisticated the mill: the hearty, wholesome, soul-warming flavor of bread or any other food made from freshly ground wholemeal. So let's start there.

INCOMPARABLE FLAVOR

Leavened bread's delicious flavor and delectable aroma have made it a favorite for 6,000 years. But opinions about what constitutes "good" bread vary drastically from one country to another and from one century to the next. It is hard to sway people from their preferences. So, when health zealots of the 1970s alerted us to the deficiencies of modern white flour, a blip resulted in purchases of commercial whole-wheat products but no enduring large-scale demand. Today, despite persistent warnings about the risks of our high-fat, nutrient-poor diet, whole wheat has not become the nutritional rage of the new millennium. Why? Because most Americans are stuck on the light, fluffy bread with which they are familiar, and they don't believe anything like it can be made from whole wheat. The truth is that American-style bread, made in a bread machine from freshly ground grain, retains what people like most about "light" breads—a soft, moist texture—while adding mouth-watering flavor and fragrance, both of which are missing from packaged store-bought bread.

But this lighter, milder-type bread is certainly not the only variety that can be created from wholemeal. In fact, the flavor road for home millers starts with something almost as benign as white bread, hits a mid-point at wholemeal potato bread and surges on to those richly flavored rye varieties that are popular in many parts of Europe. To get a better idea how a home mill can enhance and expand the flavor of ordinary baked goods, let's look first at the home miller's ability to combine different flours and then at how home-milled flour contributes flavor to the traditionally nutrient-free zone of desserts.

Mixing Flours

We learned earlier that commercial millers perform a sort of miracle by mechanically separating grain components then recombining them into bread, cake and all-purpose flours. This microscopic dissection of grain cannot be performed at home. But a flour mill provides the home miller with the next-best thing: the ability to combine flours from different grains to achieve ideal flavor, texture or performance in a particular baked good. Mixing flours for flavor is an important baking advantage unavailable to people who rely on commercial flours.

"Bread flavor [or aroma] is determined by bringing freshly cut surfaces close to the nostrils...the flavor of an ideal bread is best described as true wheat, sweet, nutty."

American Assoc. of Cereal Chemists' Journal December, 1918

Flour mixing can be subtle or flamboyant. The most basic combination is two different bread wheats, my favorite being hard red spring and soft white. But flour mixing is not restricted to wheat. Rye can replace some wheat in any bread recipe, although it should be added later in the process to avoid excessive kneading. Triticale (a hybrid of wheat and rye), spelt, corn and amaranth are just a few of the other grains that can be milled and added to bread products for flavor. Remember, flavor and aroma are inseparable and "good" isn't there until someone buries his nose in a hunk of bread and says, *"Hey, this smells good!"*

Adding Flavor to Sweets

National statistics indicate that we have lost the battle with our taste buds to eat less sugar, fat and chocolate. So, if you have not been able to beat 'em, then join 'em. A home flour mill makes it possible to add healthful wholemeal to sweet treats. But because wholemeal, with its added bran and germ, is a more complex product than white flour, it performs better in some baked goods than others. Fortunately, the products that most readily accept wholemeal are those that already include other high-fiber, high-nutrient ingredients. Excellent results can be expected when wholemeal is used in carrot cake, banana bread, gingerbread, brownies, zucchini bread, or oatmeal and peanut butter cookies. Whereas desserts made with white flour taste like the other ingredients—sugar, chocolate, nuts or vanilla—wholemeal makes a significant flavor contribution on its own. Because of this delightful added flavor, it is often possible to cut back on some sugar or fat that may be substituting for the flavor missing from white flour.

MORE THINGS TO MILL

One of the great benefits of owning a home mill is the ability to grind a wide range of items that may be overprocessed or difficult to locate if purchased commercially. Some of these items may be sold in quantities large enough to warrant their presence in a health food store or mail-order catalog but not in quantities large enough to guarantee freshness. Let's look at some ways a home mill can improve nutrition and expand your intake of other natural foods.

Rye, Corn and More

Milling at home is virtually the only way to get fresh, fragrant, unbolted corn or rye meal. This is true because the lavish oils in the germ of corn and rye are unstable when liberated from their protective layers of bran. They tend to become rancid with very little provocation so they are highly unreliable shelf items. Although you may at first plan to grind nothing but flour for bread, chances are good that all but the most time-strapped home millers will eventually wander into the sweet, fragrant world of fresh, whole cornmeal. Similarly, bakers of hearty hearth loaves will discover that home milling provides the only reliable source of fresh rye for their special loaves. And a mill that handles very oily *and* very small items can provide fresh, non-rancid flax seed meal to add to bread or sprinkle on foods.

You will learn more later about corn, rye, oats, seeds and other items that can be ground in a home mill. For the moment, be aware that buying a grain mill opens the door to a vastly expanded universe of health and flavor.

Flaked Oats, Seeds and Nuts

Some may be surprised that delectably fresh oats can be rolled at home. In fact, a burgeoning market has developed for home rollers or flakers. These inexpensive machines, often available as attachments to mills or other appliances, roll or crush oat groats and small, soft grains and seeds into flakes. (See appendix for buying sources.) Recipes are plentiful for oats, a familiar and well-liked food, which is a significant source of the soluble fiber beta-glucan, which reduces risks for heart disease and cancer. Unlike commercial rolled oats, the home-made version is inexpensive, fresh, and full of the grain's original nutrients because it is lightly processed, without water or heat, and used immediately.

Nuts and Nut Butters

All grain mills grind free-flowing dry grains like wheat, rice and barley. But some mills are designed to make nut "butters" out of almonds, acorns, chestnuts, peanuts or, in a few cases, seeds like sesame. Although making nut butters is a messy job, the payoff can be significant in terms of both health and flavor, particularly for a large, active family that uses a lot of peanut butter. Homemade peanut (or other nut) butter is far more healthful than most commercial varieties, which contain added salt, sugar or hydrogenated oils. Even "fresh" peanut butter from health food stores is often made from old nuts, thus carrying a high risk of rancidity. (If children resist the switch to unadulterated peanut butter, adding a small amount of honey can help in the transition.)

Beans

Beans offer a rich supply of minerals and vitamins, as well as soluble fiber, that are not readily available from other foods we commonly eat. Soybean, garbanzo and other bean flours can be added to dough to improve texture and, as a side benefit, improve the protein value of the bread. Many delicious foreign dishes call for bean flour or cracked beans or other legumes. Tempeh, a fermented soybean food, can be made at home from cracked beans, which is easier than soaking or cooking and removing hulls. We need to find more ways to work these neglected nutrient-rich foods into our diets.

Beer Mash

As micro breweries have exposed us to a wide variety of new beers, both home brewing and wheat beer have grown in popularity. And when an experienced brewer advances to making quality beer, he wants maximum control over the finished result. This means making mash at home. Wheat and barley, as well as the smaller quantities of specialty grains that give each beer its distinguishing characteristics, must be cracked before use in homemade mash. It won't take long for serious home brewers to recognize the importance of a home grain mill that can crack these grains or a roller mill that can flake them without producing much flour. Those with celiac disease can even brew gluten-free beers.

SURVIVAL AND SELF-SUFFICIENCY

On September 11, 2001, we came nose-to-nose with a threat many had been slow to believe even possible—mass murder by foreign enemies within our borders. The truth is, though, that many forces outside our control can wipe out individuals, households and entire communities. Hurricanes, tornadoes, floods, earthquakes, blizzards, landslides, fires, droughts, even volcanic eruption—we have seen them all in recent decades. More and more of us have decided to squirrel away some emergency rations. Although most of us will probably hoard no more than a few cans of tuna and a handful of protein bars, it is mesmerizing to watch TV clips of cellars jammed with boxes of cereal, bags of rice, flour and beans, bottles of water, jugs of cooking oil, and a long list of essentials like salt, canned meats and sugar.

But it's a shock to realize how much money is being spent on storable foods that are loaded with calories. Military-type packaged meals ("Meals Ready to Eat" or MREs), for example, which cost $6 to $10 each, are designed as short-term energy-boosters for young, healthy servicemen. Because of their heavy reliance on fat and refined carbohydrates, they may prove problematic for longer term nutritional needs. This money, as well as the enormous amounts going for freeze-dried packaged foods, could buy a lot more nutrition if some of it went for a non-electric (or convertible) grain mill and a couple of bags or more of wheat.

Being concerned about self-sufficiency doesn't mean you are paranoid. It is entirely reasonable to anticipate that you may at some time find yourself without food for a week or longer. Tuna-noodle casserole would suffice for awhile. But wouldn't it be nice to bake fresh bread, cookies, cakes, cornbread and other delicious whole grain foods? Yes, but this does present a couple of logistical problems. Since disasters are rarely announced before hand, packaged flour would need to be replaced regularly in order to make sure that it was fresh at the moment an emergency struck. And if food were scarce for a prolonged time, the nutrients that are lost in the processing of white flour could become significantly more important than during times of plenty. By contrast, if whole grains are protected from excessive heat and humidity, they can survive for years and still be ground into fresh, fragrant, fully nutritious flour as needed.

A flour mill, a bag of wheat and some powdered milk can provide a huge insurance policy at a relatively small price for anyone. So, to be prepared for the worst, consider making your grain mill manual or "convertible," (which means that it can be powered by either kilowatts or muscles). When times are good, the mill provides healthful whole-grain foods. If times get tough, it *still* provides healthful whole-grain foods to be baked in a Boy Scout or solar oven. (See inset on next page.) And if something happened to the mill, the wheat could still be sprouted for a nice serving of fresh greens, or soaked or boiled or planted, if the whole thing did crumble. If, on the other hand, all these fears proved silly, you could will the mill and wheat to your children.

BAKING WITHOUT POWER

People who want total self-sufficiency must be prepared to bake the bread they make from home-milled flour, without power if necessary. The Boy Scouts make a handy oven out of a cardboard box. Here is how to do it:

- Take a tall cardboard box with a four-flap lid. Cut the bottom flaps off the box. Line the box with long sheets of heavy aluminum foil. Gluing the aluminum to the cardboard simplifies things, but you can let the ends hang over the top flaps.

- Take four or five long, straight pieces of wire (about the diameter of a coat hanger) and poke them through opposite sides of the box about halfway up. Insert the wires through one side and out the other to make a shelf for the bread. (Make sure there's enough clearance so the top flaps of the box don't rest on top of the loaf when closed).

- Poke more holes through all sides of the box (and aluminum foil) for ventilation.

- Fill a metal or aluminum pan with approximately 18 hot charcoal briquets (or coals from a wood fire).

- Set the pan of coals on the ground where the heat will not damage anything and set the box over the pan of coals.

- Protecting your hands from the heat, place the bread on the shelf.

- Loosely close the top flaps of the box and cook the bread for 10 minutes.

- Lift the box flaps enough to peek at the bread to make sure it isn't burning. If it is, lift the box away, quickly remove a few coals, then replace the box. If burning continues, next time use a larger box, or fewer coals, or place the shelf a little higher.)

- Bake bread until browned and tapping on the bottom produces a hollow sound.

Solar cookers provide another baking option for those in sunny areas. A Global Sun Oven® or compact solar cooker are available from Kansas Wind Power (13569 214th Rd., Holton, Kansas, 66436-8138, (785) 364-4407, *http://www.kansaswindpower.net*). Or try *Cooking with Sun* by Beth Halacy (Morning Sun Press, 1992) or other books for instructions on making your own.

GLUTEN ALLERGIES

Some individuals are sensitive to certain breadmaking proteins in gluten. This sensitivity, which damages the small intestine, is called *celiac disease*. Wheat, rye and barley (and the man-made wheat/rye cross called triticale) are known offenders. Degree of sensitivity varies by individual, and spelt and Kamut have also proven toxic to many. Early on, oats also appeared harmful, but recent studies have called this into question. Oats are problematic, however, because they can be contaminated with small amounts of wheat. Fortunately, a cursory inspection of oats by home millers would quickly reveal the presence of wheat, which is identifiably different in appearance. Of course, any grain should be used in small quantities at first to test for gluten sensitivity.

Fortunately, bread is not the only delicious grain-based food to be enjoyed by celiac sufferers who mill at home. For example, literally hundreds of wonderful recipes are readily available for cornmeal. Even more have fallen out of general use but can be reclaimed from old cookbooks in libraries or used bookstores. Low or non-gluten grains like cassava (tapioca), quinoa, buckwheat, millet, and rice can be milled for use in ethnic dishes. Rice and beans are gluten-free foods that can add nutrition and variety to an otherwise boring diet. For example, falafel, a Middle Eastern dish made from garbanzo bean flour, is a wonderfully healthful and delicious food. And since flour from less popular whole grains risks degradation while waiting in barrels or on store shelves for the occasional buyer, gluten sufferers can benefit greatly from the ability to produce small, fresh, non-rancid portions of exotic grains at will.

TRAVELING WITH A MILL

If you are one of the exploding number of people traveling or living in a recreational vehicle (RV) you need not be excluded from the benefits of freshly milled whole grains. Despite space and power limitations, most RV owners can grind flour and make bread, cornmeal, falafels and other wonderful foods on the road. Here's how.

RVers who frequently "boondock," or stay in places without water and power connections, need to buy a hand-operated mill or come up with an electrical (AC) power source. A generator provides AC power but boondockers who rely exclusively on batteries (DC power) may need to install a solar or wind system and an inverter to get AC power for an electric mill.

Once AC power is available, space becomes the limiting factor. Fortunately, compact, light-weight manual and electric mills are available. A bread machine, if desired, can be carried easily in a large RV, although lifting may be necessary if it is stored in an inconvenient place. People in smaller rigs may have to make bread the old-fashioned way, but hands-on time can be reduced. A "sponge" process, wherein part of the flour and water in a recipe are left to develop overnight, actually improves flavor and texture.

Kneading, rising and proofing can all be done in the same large plastic bowl, which must then be washed only once. For rising, the covered bowl can be placed in the sun, with a blanket wrapped around it to prevent cooling by wind. When the sun is hiding, the plastic bowl can be placed in the oven with the pilot light on. The limited baking height of most RV ovens makes hearth loaves or rolls easier to manage than standard-sized loaves. Two round disposable aluminum pans fit into most ovens and can be re-used, or thrown away, if washing water is limited. (A Boy Scout oven can also mesh well with the RV lifestyle, as it takes little storage space and can be used like a barbecue in RV parks, National Parks or anywhere that open fires are not permitted.)

Wheat poses a space problem in an RV, but not an insurmountable one. No more wheat should be carried than will be needed on the trip. Multiply the number of baking days by 450 grams (or one pound), which is the amount of wheat in one loaf of bread. Pack the wheat in several easy-to-handle plastic containers with grips or handles. Do not carry grain in a large bag unless it is inside the RV, as it is too unwieldy to handle, may disrupt the weight balance of the RV and may be exposed to moisture, dust and mice. Even worse, it may spill if the bag tears. Store wheat containers near the center, above the axles, or distributed evenly on both sides of the RV. Carry at least one container in an easily accessible place.

CULINARY ZEALOTS

Perhaps culinary zealots are the most interesting people who choose to mill their own flour. Some nursemaid rich, dark loaves of rye or wheat through a long (sometimes *several-day*) breadmaking process. Certainly such a loving commitment of time merits the highest quality ingredients available. These and other devoted cooks may begin milling flour at home because they understand that high-fat flours like rye must be ground and used immediately. But this innocent start, with a good and probably very expensive mill, a small bag of rye and a bigger bag of wheat, is just that, a beginning. Soon, the new miller will buy a little soft wheat for cakes, more rye for sourdough, some corn for polenta, a bag of millet for that African dish, yellow split peas to crack for Indian vadi... Eventually, friends start commenting on the wall of shelves with quart-sized canning jars filled with colorful and exotic grains. Then barbecue parties get canceled because the patio is cluttered with bricks and mortar for the hearth oven, and the beer in the refrigerator is replaced by glass jugs of sourdough starter and the car has to go out on the driveway so the garage can be walled off for the rows of garbage cans filled with grain, and the giant stone mill, and a bench for the hand grinder, just in case the power goes...and...well, one day the zealot will shake his head and with a furrow ask, *"Why didn't I see how white flour was holding me back?"*

A FINAL WORD

To sum it up, most people will buy a mill and grind at home for one simple reason—it is a quick, easy way to get nutrition and flavor back into their daily diets. But most home millers who start with this simple intention usually end up milling other things as well. For this reason, it is important to be aware of the full range of home milling possibilities before actually purchasing a mill. It is also important to understand that each mill offers a combination of features and that some mills do more than others. But before we get to the meat of this book—everything you could possibly want to know about flour mills— let's take a look at how much time and money one can expect to spend setting up a home milling operation.

CHAPTER 6

Finding Time to Grind

The Misconception:
It takes too much time to mill flour at home.

The Truth:
Milling time is insignificant.
(But it took the bread machine
to make home milling practical
for the average working American.)

By the turn of the nineteenth century, flour milling had already slipped out the back door of most American homes, with lots of dust and little regret. Meanwhile commercial white flour was receiving a thunderous welcome at the front door from homemakers eager to cut their burden to washing, mopping, chopping, sweeping, hoeing, sewing, canning, baking and cooking three big meals a day from scratch. But that was then. It is now the twenty-first century. We have an army of labor-saving machines. And a home flour mill is the most practical and beneficial of them all.

So why can't we pick through the coffee grinders, pasta makers, toasters, can openers, bread machines and food processors on any kitchen counter in this country and find a flour mill? H-m-m-m... Of course, very few people have even heard of home milling. And when they do, it strikes them as a quaint, interesting, or mildly ludicrous idea. The real resistance, though, is lodged in a suspicion by time-conscious Americans that flour milling is a nineteenth century time hog resuscitated by *food faddists* with unrealistic schemes to get them back to some imaginary roots. "*Get real...*" is their response. "*I don't have time for new jobs...*"

How Much Time, Really?

Home milling is a minor job. Really. It is totally practical and entirely feasible for even the time-desperate to take on. Yes, it takes a little time to set up the operation. But not much. And actual milling time is inconsequential with an electric mill. Even the breadmaking process can be a long, soul-warming experience for those with time, or five minutes of throwing ingredients in a bucket while the flour is milling for those without time. But all home millers will find that time invested in selecting the ideal equipment and ingredients will be returned many times over.

Set-up Time

People who anticipate doing little more than milling small amounts of flour for bread can buy virtually any mill that does not destroy the flour with heat or excessive grinding. Basic needs can be met nicely by an inexpensive electric metal burr or impact-type mill. Be aware, however, that most of these simple mills do not provide the full range of possibilities described in the preceding chapter. People who want to grind particularly large or small or oily items like beans, corn, peanuts, or seeds, or to be independent of electricity, need to spend time in the other chapters of this book.

The *Quick-Pick Option* in this chapter provides the truly harried (and those who hate research) with a simple way to eat delicious, nutritious, wholemeal bread before they have read every line of this book. This *Quick-Pick Option* can also help eager converts set up a relatively inexpensive operation to get them by while they conduct in-depth research. By taking time to explore all mill possibilities, write manufacturers for brochures, study a good wholemeal bread book, and save up money, they can be absolutely certain they are buying the perfect mill for their lifestyle.

Milling Time

Once a home-milling operation has been set up, milling time is usually insignificant—about three minutes per loaf with most electric mills—although time will vary with the machine chosen. A small hand-operated mill may take 15 minutes per loaf or more, while a large hand-operated mill may produce flour for two loaves in 15 minutes.

Very fast electric mills take no more than three minutes per loaf. Here are some ways to shorten the job even more.

Keep wheat accessible. If wheat must be stored away from the mill or in difficult-to-reach areas, save time by keeping smaller quantities near the flour mill for quick access.

Mill weekly. If you make bread *and* pancakes, mix flours, or just need to shave minutes *everywhere*, you can mill larger quantities at one time. But do not exceed the manufacturer's recommendations for your mill. Store meal in airtight containers in a cool place. If not used within a couple of weeks, refrigerate or freeze them, then bring them to room temperature before using.

Use a food scale. Weighing is infinitely faster than measuring. Digital scales that measure in grams are best. Increments should be no greater than five grams.

Prepare food packets. Weigh (or measure) meal in one-loaf quantities then put into resealable plastic bags. Add other dry ingredients, except yeast. At breadmaking time, only liquid ingredients and yeast need to be assembled. Store as above. (Advance preparation makes pancakes a feasible breakfast, too.)

Breadmaking Time

The advent of the bread machine is of more historical significance to home milling than flour mills themselves because it reduces breadmaking to the simple task of dumping ingredients in a pan and

AN ARGUMENT FOR THE BREAD MACHINE?

In 1913 doctors hired by the Factory Investigation Commission in New York City crept around low-rent cellars in where nearly 2,400 bakeries were squirreled away. Of the 800 bakers examined, 32 percent had TB, rheumatism, anemia or venereal disease, 26 percent had chronic catarrh (inflammation of nose and throat causing excess mucus— and drippy noses?), 12 percent had optical diseases, and seven percent had eczema.

Hence, an early slogan of the commercial baking industry: *"Untouched by Human Hands."*

QUICK-PICK OPTION:
For People with No Time

- Look at Appendix A, which lists grain mills by type and price range. Select and order an electric impact-type or small electric burr mill (in your price range) or an attachment to an appliance you already own.

- If you are going to use a bread machine, buy one with a delay timer and one that makes 100 percent whole-wheat bread if possible, although any will work.

- Buy a large measuring cup with metric delineations (at least 350 ml) and a digital food scale that holds at least 3.5 cups (450 grams).

- Buy some wheat:

  Visit a local co-op or health food store that carries bulk foods. If they have or can order hard red spring wheat with 15 percent protein content or better, try five or ten pounds of it. If you get good results within three tries, buy more.

  If you can find nothing locally, call one of the high-protein wheat sources in Appendix B and order five to 50 pounds of hard red spring wheat. (Reaffirm the 15 percent protein content, as it varies from year to year. If protein is lower than 15 percent, order just five or 10 pounds to make sure it performs well.) Store wheat in plastic containers or resealable plastic bags, safe from moisture, heat, light, bugs and rodents.

- Buy a large bag of *non-instant* powdered milk and a small bag of regular or defatted soy flour, or any other bean flour, and refrigerate or freeze it. (If your mill accommodates beans, just buy whole garbanzo, soy or other beans.) Also, buy a bottle of ascorbic acid crystals from your pharmacist or health-food store.

- Follow the Basic Wholemeal Bread recipe in the breadmaking section of this book using all hard red spring wheat.

punching buttons. It is a technological miracle for the time-starved bread lover or *anyone* else who wants high-fiber carbohydrates back in their diet. The number of people in this condition is hinted at by industry estimates of well over ten million bread machines in U.S. households, with the curve sloping up and most prices drastically down. It is true that some early machines had problems. Instructions were garbled or misleading. Some machines did not handle whole-wheat bread well. Now, however, many large appliance manufacturers sell at least one model and their performance, even with whole wheat, is remarkable. Fortunately, many bread machines can be retrieved from closets where devastated bakers stuffed them after discovering that loaves made from modern white flour *still* tasted like cardboard.

But can these machines make good-tasting bread from home-ground wholemeal? The definitive answer is, *Yes!* Almost any bread machine will make fine wholemeal bread as long as the recipe is simple and high-protein wheat has been used—and it will taste great! But mixing, kneading, and rising times, as well as temperatures, are set in stone on most machines. So breads with ingredients that require special handling may not fare so well. There is no need to babysit a bread machine, but it won't call 911 if there is a problem, either.*

What about people who do not want a bread machine? Fine. After all, *a bread machine is not a necessity for home millers; it is a timesaving kitchen assistant.* Obviously, when time is not a make-or-break concern, home-milled flour can be used in a spectacular variety of delicious and tasty products that need shepherding by a concerned human. But even lucky people without time concerns can find uses for a bread machine. For example, a machine can keep kneading dough all day, leaving the cook free to turn glob after glob of fragrant dough into hearth loaves, cinnamon twists, pita bread, pizza crust, etc., etc., etc. And even the most discerning *gastronome* may find it convenient to let the bread machine oversee the baking while he makes a last-minute dash across town for lemon grass or fennel.

---

*My experience is that uncomplicated wholemeal breads containing high-protein wheat work well in any machine that I have tried—Welbilt, an old Sunbeam, Zojirushi, Breadman and Panasonic. In this matter, however, I defer to the *real* cook, Laurel Robertson, whose revised edition of *Laurel's Kitchen Bread Book* (Random house, NY, 2003) includes a new chapter on baking with bread machines that will be vital for those working with more complicated ingredients.

In any case, because this timesaving automaton is what makes home milling and baking feasible for so many people, here are a few guidelines for purchase and use:

- If at all possible, buy a machine advertised for *100 percent whole-wheat bread*, not just *whole wheat*, because a lesser motor may face a shortened life span under the added burden of kneading wholemeal dough (particularly if the dough contains too little water too many times).

- It is very helpful to have a window of some sort to check progress.

- A delay timer is almost indispensable for someone who works.

- Some machines allow the operator to adjust or create bread programs. This flexibility can turn failure to success when different ingredients assert themselves on the end product.

- Follow the manufacturer's instructions to the letter—he knows what works for his machine.

- Room temperature can affect the bread machine. If loaf results are inconsistent despite using the same recipe, temperature may be the culprit. On very hot days, less yeast may be needed. When nights are cool, breads made with the delay timer may need a little extra yeast.

- A bread machine can be a valuable teacher. Borrow a friend's and feel the dough after kneading. This will help you recognize properly developed dough.

- One compromise, for those with time, is to let the bread machine do the hard part (kneading), then manage the rising, shaping and baking yourself.

- Always test a simple recipe with wheat that contains 15 percent protein to determine if your machine can make a decent loaf of bread.

HOW MUCH MONEY?

The up-front costs of buying a flour mill, some wheat and other ingredients, and a bread machine (if desired) can be as reasonable or unreasonable as the pocketbook can tolerate. There is tremendous variation in price for both flour mills and bread machines. Lower prices often reflect compromises in quality, so an inexpensive machine may be fine in the short term but not last as long as one with a higher price tag. Very, very high prices may go with higher quality and special features, but may also reflect import duties or currency exchange losses for machines manufactured abroad. Make sure you cannot get the same features and quality for less money from a machine made in America (even if it isn't *all* made in America.) And always remember, a mill that destroys flour with heat or excessive grinding is not a good deal at any price.

Here are price ranges for various items necessary to start your home milling (and baking) operation. A flour mill can cost between $50 and $1,000 but a fast, simple one will probably be around $200. A bread machine can cost from $80 to $300, depending on quality and features. Any machine capable of making a high loaf of white bread will work with wholemeal in the short run, but the least expensive ones will wear out quickly under the added strain of kneading wholemeal.

Wheat prices can range from $12 to $25 per 50-pound bag. The price that farmers receive for field wheat varies from year to year, but has usually stayed below $5 per bushel (60 pounds). It does not hurt to check the current price of field wheat in the commodities section of the newspaper to see how it compares with prices historically.

The farther wheat gets from the farmer, the more it costs, but for many years it has been possible to buy wheat from health food stores or granaries for about double the farm price. Transportation costs are added to this price. Unless farm prices or shipping costs shoot upward, a ballpark cost (including shipping) for 50 pounds of good bread wheat should be about $25 or less, unless you are forced to ship long distances. Wheat is cheaper if purchased from a health food store, co-op, or a grain outlet near the source, which means that if you are near a growing area, even a four-hour drive *might* be worthwhile. Incidentally, buying wheat in small quantities can increase the total cost per bushel, particularly if shipping costs are tacked on.

Dough conditioners mitigate some negative effects that bran and germ have on bread. Inexpensive conditioners include egg, milk, ascorbic acid, beans or bean flour and potatoes or potato water. Commercial dough conditioners (described fully in the chapter on bread making) may be more convenient than the common household items listed above, but they are also quite expensive. One commercially produced dough conditioner that is very convenient and somewhat less expensive than the others is *non-instant* powdered milk, a form usually available only from health food stores.

 ## Summary

There is a lot of talk in this country about malnutrition, particularly in children. Malnutrition has two causes: insufficient food or improper diet. No American child is malnourished because of shortages in the grocery store, which is the case in other parts of the world. Rich and poor children alike, however, may be malnourished from an improper diet. For example, although children should eat five servings of fruits and vegetables daily, on average they eat one serving of fruit and 30 percent less than one serving of vegetables. This partial serving of vegetables is often greasy French fries. An even worse case can be made regarding whole grains.

The least expensive foods are largely unprocessed and brimming with nutrients: whole grains, milk, dry beans, potatoes, bulk oatmeal, fruits and vegetables *in season*, even meats in bulk or on sale. The most expensive foods are usually overprocessed and have many calories and a spotty supply of nutrients. Examples are potato chips, canned soup, frozen pizza, TV dinners, hot dogs, ice cream and boxed cereals. One large box of overpriced, sugar-coated, highly advertised cereal costs more than six loaves of home-made wholemeal bread while offering a fraction of the nutrients. This is just one example of real food costs. The cumulative dollar amount of these high-cost, high-calorie processed foods is astounding. In fact, the money we squander daily on expensive fast foods could quickly add up to the cost of the most expensive bread machine and grinder.

Today, a person's willingness to do the nutritionally right thing depends very much on that thing being quick and easy. In a world of preprocessed, prepackaged, practically predigested products that rely heavily on fat, sugar and salt, it is difficult to *Just say no!* But anyone can get most of their grain servings from whole grains each and every day and the mildly determined can do better than that. When the bread machine made breadmaking quick and easy, a grain mill became the tiniest added burden for a gargantuan improvement in diet. You have the time. You have the money. Only *you* can decide to spend them on home milling.

CHAPTER 7

Choosing the Right Mill

A Tool for All Reasons

Mills are frills, electric witches
grind the grain for chubby wenches
while perky, querky, lustrous girls
drop sweet sweat o'er hand-worked mills.

Noisy, dusty, grinding stuff
fiber fix for men so tough
brawn and brain embrace the rule
mills are frills but tools are cool.

Millions of people worldwide still depend on primitive milling devices for their daily flour—from two stones rubbed or pounded together to large community mills powered by water, animals, diesel and humans themselves. These mills flourished in low-technology countries out of need, primarily in rural areas with no electricity and no roads for daily bread trucks.*

By contrast, household flour mills survived in the United States and other high-technology countries because small groups of people persisted in their belief that home-ground wholemeal was superior in nutrition and flavor to commercial flour. Another important reason why

---

*Low-technology community mills are manufactured in Europe, Africa and India. The United Nations Food and Agriculture Organization (FAO) in Rome publishes some information on these mills.

home milling machines did not disappear was the desire by many to have a source of nutritious food in the event of an emergency.

If you are new to the idea of home flour grinding, you will probably be surprised at the large collection of flour mills available for purchase. Many household mills are manufactured in the United States, but high-quality mills are also being imported from Germany, Denmark, France, and Italy.

Buying a mill is a lot like buying a new puppy: so many to choose from but oh, what fun! And what a nightmare if it barks all night, bites the kids or makes messes. To do this right, you must begin to visualize a flour mill in your home. How big can it be? Can you tolerate a little noise? A little mess? Will you grind a loaf's worth of flour or a week's worth in one stretch? Do you want to make peanut butter, or just grind flour? Do you want to crack grain to make mash for your home brewing operation, or just grind flour? The following pages will raise many such questions in your mind, and introduce potential pitfalls in the purchase of a home flour mill. As you read, remember that you may have to compromise by accepting some problem areas in order to get a mill in your price range that will do the things you want it to do. Remember also that a very useful feature on a flour mill will not be useful to *you* if you haven't the time or inclination to use it.

Without this book, tracking down and buying a home flour mill can be complex and confusing. Why? Because most are not yet available at local stores and because no single milling machine is perfect for all purposes. But if there *were* an ideal grain mill, here are the features it would have.

- It would have a milling mechanism that never wore out.

- It would not heat the flour excessively.

- It would be convertible—manual *and* electric.

- It would come apart easily for repair, cleaning or parts replacement.

- It would have a grinding range from powder to chunks.

- It would grind dry or oily things.

- It would have a large hopper.

- It would have a feeder that could handle anything from seeds to corn

- It would have a large, convenient flour catcher.

- It would not spew flour dust.

- It would be easy to clean.

- It would be very quiet with little vibration.

- It would be small and lightweight yet durable.

- It would be attractive.

- It would be reasonably priced.

And to make it *really* convenient, this mill would be available in a nearby store for examination and testing before purchase.

Unfortunately, at the time of writing, no single mill has all of these features. And most mills must still be ordered by phone, mail or on the Internet. This should not discourage you. When you have finished this book, you will be better qualified to compare and evaluate grain mills than most clerks who sell them in stores.

Now, let's get into the soul of this book—basic technical information as well as hints from my personal experience to help you decide which is the best mill for your individual circumstances. We will start with an introduction to the most common milling mechanisms used in home flour mills, with summaries of their advantages and disadvantages. Then, because it is such an important—and misunderstood—issue, we will again take up the issue of heat damage to flour during milling. We will also look at power options, from electric to manual to convertible, and at choosing a machine that offers maximum versatility. Then, after considering convenience features that make a mill easier to use or integrate into your lifestyle, we will peek at community mills and, finally, get a road map for tracking down an ideal mill for your purposes. At the end of the chapter you will find a comprehensive form that can be helpful in evaluating *any* machine you encounter. So, let's get started with this important information.

STONE-GROUND THEORY

Stone-ground flour advocates will fight before they switch. But the scientific literature is virtually silent on technical factors that might support this dogged preference, which is not to say that none exists. But here is a theory.

By the time roller mills replaced stone mills, millers were already highly accomplished at sifting the nutritious parts out of their flour. But when the nutrition losses in white flour became an issue again in the 1960s and 1970s, few people still knew that millers using huge stone mills had produced a less-than-healthful product by bolting out as much bran and germ as they could. Conceivably, modern stone milling advocates were familiar only with existing stone mills, which had survived by producing unbolted flour as an alternative to roller milled flour. Thus, it is possible that "stone-milled flour" simply became synonymous with unbolted meal, and is viewed as more healthful for that reason.

On the other hand, two reasons why large, solid (rather than composite) stones may be superior to other burrs is that they heat up more slowly and that they crush grains rather than breaking them. Crushing may have advantages that we are no longer aware of. Unfortunately, only a few modern manufacturers offer solid stone burrs and the prices are understandably high for these exceptional pieces of equipment.

COMMON MILLING MECHANISMS

Each grain mill has some mechanism for crushing or beating or grinding grain into a meal. In most cases, some provision has been made to create a range of textures, from coarse to fine. Some mechanisms are more versatile than others: they grind hard, soft, oily or wet items. All home-sized mills produce a single meal containing all the bran, all the germ, and all the endosperm, as compared to the sifted or bolted flour produced by roller mill factories. Most home grain mills use one of four basic milling mechanisms: solid stone burrs, composite stone burrs, metal burrs, or metal impact "teeth" (or pins). Included in this review for information are two additional mechanisms—small roller mills that flake oats and seeds or crack grains for mash in home brewing, and hammer mills, which can damage flour and are, therefore, rarely used to mill grains for human consumption.

Solid Stone Burrs

Man has crushed grains between stones for at least 25,000 years. But mechanical *mills* began to replace rocks as soon as the wheel was invented. Since then, all stone mills have employed two circular surfaces of identical size. One stone (or *burr*) is fixed, while the other rotates on a drive shaft connected to a power source. Vertical placement is more common now than horizontal. Grain drops from a hopper through a feed valve at the center of the stones. As the stone turns, grain is *sheared* and crushed as it works its way from the center to the outer edges (as opposed to the breaking action of roller mills). Grooves in the stones help move the grain along. The depth of the grooves decreases gradually from the center outward, allowing for gradual reduction of grain into smaller and smaller fragments. The gap between the stones can be adjusted to produce different textures. The best solid stones (which are now rare) came from France until that supply was exhausted, then from Greece. Two American companies currently make stone mills using native American granite. An Internet website in the Ukraine sells large wooden mills with solid natural stones (described as "Sexten primary rock") mined from cliffs in the south Tirol area of Austria. (See "Community Mills" in the Appendix for more information.)

Composite Stone Burrs

Most "stone" flour mills today actually use manufactured burrs, constructed by pressing natural or artificial stones in a bed of cement. While smaller, these mills generally have a design similar to that just described for solid stone mills. Many (but not all) of these composite stone burrs are mass-produced in Asia. Most are made from one of the following.

Artificial stone. These stone burrs have surfaces with composites of abrasive materials (such as corundum, emery or a mixture of materials) in a matrix of magnesium oxychloride cement or other material. They may be heat-treated or vitrified to increase durability (which may be reflected in the price). Some have razor-sharp stainless steel (or other metal) cutting edges imbedded in the other materials to cut the grain and reduce wear. Most composite stones do not require cleaning or sharpening, and do not get out of alignment.

Natural stone. These composite stone burrs consist of small pieces of natural stone imbedded in cement or other suitable material. Emery, metal cutting edges or other materials may also be combined with the natural stone.

Arguments For and Against Stone Grinding

Solid stone burrs. Possibly the greatest advantage to using solid stone burrs is that when properly adjusted and driven at slow speeds, they can produce large amounts of flour before heat builds up to unacceptable levels. Some machines require dressing (or sharpening) to keep them functioning properly. Solid stones are softer and require more sharpening and cleaning than newer composite materials.

Composite stone burrs. These modern burrs are hard, durable and require little maintenance. They can produce a finely ground, uniform flour. The gap between the stones of most mills can be adjusted for a range of fine to coarse meals. Burr diameter may vary from one mill to another, and very small burrs grind less flour per minute than larger ones. Although solid stone burrs take a long time to heat up, this is not true for composite stone burrs, particularly in machines that are driven at high speeds without a cooling mechanism and those with imbedded metal.

Very fine (and expensive) mills are available for stone milling advocates. But detractors (some of whom sell competing products) lodge various complaints against solid and composite stones. How much credence should be given to these arguments must be determined by the individual, in view of the fact that man has successfully used stones since he put his first fistful of grain between two rocks. Here, so you can ask questions of stone mill manufacturers, is what detractors claim is wrong with stone milling:

- You *eat* the stone too. As stones wear, tiny pebbles end up in the flour, which could damage teeth.

- Solid stones are heavy, get out of alignment easily, and few experts remain to repair them.

- Dressing of solid stones (sharpening the grooves) requires time and a high skill level. Improperly maintained stones can cause friction, which generates heat that can damage flour, or damage starch excessively, which affects the water-absorbing capacity of flour and reduces loaf size.

- Solid or composite stones require cleaning and may gum up when milling oily items like corn, rye and soft wheat. Stones may not be able to grind soybeans, hard popcorn, beans or legumes, either.

- Bacteria can grow on solid or composite stones that are not cleaned regularly.

- Excessive heat can build up with high speeds or prolonged grinding (particularly with composite stone burrs).

Metal Burrs

Metal burrs (also called *plates*) are used in a wide range of mills, from very small to large. These mills have two grinding burrs of hardened cast steel or other metal, one fixed and the other rotated by a power source. Most of these burrs are flat, but several have a nested-cone shape. The grain is fed by auger or dropped directly from a hopper into the gap between the burrs, which are grooved to aid the shearing and crushing of the grain. The gap between the burrs can be adjusted to vary fineness of grind. The diameter of the burrs varies from one machine to the next. Like composite stone burrs, many metal burrs are mass-produced in Asia.

Arguments For and Against Metal Burrs

Because steel tends to be sanitary, durable and maintenance-free, there are few complaints about the newer metal burrs themselves. Most metal burrs can grind anything: dry grains, beans, corn, soybeans, and sometimes nut butters. Most produce a full range of textures from cracked to very fine. Some mills, however, require changing burrs to achieve different textures of meal or changing augers before larger items like beans or corn can be fed smoothly into the grinding mechanism. Some manufacturers offer a choice of stone or metal burrs for the same mill. When metal burrs are washed after grinding wet or oily things (such as peanut butter), they must be dried completely before reassembly to prevent rusting. One vital exception to the problem-free reputation of metal burrs is that milling friction creates heat that can build up with high speeds or lengthy milling time. This can be a significant problem with some electric burr mills.

Impact Mills

This newest innovation in milling technology employs two stainless steel heads with concentric rows of "teeth" that spin within each other at high speeds. Grains drop in and hit the whirling teeth (repeatedly) to produce a very fine, uniform meal that is then expelled from the milling chamber. This mechanism was developed for the pharmaceuticals industry then adapted to grain milling.

Arguments For and Against Impact Mills

Impact mills do a fast, efficient, neat job of milling flour with somewhat less friction than burr mills. They are small, easy to clean, moderately priced and easy to locate. Variations in price reflect added features such as extra insulation for quietness or a flour cannister that minimizes airborne flour dust.

These mills are widely available and will be the first choice for many people who are looking for a quick, easy, relatively inexpensive way to mill flour. Drawbacks are that despite machine settings to vary the fineness of the meal, little difference in grades is apparent. Impact mills cannot grind oily items like peanuts. They cannot be converted to hand power, so they cannot be used without electricity. Manufacturers claim low milling temperatures but beware of heat build-up when milling more than household quantities.

Roller Mills

Commercial roller mills (more fully described in Chapter 1) consist of two large rollers that, when properly adjusted, can break, rather than crush, grains without producing much flour. Although the roller mill mechanism is rarely encountered in smaller flour mills, there are exceptions. One firm in India manufactures a reduced-size roller mill for community use. Smaller roller mills, both hand and motorized, are designed to properly crack wheat or barley to make mash for beer. These functional machines may have two or more textured stainless steel rollers with fixed or adjustable gaps. They can be manual, drill driven, or electric. The goal is to discretely crack the grains while producing a minimum of flour, a task not achievable by most other appliances.

Oat Flakers

Roller technology is also used to turn oats and other small grains or seeds into flakes, which we can then digest. These machines, called *flakers* or *rollers*, employ two textured rollers made of steel or composite stone that may or may not be adjustable for flake thickness. Grains or other items are flattened as they pass between the rollers. These simple machines, which may be manual or electric, are growing in popularity and widely available. Many flaker add-ons are available for existing appliances or mills, and one expensive and beautiful imported mill incorporates a mechanism for grinding flour *and* one for rolling oats. Prices range from very low to fairly high. The manual ones are easy to operate and fun for kids. All offer a pretty reasonable way to roll fresh oats and other items that may include wheat, rye, rice, spelt, oily seeds, nuts and beans, but this varies by individual flaker. Although oats are soft and require no processing beyond rolling, harder grains and seeds must be soaked before or after flaking to enhance digestibility. (For more, see the section on oats in the chapter entitled *More Grist for Your Mill*.)

Hammer Mills

Hammer mills are high-output machines used to produce animal feed in African countries like Tanzania, Kenya and Malawi. In this country they are used primarily to reduce or pulverize products like chemicals, minerals, wood chips, livestock feed, herbs and spices, paints and varnishes, graphite, and many, many more. Hammer mill designs vary, but most have a steel disc or discs with from 1 to 32 hammer-like plates projecting outward. Grain is gravity-fed from a conical hopper at the top and then hammered around the milling chamber until small enough to pass through an exit screen. The size of the screen mesh may be changed to produce different grades of meal or flour. These machines usually have a device to blow the crushed material out and cool the machinery. The beating given grains by hammer mills can cause too much starch damage, making the flour absorb too much water and produce a wet, sticky dough. For this reason, hammer mills are rarely used in this country for flours intended for human consumption. They are described for information or for a chance encounter with a home mill employing this mechanism.

AVOIDING EXCESSIVE HEAT

Heat build-up is a very important factor to consider in selecting a grain mill because excessive heat can damage the breadmaking quality of gluten or push lipids in the germ toward rancidity. Some heat-sensitive vitamins may also be damaged and enzymes made inactive or destroyed at specific heat levels.

Heat is generated when grains are crushed between burrs or slammed around by metal pins. As milling time or speed increases, the amount of heat also increases. Unless this heat leaves the area voluntarily or is assisted away, the milling mechanism will heat up. Flour that touches the hot mechanism will also heat up. A slow machine may lose heat nearly as quickly as it is generated. A moderately fast machine can produce household quantities of flour before excessive heat builds up. Very fast machines, however, run the risk of generating very high temperatures very quickly unless some provision is made to conduct the heat away. Three components of grain are at particular risk regarding heat: gluten, lipids and nutrients.

Gluten Damage

The elements in wheat that contribute most significantly to breadmaking quality are the gluten-forming prolamins, *gliadin* and *glute-*

nin, generally referred to simply as gluten. In order to do its breadmaking job, gluten must retain the unique elastic qualities that allow gas retention during the fermentation period. Low milling heat generates changes in gluten that are deemed beneficial in this respect by commercial bakers. Excessive heat, however, can cause gluten to lose its elastic properties. The question is, *When does heat become excessive?*

One study of the commercial production and drying of "vital" gluten (using driers operating between 122 degrees and 167 degrees)* showed that the *baking performance of gluten declined progressively between 122 degrees and 158 degrees.* Virtually all functionality had been lost by 167 degrees. Further, a basic textbook on cereal processing states that "warm conditioning" of bread wheat (1 to 1½ hours at up to 115 degrees) is preferred over "hot conditioning" (115 degrees to 140 degrees for less time) *because there is less risk of damaging the baking quality of flour.* Ideally, then, milling temperatures should remain below the 115-degree mark at which baking quality *may* be at risk, although some may feel safe up to the 122-degree level at which damage to gluten has been documented.**

Lipid Damage

Another vulnerable wheat component that can affect flour quality is the volatile fats (lipids) that are abundant in the wheat germ. The moment a kernel of wheat is broken apart, the cells are rearranged and exposed to new elements and a very complex set of interactions begins to take place. Variables involved are the fats in the grain, heat, oxygen, water, enzymes, substrates, and time. Ultimately, these changes relate to the oxidation of fats, a process that leads to fat spoilage, or rancidity. Rancid oils are a health danger because, among other things, they destroy vitamin A in the body. Preventing rancidity was the primary reason that millers of white flour removed the germ from wheat and other grains as soon as it became technically feasible. Home millers must be cautious not to revive this health risk.

---

*"Thermal Modification of Gluten as Related to End-Use Properties," Autran, Ait-Moh, & Feillet, in *Wheat is Unique*, Y. Pomeranz, (American Assoc. of Cereal Chemists, St. Paul, MN, 1988)

**Technology of Cereals, 3d Ed., N.L. Kent (Pergamon Press, Oxford, 1994)

Although lipids begin degrading the moment they are released from the grain's protective shell, the process is very slow. The progression to rancidity can be accelerated, however, by factors such as oxygen, moisture and heat. There appears to be little risk of rancidity for home millers who mill household quantities at reasonable temperatures and consume their flour within a week or two of grinding. But for those who mill oily products like corn and rye but do not use them immediately, or who want to "age" their breadmaking flour, heat build-up should be a primary consideration when selecting a mill.

On a related topic, I have found no scientific evidence that mills with cooling mechanisms that expose flour to massive amounts of oxygen damage flour or lipids, probably because the oxidation process is so slow. Still, cautious home millers who want a cooling mechanism to reduce milling heat may choose to limit storage time for air-cooled flour.

Vitamin or Enzyme Damage

Although claims have been made that the vitamins in flour begin to deteriorate at 115 degrees, this is not easily verified. Most of the vitamins that occur in whole grains are relatively stable to heat in the short run, although other factors such as moisture and pH can exacerbate the effects of heat. In any case, people are usually not very concerned about heat damage to vitamins during milling, because they believe baking temperatures will destroy them anyway. This is not necessarily true. The heat-sensitive vitamin thiamin, for example, is partially protected by starch during baking, which keeps losses at 5 to 35 percent. Of possible additional concern, however, some enzymes become inactive or unstable above 122 degrees. Because much remains to be discovered about the effects of heat on other health-promoting components in food, such as phytochemicals and antioxidants, people very concerned with nutrition may wish to keep temperatures as low as possible, just in case.

In the past, home flour mill manufacturers selling fast machines found acceptable any heat short of the 140-degree mark at which gluten deterioration became obvious. Manufacturers of cooler-running hand mills considered the top temperature to be the 115-degree mark at which they thought vitamins deteriorated. In the end, the acceptable level of milling heat remains the choice of each individual home miller. The nutritionally fastidious may set a heat limit at 115 degrees, where heat-sensitive vitamins may begin to be destroyed and gluten might possibly be at risk. Others may set a limit at 122 degrees, the point at which enzymes begin to be rendered inactive and some deterioration of gluten has been observed. Some may be satisfied with any temperature short of the 140 degrees where bread quality losses are clearly apparent, since heat has no effect on fiber or minerals.

But once the maximum heat level has been set, how can one know whether or not a specific mill generates more heat than is desirable? The only absolutely reliable way to judge the temperature of flour produced by a given mill is to test it. Stick a candy thermometer in the flour during or immediately after milling and wait. Be sure to mill a sufficient quantity—a full hopper or six cups, if possible—to determine whether household amounts of flour can be milled before excessive heat builds up.

Frequently, though, no test will be possible. Then you must rely on information provided by brochures, manufacturers or sales people. Ask questions, but be aware that even well-intentioned, otherwise well-informed people may be poorly informed about the full range of temperatures at which damage can occur. Here are additional factors that may be helpful in evaluating manufacturer claims regarding heat when a machine cannot be tested. All friction, including rapid movement of grain, generates heat. Metal conducts heat well; it will heat up and cool down relatively quickly. A large, solid stone burr will take longer to heat up, but will also cool down more slowly. Burr size may vary from one mill to another; large burrs will produce more meal before heating up than identical but smaller burrs. Special mill features such as a reduction gear or air blower reduce or eliminate heat build-up.

The following details about heat build-up in five sample mills may be helpful in evaluating other mills.

- One large hand-operated mill with standard-sized metal burrs and a flywheel produces about a half cup of fine flour per minute without exceeding 105 degrees no matter how long grinding continues. (Speed depends on user effort.)

- One slow electric mill offering standard-sized composite stone or metal burrs and a ¼HP (horsepower) motor reduced to 60RPM (revolutions per minute) produces one-half cup of fine flour per minute. Flour temperature does not exceed 115 degrees as long as the mill is used for short periods.

One large electric mill with solid stones (12.5-inch face width) and a 1HP motor turning at 1750RPM produces three and one-half cups of fine flour per minute. According to the manufacturer, flour temperature never exceeds 110 degrees.

One high-speed electric mill with a ½HP motor that turns its composite stone burrs at 1725RPM produces three cups of fine flour per minute. According to the manufacturer, flour temperature never exceeds 140 degrees.

One electric impact mill with a 1¾HP, eight-amp motor that turns the pinned discs at 28,000RPM produces three cups of fine flour per minute. According to the manufacturer, flour temperature never exceeds 135 degrees.

 ## CHOOSING A POWER SOURCE

One very basic decision for every home miller to wrestle with early on is the power source for their grain mill. There are three power options: electric only, manual only or convertible from manual to electric or vice versa.

Electric Mills

The main drawback to an electric-only mill is that it cannot be used when power is lost. But for people whose primary concern is getting the flour ground and the bread on the table without any fuss, frills or fanfare, this may be an acceptably rare event. The zippiest, cleanest, easiest mills in this category are relatively inexpensive. They do one heck of a job and then go back in the cupboard. Anyone determined to have greater versatility, however, must compare different mills.

Although almost every mill has its own style and features, electric mills fall into four basic categories: old-fashioned mills, modern mills, attachments to existing appliances, and all the rest.

Big Old Mills ($250 to $1,000). Most older-style electric burr mills are sold by mail order, but more and more are appearing on the Internet. They are heavy, noisy, vibrate seriously and hog space. Many also have exceptional performance, some updated features, a proven track record, and long warranties. Several of these mills are housed in wood cabinets, while others are bare-motor models. Most are not decorator items, but may be the greatest deal available. Their value, compared with many sleeker, more modern mills, often lies in the size, quality and durability of the motor. So, if you find one that does not heat the flour beyond acceptable levels and you have a garage or utility room with enough space for a large, noisy, possibly dusty machine, you may have found the very best bang for your buck. It may keep going long after a smaller, prettier (and possibly less expensive) one whines to a halt. I include in this group the large, solid stone mills because of their size.

Sleek New Mills ($60 to $900). The category of newer style all-electric mills includes a full range of machines with different combinations of features and diverse prices. The smallest, least expensive electric mills tend to have plastic housings, small motors and small metal or composite stone burrs. They do one job—milling wheat into flour—and some do it well. They definitely make flour milling affordable for anyone. Remember, though, that you generally get what you pay for. Chances are good that the least expensive among these mills will not survive longer than a year or two because the motor burns out, or the burrs get dull and the machine cannot be dismantled to replace them. The larger mills in this category generally offer features that consumers are willing to pay for, such as greater milling versatility, lots of attachments, less noise or vibration, a cooling device, exquisite wood housing, industrial motor, filters to reduce flour dust, bigger grinding plates, enclosed flour catcher, the option of milling larger items, etc. Many, if not most, people will find a mill they like in this group.

Convenient Add-Ons ($100 to $200). A growing number of kitchen appliances accept grain mill attachments. This is a practical and inexpensive option if you happen to own (or intend to buy) an appliance for which a grain mill attachment exists. But be aware that wheat is a very hard substance and a substantial motor is required to grind it. A milling attachment can put a lot of strain on a motor that is not big enough for the job. The machine could even hang up on large items like beans or kernels of corn, causing an inadequate motor to burn out much more quickly than it otherwise would. Beyond saving money, an attachment to an existing appliance has the advantage of saving counter space. But remember that an attachment will not be convertible to manual use in case of power failure (unless the appliance itself is convertible, of course.)

Oddballs ($50 and up). A number of electric mills do not fit neatly into the above categories. Some are patterned after coffee mills. Some have blades, like a blender. One has a blender-like mechanism that acts like a hammer mill. These mills tend to have hoppers designed for small amounts of grain. Some are portable. One thing is certain: if a mill is on the market, somebody must need it. Thus, if you have a need that is not met by any of the mills mentioned in this chapter or listed in the Appendix, there may still be an oddball out there that can do the job. Keep looking, particularly in health-food stores, kitchen specialty stores, alternative-lifestyle magazines where grain mills are often advertised, and on the Internet.

Manual Mills

Please do not just automatically dismiss a manual mill. But do be prudent and very realistic in deciding whether you have the time and energy to integrate one into your household. They provide exercise and, when used manually, are virtually impossible to speed up enough to damage flour. Here is a run-down on manual mills.

Small Hand Grinders ($60 to $300). These mills are numerous, inexpensive, and the newer varieties grind both coarse and fairly fine flours. Several small manual mills, patterned after an early silver-colored mill called the Corona, look like old metal meat grinders with long handles. They must be clamped onto a table or bench. Several slightly larger, more modern white mills with long handles have recently appeared on the market. Some accommodate a separate mechanism for rolling oats and cracking wheat and some are easy to operate.

Most manufacturers do admit, however, that these mills are not easy to operate. In the past, people bought them because they were cheap (when most mills were expensive), required no electricity, and could crack enough grain to make mash for home beer or mill enough flour for a loaf of bread. In fact, a small hand-operated grain mill might be an inexpensive back-up to an electric mill in case of power loss; but be prepared to work a bit.

Large Hand Grinders ($250 to $600). These mills are in another category altogether. Some are rather expensive but the ones with flywheels are infinitely easier to operate than most of the smaller mills described above. They are also attractive, efficient, and great conversation pieces. Most large hand-operated mills have metal burrs, which can grind almost anything from grain to peanuts, as coarsely or finely as desired. On the negative side, they are noisy (although many electric mills are even noisier), they require space (particularly if a motor or exercise bicycle is attached), and they must be attached to something very substantial. Some require changing burrs or augers to grind different-sized items.

Although a hand grinder is a hard sell to anybody with time problems, large flywheel-type mills continue to be among the best mills ever made. Most are updated versions of metal-burr mills used by the pioneers. They provide excellent exercise, build muscles and burn fat from the back and upper arms of the mill operator. Children love them. They produce a cool flour and usually grind many different items. These mills are an excellent choice for organized, self-disciplined individuals who have demonstrated that they can stick to an exercise program. But, again, be realistic. It can take up to 15 minutes of energetic work to grind enough flour for two loaves of bread. And you cannot make the bread unless the flour has been ground.

Convertible Mills

Historically, Americans bought home flour mills for many different reasons. But those who wanted an electric mill for daily use also wanted the ability to use it manually when they lost electricity. Conversely, those who chose manual mills wanted to have the convenience of electricity when they were in a rush. In response, mill manufacturers who had the capacity devised ways to make their mills convertible. For this reason, you will encounter electric mills that can be converted to manual use by adding a handle. If you are considering an electric mill that also works manually, ensure that it works well either way. Some don't. Also, make sure that the handle provided is sturdy enough, or designed well enough, to be used manually. Try it out, if at all possible. Most sleek, new electric mills cannot be converted.

Many manual mills can be converted to power use, generally by adding a pulley and gasoline or electric motor. The flywheel on large manual mills often has a groove to accommodate a belt that can be attached to a motor (or, theoretically, a stationary bicycle). Although a few manufacturers offer motors as add-on items, most merely offer suggestions for making the conversion. If you buy a manual mill with the intention of converting it to electric use, get exact specifications from the manufacturer for the appropriate motor and belt to use and consider carefully how adept you are at troubleshooting mechanical retrofits.

 ## MILLING VERSATILITY

You are going to grind flour for bread, of course. But a home mill opens up a culinary Disney World for anyone with a spirit for adventure. The most basic versatility lies in the ability to grind grain to a desired degree of fineness or coarseness. But with the right equipment, it is also possible to grind oily items like soy, rye, soft wheat and even peanut butter or large items like corn and beans. Some mills even hull sunflower seeds. So remember, where there's a will, there's probably a mill, so if you have special needs, keep looking.

How fine is fine?

Most home flour mills offer a range of texture settings, from cracked grain to very fine flour. This does not guarantee high performance at both ends of the range. High-speed impact mills, for example, have several settings but actually produce only a few grades of fine flour. Some small manual mills, on the other hand, are unable to produce a very fine flour with a single run through the mill.

How finely or coarsely the meal is ground has important consequences to the quality of the products made from it. Very fine wholemeal is at one end of the spectrum. It tends to have a brownish tinge because all the grain parts have been reduced to a uniformly small size. Since smaller bits of bran interfere less with gluten and other baking components, very fine meal makes the lightest possible bread. Very fine meal is also preferred for most pastries and many cakes. A medium-to-coarse grind may be best for a hearty hearth loaf, will make an adequately high loaf of regular bread and will not hurt muffins or oatmeal cookies.

Cracked grain is at the other end of the grinding spectrum. Coarsely cracked corn with little flour makes good polenta. Cracked wheat with little flour is the base for wheat beer mash. Bulgur is a commercial form of cracked wheat that can replace couscous in recipes and be cooked into a cereal. In my opinion, neither metal nor stone burr mills crack grains well. They crush it, producing a lot of flour in the process. Impact mills whirl at such tremendous speeds that the grain is pulverized rather than cracked. If you are adamant about having discretely cracked corn for polenta or cracked wheat for beer mash, investigate the roller mills listed in the Appendix.

The large-fleck, small-fleck factor in bran has important health implications. As pointed out in the chapter on fiber, large flecks of bran are 75 percent more effective than powdered bran at bulking up the stool. If the primary objective of home grinding is to prevent the many constipation-related diseases that plague modern industrialized societies, a supersonic machine that turns grain to flour dust in seconds but can't do anything coarser, probably should be avoided. If, on the other hand, you eat lots of vegetables, fruits, legumes and other whole grains every day, bran fleck size may be of less concern. (Just for reference, I successfully use a moderately fine meal for bread, pancakes, cookies and breading for meat and vegetables. I use a fine meal for cornmeal, cakes and muffins which can be gritty if a coarser meal is used.)

Grinding Oily Things

Mills must be evaluated individually to determine if they can accommodate all the items you anticipate using. Mill only items recommended by manufacturer to avoid damaging your mill. Stone burrs are often not recommended for milling oily items like soybeans, rye, corn or nuts because they tend to leave a residue on the stone, known as *glazing*. At the very least, stone burrs need cleaning after milling oily items, as instructed by manufacturer. (Cleaning may involve no more than grinding half-a-cup of hard wheat.)

Metals burrs are very versatile, capable even of grinding nut butters, if the machine is designed for that purpose. But cleaning may be quite a job. Find out whether you must dismantle the entire machine to change burrs *before* you can grind wet or very oily items because you will certainly have to dismantle it afterwards for cleaning. All this dismantling and reassembly work can be time-consuming.

 ## CONVENIENCE FEATURES

All mills have basic features such as a grinding mechanism, hopper, feeder, flour catcher, etc. The design of these features may be more convenient on some mills than on others. All mills also have some problems with noise, vibration, spewing flour dust, size, etc. Some manufacturers design their machines, or add features, to reduce the impact of these problems. Following is a run-down of the features you must consider in selecting a mill that is appropriate to your lifestyle and one that will make milling a pleasant and convenient activity.

Hoppers and Feeders

Each grain mill has a *hopper* that holds grain until it drops or is fed into the grinding mechanism. In some mills, kernels drop from the hopper into a *feeder*, which is a rotating auger that moves grain toward the grinding mechanism. In other mills, the kernels drop directly into the grinding mechanism. Although the hopper and feeder are not the most important features of a grain mill, problems with them can be irritating. For example, if the hopper is too small, you may waste time watching and refilling it. (Most manufacturers recommend operating a mill only when it contains grain.) Or, if you twitch while filling the hopper, you may waste precious time retrieving stray kernels.

Large nuggets like corn and beans cannot be ground if the opening between the hopper and grinding mechanism is too small to accept them. Or, if the auger is designed for small grains, large items bounce around rather than feeding freely into the grinding mechanism, which can significantly increase grinding time. Some manufacturers solve this problem with a separate "bean auger"designed to properly feed larger items. Ask if the mill, as sold, can handle each of the grains, seeds, nuts or beans you might want to grind. On the other hand, if you find a machine that meets all your other needs but is impaired when it comes to large nuggets, you can do a preliminary "break" by milling grain into the largest chunks possible, or crack it first in a blender, then re-grind the pieces in your mill. Break only small quantities at a time in the blender to avoid producing excess flour, which can compact in the grooves of *any* burrs, whether metal or stone. In fact, no matter how you do it, to be on the safe side, sift out as much floury material as possible. If the mill cannot be dismantled to remove flour residue, it may be ruined.

Flour Catchers

A flour mill must have some provision for catching what it grinds. Sometimes the manufacturer provides a flour catcher; sometimes this is left to the purchaser. If flour simply falls into an open container, small amounts will also billow up and stick to walls and everything else, including the mill operator. It can be vacuumed up, of course, but this takes time. A great deal of engineering has gone into this problem and many solutions will be encountered. Some modern mills offer enclosed flour catchers; this is a definite bonus.

Generally speaking, a flour catcher should be large, convenient, easily cleanable, and efficient. If it looks like you can drop it, you will. If it looks like flour will escape, it will. If it looks like it will bounce off the mill, it will. If the manufacturer leaves the solution to you, some ingenuity may be required. The basic rule is to get the catcher as close to the flour as possible, so less wanders off. One option is to put the mill in the garage or another place where flour dust is not an issue. It is unwise, however, to place a mill with an open flour catcher near an open window or fan.

Flour dust may cause more trouble than a little extra vacuuming. It is one reason we have a shortage of gorgeous old wind mills and water mills. Why? Because it takes no more than 20 grams of flour in a square yard of air and a spark to ignite one of the explosions that destroyed more old mills than any other misfortune. The point here is not safety, since your kitchen is not an enclosed box, but quantity. Some machines generate a lot of flour dust, which may be of concern if you suffer from allergies. Several mills offer a filter that exhausts clean air into your kitchen (and a blower that cools the machine as well). If allergies are a concern, look for a mill with features that solve the dust problem.

Noise

One thing few sales people volunteer is that grinding grain is a very noisy business. Some mills are even noisier than others. Milling noise results when hard grains are hurled around inside a chamber or crushed between two hard burrs. This means that even hand-operated mills are noisy. But electric mills have additional noise from the motor, plus vibrations. On the other hand, electric milling is faster, so the duration of the noise is reduced.

Noise can be a problem if you have close neighbors and you need to mill at odd hours. But even family members may be cranky about noise when they are sleeping, watching television or talking on the phone. If noise is a concern, operate the mill in the garage or buy a machine with noise-reduction features. Ask manufacturers, dealers or sales people to describe any design features that are supposed to make their mill quieter.

Kitchen Space

Not only are many grinders noisy, but they can also be *large*. You may not want a big, noisy hunk of metal that must be permanently bolted down, but you may be surprised to find out that you do. Your grinder choice may come down to flour temperatures, power convertibility and...well, who knows what your bottom line will be. Harried apartment dwellers can find a small, stowable mill or an attachment to an existing appliance. Gourmands and urban farmers can find a mill that does everything except make soup, but it may take up counter or garage space. People in RVs can find mini-mills that weigh less than a pound. Fortunately, size is one area where there is a mill for everyone.

Beauty or Beast?

Now we get to a truly subjective feature—beauty. Flour mills run the beauty gamut from hogs to peacocks. But you can love a hog and hate a peacock (really...), so resist the temptation of beauty long enough to evaluate the mill's other features. Some top-of-the-heap German mills offer an exquisite wood housing with enough style for a million dollar log house or a Fifth Avenue penthouse. Other mills have a functional beauty—tidy, smooth, cleanable plastic boxes. Some mills have an old-fashioned charm about them—large machines concealed in country-style wooden boxes. Then there is the pioneer look—hand-operated mills with large flywheels that look exactly like antiques, or like polished white, red or green replicas of antiques—truly lovely, totally functional conversation pieces that do a great job of grinding (for those with time and energy). Finally, there are functional black models—although paint colors actually vary—that continue to find a market. However smitten you are with the appearance of a mill, it remains important that you consider milling speed (and possible heat build-up), bran fleck size, price, versatility, and any other features that make a mill ideal for *your* purposes. *

Cleaning up

After grinding, you must (occasionally) clean the mill. Frequency and extensiveness of cleaning vary with the type of grinding mechanism and manufacturer recommendations. Milling with a machine that must be dismantled and cleaned frequently is not practical for most people. But if you can't get inside a mill, you can't clean it and that may be a bigger problem.

Metal impact mills require no cleaning. But metal burrs used to mill soft white wheat or cornmeal may require periodic cleaning. Usually a once-over with a soft pastry brush is sufficient. But if a hardened residue is discovered in the burr grooves or flour production becomes noticeably reduced, more diligent cleaning is needed. Toothpicks or small wooden barbecue skewers do a safe and thorough job. *Never clean the grooves with metal or anything sharp.* If your mill grinds nuts into butter, you will have a sticky, gooey mess to clean up every time. Be sure to let the metal burrs dry totally before reassembly to prevent rust. If the manufacturer of a stone mill indicates that milling oily items is okay (and not all of them do), it is still a wise precaution to mill a cup or more of hard wheat afterwards to prevent grain oils from building up on burrs.

Once you have determined whether a mill can handle each and every grain, kernel, seed, or bean you may desire, ask these three questions at least: *How long does it take to clean the machine? How often must*

---

* It is always wise to ensure that any parts that might touch food be made from safe, inert, non-toxic materials.

it be cleaned? Does anything have to be taken apart to clean it? If a manufacturer claims that his stone burrs do not gum up when milling oily items (such as flax seeds or even soft white wheat), ask what makes them different from other stone burrs.

Accessability

Being able to dismantle a mill to repair it, clean it or replace parts can make the difference between a long, pleasant relationship and a short, frustrating one. I once had a sweet little electric mill that cost about $30, weighed less than a pound and seemed destined to return milling to every American home. It faithfully milled a wide variety of small, dry grains for over a year until I foolishly re-ground some flour-laden corn chunks for a finer meal and managed to clog up whatever milling mechanism was locked inside. Despite an hour with my screwdriver, I never got near the burrs and ended up throwing all the parts away. Unfortunately, the company had by that time taken the inexpensive little mill off the market and I've never encountered another like it. To avoid a similar heartbreak, try to buy a mill that can be taken apart.

 COMMUNITY MILLS

The sparsely driven commuter lanes on Los Angeles freeways demonstrate how loathe we are to team up with others, even to save time and money. But it is still quite plausible to think of a group (churchgoers, dieters, neighbors, survivalists, culinary zealots) joining together to buy a community mill. The money spent on several individual mills might buy more versatility and self-sufficiency if combined to buy a larger, but more expensive ($1,000 to $3,000+) community mill. Solid stone mills, as previously pointed out, have the capacity to mill significant quantities before generating enough heat to damage flour, but they tend to be larger, heavier and more expensive than average household needs can justify and they cannot mill all items. If the group's needs could not be met with a single mill, two mills with different features would surely do the job. On another front, a large commercial mill designed to run on an alternative power source (diesel, water, bicycle) might provide a group with the ultimate in self-sufficiency. It should be mentioned that a very high level of cooperation would be required to share a community mill. And (yet again...) any mill selected should be capable of milling large quantities without generating enough heat to damage the flour.

Another possible use for a larger mill would be semicommercial. An individual could make a capital investment of, say, $1,000, and sell milled wholemeal to others who did not want to bother grinding their own. It is unlikely that flour milling by itself would generate high profits. But a small bakery, health food store, country store or produce market with an existing customer base and room to expand a bit might add a mill to attract new clientele.

BUYING THE IDEAL MILL

Once you have a general idea what features you want in a mill, start the search. Here's how.

- Review the section on mill sources in the Appendix. Select the mills that are likely to meet your needs, then write, Fax, e-mail or call for brochures and dealer lists.

- Search the Internet for grain mills, health appliances, bread machines, flour mills, milling machines. Use your imagination. Internet grain mill sales have exploded, so a growing number of manufacturers and dealers have web sites or offer their products through on-line merchants.

- Call health food stores in your area. If they carry grain mills, go in to look at them. Buy grain and test them, if possible. Stick a candy thermometer in the freshly ground flour. Do a careful evaluation of the mill's features.

- Call local kitchen specialty stores. Most have grain mills or grain mill attachments.

- Scour department store shelves for mills or attachments to existing appliances, probably near the bread machines.

- Go to the library, or check the magazine rack at the health-food store or bookstore. Vegetarian and alternative-lifestyle magazines are popular places for mill advertisements. Write to any mail-order house that offers a catalog for grains, flour or health-food products. Many also carry grain mills.

If your search is in its infancy or you like lots of choices, do a mass mailing to every address you can locate. Ask if a mill has been sold in your vicinity that you could test. Ask if you can return the mill for a full refund should it fail to meet your expectations. And keep your wits sharpened. Don't be unduly swayed by good looks or smooth talk. Most sales people believe heartily in their products. But when it comes to mills, they may actually know less than you now do about the full range of home grain mills available. Theirs may be perfect for someone. But is that someone *you?*

Because many people will pore over every brochure they can get their mitts on and then select a mill that for an almost magical combination of reasons exactly fits their needs, at the end of this chapter is a questionnaire that will facilitate an in-depth comparison of mills. Whether you use this form or select the *Quick-Pick Option* presented earlier in this book, very soon you will begin one of the most important lifestyle changes you can ever make, by becoming a home miller. My fond advice is to *Enjoy the nutrition! Enjoy the flavor! And tell a friend.*

Ultimately, each person will research and buy a home flour mill in his or her own way. It is vital to treat the purchase of such an important appliance as a lifestyle investment, something you are willing to save for, like a new coat, a refrigerator, or the down payment on a new car. In fact, many of the sturdier, more expensive mills (both manual and electric) are so durable that they will become heirlooms, passed down for generations. Anyone can locate and purchase an adequate mill at a reasonable price. But if you have settled on the very best milling machine only to discover that it exceeds your budget, get out an envelope and start tucking spare money into it. Some things improve life so much that they are worth waiting for, worth doing at any price. Home-ground flour has to be at the top of that list! So set your sights high, because *one rarely goes farther than the distance planned.*

GRAIN MILL QUESTIONNAIRE

MANUFACTURER/DEALER INFORMATION
Seller name and address: _____

_____

Tel: (____)_____Fax: (____)_____E-mail_____

Years in business_____ No. of mills sold this year_____

Years mill has been manufactured_____No. of mills in existence_____

GRINDER/MILL INFORMATION
Mill name and Model No._____

Price $ _____ Assembly required?   ☐ yes   ☐ no

    ☐ discount if bought unassembled

Shipping weight_____ Approximate shipping cost $ _____

Is this mill:

☐ *Hand-operated?*

    Convertible? To: ☐ Motor ☐ Bicycle

    Conversion kit price $_____

☐ *Electric?*

    Horsepower_____RPMS_____Volts_____

    Convertible? To: ☐ 110V ☐ 220V ☐ Hand ☐ Bicycle

    Conversion kit price $_____

Dimensions L: _____W: _____H: _____

Warranty: Heads/plates/burrs_____years Motor and body_____years

Any features that make this mill quieter than others? ☐no ☐ yes *(If yes, describe)* _____

Does mill need to be bolted down?   ☐ yes ☐ no

No. of grinder settings on mill (fine to coarse)_____

How are settings changed? _____

Is it possible to crack grains, instead of grinding?   ☐ yes   ☐ no

Is mill equipped to grind oily items, like nuts? ☐ yes ☐ no

    with attachment (Price $_____)

Is this mill recommended for oily grains such as soybeans, corn? ☐ yes ☐ no

Is this mill recommended for grinding nuts into nut butters? ☐ yes ☐ no

Could a pebble in the grain damage machine? ☐ yes ☐ no

Why not? _____

GRINDER/MILL CONSTRUCTION

Heads/plates/burrs Material Used:

☐ Stainless steel burr
☐ Solid stone burr (What kind of stone?)
☐ Real stone composite burr (What kind of stone?)
☐ Artificial stone composite burr (What materials?)
☐ Stainless steel impact teeth
☐ Aluminum burr
☐ Other (Describe) _____

Body:

☐ Metal (What kind?)_____
☐ Plastic
☐ Other (Describe)_____
☐ Superior Design Features? _____
_____

Are all parts of this mill made from food-safe materials? ☐ yes ☐ no
Hopper Capacity_____
Flour Catcher ☐ flour bag ☐ drawer ☐ user must provide
     Capacity (in
cups)_____

Cleaning:

Disassembly required? ☐ yes ☐ no
Clean how often?_____
Time required to clean _____
Describe cleaning process in detail _____
_____

Use this table to document fineness of flour; milling speed; and any rise in flour temperature:

Grain	Coarseness	Max RPMS	Lbs/Hour or Time/Cup for Six Cups	Maximum Flour Temp.	Not Recommended
Hard Wheat					
Soft Wheat					
Corn					
Durum Wheat					
Rye					
Soy or other Beans					
Flax seeds					

Chapter 8

Grist for Your Mill

Mother Nature's Gift

All grain was grass, all flour once grain,
a vibrant, valiant, victorious vein
of amber, inspiring immigrants to reign
reverently o'er Her fields of nourishing grain.

Now the millennium's gone, She scorns our fame,
our bread gone fallow, we plunge in shame,
sorrowful, shabby, selfish blame;
for the hot steel curse on Her favored grain.

Every month of the year a crop of wheat is harvested somewhere in the world: at the edge of the arctic, near the equator, at sea level or above 15,000 feet, in Tibet. With 22,000 varieties in existence, wheat has garnered more land than any other crop. It is the fourth-largest field crop and leading export crop of the United States. It is grown in 41 out of 50 states, and one day Apogee—a short, high-yielding wheat developed at Utah State University—may be a food crop for astronauts on long missions into space.

Like us, wheat has become more civilized over the millennia. All along its 17,000 to 25,000-year trek from wild grass to modern high-yield crop, wheat has been "improved" by man to better serve his needs. In fact, early attempts to cultivate wheat as a crop failed until man could engineer plants with kernels that did not sail off with the first wisp of air that passed. In the end, his improved wheats cling so tenaciously to the stalk that they are incapable of self-propagation.

Man's next great wheat-breeding triumph was turning old wheats, which were wrapped in troublesome husks that had to be beaten or pounded off, into "naked" wheats, which had no husk. For thousands of years innovative farmers continued their crop breeding efforts, to boost yields, improve the breadmaking quality of wheat, or develop varieties that could feed more people or be used in new and useful products. By 1897, wheat improvement was so important in the United States that the Department of Agriculture (USDA) set up a formal wheat research and development program through specified state agricultural college and university systems. This program survives today.

Although America's wheat lands are dominated by just a few varieties, seed companies offer thousands of varieties and farmers grow hundreds, each with characteristics that make it suitable for specific commercial products, such as bread, noodles, cakes, animal food, grain distillation, and many more. This means that not all wheats can be expected to produce spectacular, good-tasting bread. In fact, most home millers eventually buy wheat that will not knead up beyond a wet, sticky lump or produce anything but a squat, holey loaf of bread. When they finally realize the problem is not the recipe, yeast, or weather, they assume they have been sold a lousy bag of wheat or, worse yet, they give up altogether on wholemeal bread. In truth, they have gotten a wheat that is inappropriate for making the light bread that most Americans are familiar with and, therefore, prefer.

This is a sad but common disappointment. Far too few people understand that, because of wheat improvements, modern, high-protein bread wheats can produce wholemeal loaves so superior to the cannon balls of history that fiber, nutrition and superb flavor can be added to any diet without sacrificing a light, fluffy texture. It is a happier fact that virtually anyone can afford a bushel of wheat that will produce up to 60 nicely textured, flavorful loaves of bread, even with all the bran and germ left in the flour. This bushel bag of wheat costs less than a carton of cigarettes, less than two pounds of freshly roasted coffee beans, and less than a case of imported beer.

So, good breadmaking wheat is available, the price is right, but people aren't sweeping store shelves clear of home flour mills. Why? Because home milling usually strikes people as a *curiosity* rather than a practical means of improving health. After all, when milling and baking moved to commercial enterprises, household familiarity with wheat, flour and bread virtually disappeared. Now that modern appliances have made it feasible for milling and baking to return to even the busiest home, this important base of knowledge must be reconstructed. To that end, this chapter presents basic information about the characteristics in wheat that play a role in making breads and desserts. Without this simple education, bread disappointments are almost inevitable, no matter how fantastic your appliances are. Before we get to this important education, however, let's look at how wheat progressed from the wild grasses that flourished around the fertile crescent area of the Middle East into the wonderful bread wheats that we are blessed with today.

 ## THE WHEAT FAMILY SAGA

Man always munched on wild grass seeds, but wheat cultivation on dry land didn't start until sometime between 7,000 and 8,000 years before Christ. Large-scale agriculture had to wait until our ancestors could cultivate some wild grasses that would stay on the stalks when the wind blew and until some unknown genius could invent the plow. Precisely where and when this all happened is speculation, but the roots of serious wheat cultivation almost certainly lie in some fertile river valley of Syria and Palestine 5,000 to 7,000 years before Christ. Iran and later the Danube Valley became hubs from which wheat spread throughout the world. Even the Chinese considered wheat one of the Five Sacred Crops (with rice, barley, soybean and millet) by 2800 B.C.

The first wheats, called *einkorn*, were little more than wild grasses. They still grow today and are distinguished from other wheat families by their 14-chromosome genetic code. Einkorn was certainly a good beginning. But it was dark and somewhat bitter, so the Romans, the first in a long history of plant breeders, selectively cultivated einkorn to become a second family of wheats, called *emmer*, identified by its 28-chromosome structure.* Emmer was a big improvement over einkorn. It produced a softer, lighter, sweeter flour, and soon became the most widely spread wheat in agricultural antiquity. Still, both of these old wheats had a hair problem. Well, husks anyway, pesky husks that had to be beaten or pounded off.

---

*This 28-chromosome emmer group also includes a wheat commonly used today for pasta, *t. durum*, which would seem to belong in the 42-chromosome "naked" wheats family discussed below because it lacks a husk.

With more tinkering, the Romans produced a third group of wheats, ancestors of the 42-chromosome bread wheats that we use today. The wheats in this family, which showed up around 5,500 to 5,000 B.C. in the Middle East, were *naked*, in that they had no troublesome husks to be pounded off by mortars prior to grinding. This modern bread wheat group includes *t. aestivum* or common bread wheat (the most widely cultivated species today); *t. compactum* or club wheat (used for noodles and cookies); *t. sphaerococcum*, a high-yield Indian wheat (developed during the green revolution of the 1960s*); and *t. spelta* (or spelt), a low-gluten alternative we will learn more about in the chapter on other grains. We love the modern bread wheats for the same reason that our ancestors did: because their starchy kernels produce lighter, whiter bread than the wheats that preceded them.

Now that we have met the wheat family, let's start learning about the individual characteristics that determine whether or not a given wheat will perform well in bread.

 ## BREADMAKING CHARACTERISTICS

As you learn about the different characteristics of wheat with baking implications, you will encounter some potentially confusing terms used by the farming, milling and baking industries to categorize or identify wheats. Farmers, for example, describe wheat in terms of type or class, such as "hard red," and the time of year, "winter" or "spring," in which it is grown. Commercial millers use terms such as "hard" or "soft," which describe factors important to the milling process. Bakers and other food processors generally discuss wheat in terms of its suitability for a specific product, such as a "strong" wheat for making bread and a "weak" wheat for making cakes.

All of these terms, which you will learn more about shortly, describe different characteristic of the same wheats and can be used somewhat interchangeably within the agribusiness sector of our huge economy without causing confusion. But they can frustrate new home millers who try to rush out with the simple purpose of buying a bag of

---

*During the "green revolution," crop scientists doubled wheat and rice yields on existing lands, thus saving millions of Asian citizens from the looming catastrophe of the time, widespread famines.

good bread wheat. Before we get to those terms, however, let's start with one you have already encountered in this book—protein content—because it is the consumer's best indicator of how a given wheat will perform in a particular baked item.

Protein Content

Wheat protein is located in the endosperm of the kernel and is expressed in percentages, with a range from 6 to 21 percent, or even higher in experimental varieties. In general, wheats containing a large amount of protein make the best breads, whereas low-protein wheats are ideal for non-yeasted products like cookies, doughnuts, some cakes and pastries. How much protein is required depends on the kind of bread desired and the process used. Consistently high, finely textured loaves of wholemeal bread (reminiscent of white bread) can be made from wheats containing 15 percent or more protein. As protein levels drop, loaf volume begins to decrease, although alterations in ingredients and process can mitigate these changes. How low the protein content can drop before the loaf becomes unacceptable will depend on the breadmaking process, other ingredients, and the objectives and tastes of the baker.* Since breadmaking with white flour becomes impossible at protein levels below 7 to 8 percent,

START WITH THE BEST

Most unsatisfactory loaves of wholemeal bread result from inexperienced bakers using wheat with too little breadmaking protein. For this reason, beginners who like American-style light breads should start with the highest-protein wheats (at least 15 percent) so the tallest, fluffiest, best-textured loaves are achieved right away. Otherwise, while the cook learns to adjust recipes or track down better wheat, potential converts from white bread to wholemeal may be lost forever.

---

*Rye, for example, has very little breadmaking gluten, but an endless variety of rye breads exists. Additionally, people in winter wheat growing areas may tolerate slightly smaller loaves because they prefer the flavor of their local wheats, which may have protein levels of only 14 to 14.5 percent.

wholemeal's bottom limit is probably higher than this, due to added influence from bran and germ.

The amount of protein in a given variety of wheat can vary from one year to the next, from one field to the next, or even from one corner of a field to the next. This is because soil, farming techniques (such as nitrogen fertilizing) and weather have much more impact on protein content than genetics. For this reason, the wheat from a reliable source may perform differently in bread from one year to the next.

Gluten Content

Now that you know the general rule (the more protein, the lighter the bread) we must discuss the caveat. Although protein content is a reasonable indicator of breadmaking potential, bread performance actually depends on the balance of individual components within the protein structure. The elements in wheat protein that most affect bread quality are the gluten-forming *prolamins*, usually referred to simply as gluten. In breadmaking, this group of water-*in*soluble proteins combines with water to form a strong, elastic structure capable of expanding as it traps yeast-generated gasses within its walls. The two types of protein that make up this gluten group are *glutenins* and *gliadins*.

Glutenins provide the elastic quality that allows bread dough to expand, so the quantity of glutenins in the protein of a given wheat determines its breadmaking capacity. Gliadins play an important secondary role by contributing to the viscosity and extensibility of bread dough, but they are better known for their importance as pasta's strength proteins. Although both protein components are important to bread quality, the presence of adequate glutenins determines whether or not the wheat will make good bread. The quantity of both glutenins and gliadins in the grain is genetically determined.

Strong vs. Weak Wheats

Not all high-protein wheats have enough glutenins to make pretty, puffy brown loaves of finely textured yeasted bread. For this reason, bakers use the terms *strong* and *weak* to indicate a wheat or flour's "baking strength," or suitability for specific baked products. Strong wheats have an abundance of glutenins, so they are suited to breadmaking. They make tall loaves of yeasted bread with a tight, non-crumbly texture and good keeping qualities. Weak wheats, by contrast, have a deficiency of glutenins, so they can produce only squat loaves of yeasted bread with dense or crumbly textures. Weak flours are better suited to cookies, some pastries and cakes, and other products that would be tough if made from a stronger flour.

Very strong wheats are required for long-fermentation breads, wholemeal breads, and crusty breads. Wholemeal bakers who like light, fluffy bread should rely on very strong, high-protein wheat (15 percent or more), especially in the beginning when they are perfecting a recipe or trying to learn what a good loaf of wholemeal should look like. Incidentally, white bread flours, which have no bran or germ in the equation, are made from medium-strength wheats, generally about 12 percent protein, as any more would make them rubbery.

Hard vs. Soft Wheats

Hard and soft are terms of primary interest to millers in describing the texture of the endosperm and how it breaks down in milling but are also related to breadmaking strength.

Hard wheat kernels are small, hard and tend to be translucent when held up to a bright light. The endosperm tends to be vitreous, so it grinds into a coarse, gritty meal of relatively standard-sized particles. The more vitreous the kernels are, the more protein they contain, and the more grainy or sandy the flour feels when rubbed between the fingers. Hard wheats are generally strong, high-protein (11 to 17 percent) breadmaking wheats.* They are also used for hard rolls, Indian chapatis, hot breakfast cereals, farina and wheat germ. Products made from the hardest wheat, durum, are macaroni, spaghetti, puffed breakfast cereals and wheat germ. Hard grains require more milling energy than soft grains and may cause home mills to heat up quickly. Some small hand mills may require more than one grinding to make meal from hard grains.

----

*Grain hardness does not relate to baking quality in wheat varieties grown in France, and may not always relate in American wheats. For example, the hardest wheat, durum, generally has more gliadins than glutenins and is used primarily in pasta products. But durum is commonly used for leavened and unleavened breads in other parts of the world and some durum varieties grown in the United States make excellent yeasted bread.

Soft wheat kernels are generally more plump than hard wheat kernels and appear opaque against a bright light. The endosperm produces a very fine flour that feels powdery (also described as starchy, mealy or chalky) when rubbed between the fingers. Mealiness is a genetic trait that may also be induced by heavy rain, light sandy soils, or crowded planting. Mealiness correlates to high grain yield and lower protein content. Soft wheats are generally weak, low-protein (6 to 11 percent) pastry wheats. Some commercial uses for soft wheat are: crackers, cookies, cakes, doughnuts, pancakes, waffles, muffins, soft noodles, ice cream cones, pizzas, puffed and flaked breakfast cereals, granola, soup thickeners, gravy thickeners and wheat germ. Some home grain mills are not recommended for milling soft, oily grains, which can leave a residue on stone burrs.

Starch Damage

The term *starch damage* is important in milling and baking and is related to the hardness of grain. Damage caused to starch during the milling process increases the capacity of the flour to absorb water, an essential characteristic of good bread wheat that improves loaf size and performance. Of course, excessive milling is to be avoided, because too much starch damage causes the flour to absorb too much water, which results in a wet, sticky dough. Since more mechanical force is required to break hard grains apart, more starch damage is sustained in milling hard wheats. By contrast, the low starch damage and low water absorption capacities of soft wheats benefit cakes and cookies because these characteristics reduce baking time and lessen the risk of cracking during cooling.

JUDGING WHEAT HARDNESS

If you have unidentified wheat, grind some and rub the flour between your fingers. If it is gritty (like fine sand), it is most likely hard wheat, which probably will make good bread. If it has a moist, softer texture that clumps when you tighten your fingers around it, you probably have soft wheat, which is better for cakes and cookies.

Spring vs. Winter Wheats

Because soil, weather and farming practices have profound impact on the protein content of wheat, the time of year in which a particular variety is grown is also an important indicator of breadmaking potential.

Spring wheat varieties are planted in spring. They benefit from a short but intense growing season with heavy rainfall (or irrigation) in the early stages of development and high temperatures later. Rapid development favors a vitreous texture and high protein content, characteristics generally present in good bread wheats. Spring wheat is harvested in late summer. Hard spring wheats generally are the strongest bread wheats.

Winter wheat varieties are planted in autumn, for the most part on nonirrigated lands. They germinate then grow slowly in the fall, go dormant for the winter, then resume growth in the spring and are harvested in summer. The prolonged growing period results in greater grain yield but lower protein content. Because of variability in weather and other growing conditions, the protein content of winter wheats varies more than that of spring wheats. Hard winter wheats are generally medium-strength bread wheats.

Although the government classifies wheat in terms of spring or winter growing season, farmers can plant many different *varieties* of wheat during these seasons. Nine wheat varieties dominate the United States wheat crop, but seed companies market hundreds of varieties to farmers.

 ## WHEAT CLASSES

In 1916 the United States Grain Standards Act (USGSA) established a uniform system for identifying and grading wheat. This system divided wheat into six *classes* and several *subclasses* reflecting the location where it was traditionally grown and the unique properties that made it suitable for a specific end use. Two additional classes cover all wheats that do not fit into these categories. In 1976, Congress created the Federal Grain Inspection Service (FGIS) to apply these standards uniformly to all areas.

For now, inspectors use visual characteristics to help identify wheats by class: hardness, color, length, width and slope of the back of the kernel, germ size, germ angle, brush size, cheek shape, crease and surface texture. But the increasing presence of interclass crosses has made visual identification less reliable. FGIS is intent on finding a less subjective way to identify and classify wheat. Some sort of technology-based identification system (such as protein fingerprinting) will eventually replace the current one. This should provide small-quantity buyers with better information than is currently available about the breadmaking strength of any wheat.

Listed below are the eight official wheat classes into which American varieties fall. Home millers will encounter these classes when selecting and ordering wheat for home grinding.

Hard Red Winter (t. aestivum)

Hard red winter is the dominant wheat class in the United States, usually representing around 45 percent of the annual wheat crop and 60 percent of all winter wheat. This "pride of the great plains" came from Ukrainian varieties of *Turkey Red* that crossed the ocean with Mennonites late in the nineteenth century. Hard red winter is grown primarily in the large pocket of land extending from the Rockies east to the Mississippi River and from the Dakotas and Montana south to Texas. This is a hard, vitreous, medium-strength wheat (9 to 14.5 percent protein) used primarily in commercial bread, hard rolls and all-purpose flour. The distinctive flavor of hard red winter is preferred by many wholemeal bread bakers, particularly those living near its growing areas. Home millers who like wholemeal bread on the light and fluffy side should know that winter wheat produces slightly lower loaves, with more robust wheat flavor, than loaves made from spring wheats. *Turkey Red* remains popular in growing areas for its flavor.

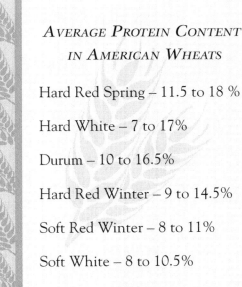

AVERAGE PROTEIN CONTENT

IN AMERICAN WHEATS

Hard Red Spring – 11.5 to 18 %

Hard White – 7 to 17%

Durum – 10 to 16.5%

Hard Red Winter – 9 to 14.5%

Soft Red Winter – 8 to 11%

Soft White – 8 to 10.5%

Hard Red Spring (t. aestivum)

Hard red spring, which represents 22 percent of the United States wheat crop, is grown principally in the upper midwest states of the Dakotas, Minnesota and Montana, with smaller quantities grown in states such as Washington and Oregon. Hard red spring is a hard, vitreous, high-protein (11.5 to 18 percent) wheat. It is divided into three subclasses, according to the percentage of dark, hard, and vitreous kernels present: *dark northern spring* (with 75 percent or more), *northern spring* (with 25 percent or more but less than 75 percent), and *red spring* (with less than 25 percent). Hard red spring is used commercially for quality yeasted bread and hard rolls. It should be the first choice for home bakers who like light-textured, high-volume bread. It is particularly reliable in bread machines. Dark northern spring is the optimum hard red spring wheat for American-type bread.

Soft Red Winter (t. aestivum)

Soft red winter is the third largest wheat class, representing 19 percent of the United States crop. This wheat is grown significantly in Missouri, Illinois, Ohio, Indiana, Arkansas and Michigan. It is a soft, weak wheat (8 to 11 percent protein) used for flatbreads, cakes, pastries, crackers and snack foods. Soft red winter is not widely available for small-quantity purchases, but is used by commercial bakers in non-bread white flour products. (French bakers use soft red French wheats, which are different from American soft red wheats, for bread, but the endearing quality of French bread is generally attributed to French fermentation processes.)

Soft White (t. aestivum, t. compactum)

Soft white includes all soft endosperm white wheat varieties. These wheats are grown mainly in the Pacific Northwest, with lesser quantities grown in California, Michigan, Wisconsin and New York. Similar in protein content to soft red (8 to 10.5 percent), soft white wheat is considered too weak by itself for breadmaking, but is used commercially for cookies, some pastries and cakes, crackers, some noodles and flatbread. Club wheats (*t. compactum*), which are included in this class, are low-protein, soft white winter wheats used primarily for noodles and cookies. Club wheats are grown principally in Washington State. The soft white wheat class has three subclasses: *soft white* (containing no more than 10 percent white club wheat); *white club* wheat (with no more than 10 percent other soft white wheats) and *western white* (with no more than 10 percent white club wheat and at least 10 percent other soft white wheats). Soft white adds a distinctive and delicious flavor to wholemeal desserts. Soft white winter wheats were strongly preferred for bread before 1860, when they were replaced by hard red wheats. (In fact, my standard bread includes 150 to 200 grams of soft white wheat because I like the flavor.)

Hard White (t.aestivum)

Hard white is the newest wheat class in the United States, grown principally in Kansas, Idaho and Montana. Although it was originally developed to capture the Asian noodle market, hard white has a growing market in tortillas, Middle Eastern flatbreads, yeast breads, and hard rolls. This hard, vitreous, usually strong wheat (8 to 17 percent protein) is likely to become a more common winter-grown wheat because it is less expensive to grow and has a higher extraction rate than the winter wheat that has reigned supreme since its introduction in 1874, *Turkey Red*. Home millers will find that high-protein varieties of hard white perform very well in bread, but lack the distinctive flavor of red wheat varieties. White-bread lovers will want to try it.

Durum Wheat (t. durum)

Durum, which came to the United States from south Russia in the late nineteenth century, represents only five percent of the United States wheat crop. It is the hardest of all U.S. wheats, with a high protein content (10 to 17 percent). Seventy to 80 percent of America's durum comes from spring-seeded fields in North Dakota, but smaller winter-sown crops are also grown in Montana, Arizona and California. Ninety-eight percent of America's durum is processed like white flour, with the bran and germ separated out and the endosperm milled into a gritty meal called semolina, for use in macaroni and spaghetti. When other hard wheats are mixed with durum, pasta quality suffers. The largest markets for durum exports are Italy, for pasta, and several North African countries, where it is used for leavened and unleavened bread as well as pasta.

Durum includes all classes of white (amber) durum wheat and has three subclasses reflecting the percentage of hard and vitreous kernels of amber color present in the wheat: *hard amber durum*, (with 75 percent or more); *amber durum* (with 60 to 75 percent); and *durum* (with less than 60 percent). Hard amber durum varieties containing sufficient glutenins to qualify as good breadmaking wheat produce tall, slightly yellow loaves that keep better than those made from other wheat flours. The flavor is somewhat unusual by itself but durum is delicious and improves bread texture when combined with other flours. Home millers will find that durum makes the best pasta. An identifying characteristic of good durum wheat is a yellow color in the flour and bread. Red durum, included in the unclassed group below, is sometimes passed off as durum but is not in the durum wheat class.

Mixed and Unclassed

There are two remaining classes of wheat. Mixed wheat includes any mixture of wheat with less than 90 percent of one class and more than 10 percent of another, or any cross that still meets the definition of wheat. Unclassed wheat includes anything that does not fit in the above categories, including red durum, and any wheat that is not red or white, such as purple wheat.

 ## SUMMARY

The foregoing will probably require more than one reading, as it is inherently complex and confusing, so here is a snapshot of the important factors for selecting good bread wheat. Although the quantity of glutenins in a wheat determines its breadmaking potential, this information is rarely available to consumers, who are left to rely on protein content. The general rule is: the more protein, the better the bread. Hard wheats and spring wheats tend to have more protein than soft wheats or winter wheats. Thus, the ideal breadmaking choices for people who like light-textured bread are hard red spring (dark northern spring, if possible) or hard white spring with a protein content of 15 percent or more. These wheats can usually be depended on to make spectacular loaves of light bread with very good texture. For hearty wheat flavor, hard red winter wheat with the highest protein content possible (probably 14.5 percent) is an ideal choice, although loaves made in a bread machine will be slightly lower than those using high-protein hard red spring.

Although the more-protein-lighter-bread rule generally holds, on occasion a wheat may perform differently than the rules would indicate. For example, a traditionally weak variety may have been reengineered for better breadmaking strength. Also, hard red wheats of any variety and protein level make better bread when the wheat is grown on dry as opposed to irrigated land. To complicate matters, as varieties are crossed and recrossed, strict classification of wheats has become more difficult. Until a system evolves to scientifically evaluate and label individual bags of grain with protein content and baking strength, breadmaking results may actually be better or worse than the known factors predict. Suppliers of high-protein wheat listed in Appendix B can be relied on for high-quality products.

It cannot be overstressed that the requirement stressed in this book for high-protein content is not absolute, but relative to the type of bread being made. Highest-protein wheats are best for tall, soft, fluffy loaves that mimic white bread. Slightly lower protein levels are quite satisfactory for the heartier loaves favored by established wholemeal addicts and lovers of European-style wholemeal bread.

Test data indicating the breadmaking capacity of given varieties of wheat is available from growers and seed merchants. But if you have an unknown wheat, there are ways to estimate its breadmaking strength. An old baker's test was to knead up a slack (not too firm) dough, wrap it in fine muslin, and knead it lightly in a bowl constantly filling with water. Eventually the starch dissolves away and the water runs clear. Carefully open the muslin and meticulously discard the bran by gently washing the glob of gluten while being careful that it does not slip away. By squeezing the remaining gooey mess (gluten) between the fingers, bakers could evaluate the flour's baking strength.

This is not only messy but may be impractical today, since few people have enough experience to discern quality in the glob of gluten. This leaves the test relied upon by centuries (if not millennia) of bakers: baking a few loaves using a recipe that has succeeded before. Once one has a proven recipe and is familiar with the spectacular results of a strong wheat, judging loaf quality is swift and absolute. But unless you are buying from a proven source like the breadmaking wheat providers listed in Appendix B, *buy only small amounts of any wheat until its performance has been proven.*

CHAPTER 9

More Grist for Your Mill

Embarrassment of Riches

Buckwheat, millet, barley and oats
flour to mush to kasha to groats,
Africans, Asians, Arabs and Swedes,
down through millennia served their needs.

But I love only familiar grains,
forget the rest, ah more, disdain,
so prim and grim and prissy am I
I'll eat my wheat, corn, rice or die.

      Six cereal grains fed most of the world for almost 10,000 years: millet, oats, barley, wheat, rye and corn. As long as the Greeks baked flat cakes over wood coals and rolled them up like manuscripts, and the Romans ate porridge from pottery bowls, grains like oats, millet and barley could hold their own in the popularity race with wheat. But once leavened bread dazzled the palates of our ancestors, wheat shot ahead in any area where it grew well as a cultivated crop. Corn (which dominated the Americas) and rice (which pervaded Asia) had their own fascinating and initially separate histories. Today they lag only slightly behind wheat as the great taste toppers of the century. But limiting ourselves to just these three grains means missing many exotic and flavorful comfort foods that have evolved throughout the rest of the world.

Whether the objective of home milling is to increase whole-grain intake, to provide variety for gluten sufferers, or for sheer culinary thrill-seeking, the grain repertoire inevitably must swirl beyond wheat, corn and rice. Home millers can learn to delight themselves and their guests with family food from around the world, such as amaranth and wheat chapatis from Nepal, durum breads from Africa, or Thai dishes flavored with rice flour. After all, many delicious recipes have been perpetuated by people in low-technology countries who still eat the grain, the whole grain and nothing but the grain. Let's explore some of the new grains you can enjoy once you have the capacity to mill, crack or flake them at home.

 ## RYE

Wild rye grasses probably originated in the same area as wheat, oats and barley, but much later. One story has it that rye was first cultivated by accident. Some weeds got in with wheat loaded on grain ships leaving the city of Pontos, by the Black Sea, destined for Russia. When the wheat was planted in the exhausted fields of Russia, only the weeds survived—weeds that became a cultivated crop called rye. True story or not, there is no record of rye before the Christian era.

Rye's hardiness under conditions too harsh for winter wheat makes it a world crop, from Argentina to Tanzania. It is an important bread grain throughout Europe and is used alone in the black bread of eastern Europe and parts of Asia. Rye is the only cereal grain with protein properties similar enough to wheat to make yeasted bread. Since it has considerably inferior elasticity and gas retention capacities, however, it is usually combined with wheat rather than used alone. It has a distinctive flavor, apart from the caraway usually added to rye bread. Rye enjoys great fame as a sourdough starter, no doubt because rye dough must be acidified to improve the swelling qualities of the proteins and to inactivate the detrimental enzyme amylase. Rye has complicated baking rules, but is loved by many because it makes a moist, dark, dense, very delicious and better-keeping bread. Because of rye's special handling requirements, home millers who want to experiment with it should buy a breadmaking book that includes instructions for whole rye products.

While rye may be deficient in breadmaking potential, it is certainly not inferior in its ability to prevent disease. Whole-kernel rye bread lowers glucose response in diabetics. And a study of elderly Finnish men concluded that adding about three slices of traditional rye bread to the diet (about 10 additional grams of fiber per day) reduced the risk of death from coronary heart disease by 17 percent. Nutrition is an important reason to include rye in wheat bread. It is high in protein, vitamins B2 and B3, potassium and magnesium. And rye is higher in the amino acid lysine than either wheat or triticale (a hybrid of rye and wheat), so it can improve the protein quality of wheat bread for vegans or individuals with special dietary needs.

Because rye's high lipid content poses a risk of rancidity, commercial rye flours generally have most, or all, of the bran and germ removed. The only exceptions are *rye meal* and *pumpernickel*. In any case, commercial rye flour is milled like white flour, with the endosperm, bran and germ mechanically separated, then recombined according to formulas for light, medium, or dark rye flours. This means that only home millers can be certain that their wholemeal rye is as nutritious and complete as the rye berry from which it was milled.

 ## TRITICALE

Triticale is a cross between wheat and rye. First produced in 1888 but not a viable food crop until very recently, triticale combines wheat's high yields with rye's ability to survive adverse growing conditions. It is a highly nutritious crop for humans and livestock, with up to 17 percent protein and nearly double the lysine content of wheat. Some varieties of triticale are better used for products usually made from soft wheats, such as cookies, cakes, waffles, noodles and flour tortillas. Recent strains have, however, produced breads equal in height and texture to those produced by wheat. Poland has taken the lead in testing triticale for bread, with the best blends at 90 percent triticale and 10 percent rye. To make triticale and wheat bread, start with small amounts of triticale and be cautious not to overknead it because of the rye content. Once you are convinced that you have a good breadmaking strain of triticale, gradually increase the percentage of triticale to 60 percent.

SPELT

T. spelta is not a new grain but a resuscitated species of wheat that fell out of general usage because of its low gluten content. In fact, this grain has remained in use in a few central and northern Italian regions where it is known as *farro* and in Germany where it is known as *dinkle*. It may well be one of the hairy ancestors of our modern bread wheats, even today retaining a troublesome husk that must be removed. It is possible that the spelt husk protects the kernel from pollutants and insects, which means fewer pesticides. Presumably, pesticides might be discarded with the husk, as well, making it a more healthful food. Spelt has received a lot of attention recently because it is tolerated by some, but not all, people with gluten allergies. It can be combined with wheat for bread or substituted for wheat in a wide range of recipes.

RICE

Rice has a rich history. It was probably first cultivated in the orient 7,000 years ago, based on artifacts that show the Chinese of the period storing rice in sealed containers. Although rice almost ties wheat and corn for world cereal production, it is far more important than the others as food for humans. Over one-and-a-half billion people get half their food from rice and another 400 million eat a diet of 25 percent to 50 percent rice.

There are two main kinds of rice—short grain and long grain. Different varieties of these rices have become favorites with different peoples of the world, such as Jasmine in Thailand or Basmati in Pakistan*. White rice, like white flour, starts out brown. In processing, rice is cleaned, the hulls are removed, and the bran and germ are separated by abrasive scouring. The rice is then usually polished. The hulls are used primarily as animal food. The bran and germ may be sold as rice polish, a great source of B vitamins, minerals and protein. Raw rice milling and polishing severely reduce vitamin con-

---

*Parboiling before milling (as practiced in India and Pakistan) actually reduces nutrient losses because the minerals and vitamins in the hulls and bran are dissolved and carried into the endosperm. At the same time, rice oil moves outward and much of it is milled away with the husks, which makes it a lower fat food.

tent. While rice is consumed mostly as whole kernels, in Japan it is also used to make sake.

Unfortunates who are allergic to gluten may find rice an important alternative grain for variety. Toasted ground rice is used as a flavoring in oriental dishes. Some health-oriented recipes call for rice flour. It is difficult to locate brown rice flour for these recipes. But rice can be ground in most home mills and it is quite feasible to keep small quantities of short- or medium-grain brown rice on hand for occasional use in breads or other dishes. But be aware that unmilled brown rice has a rancidity problem similar to rye and corn, thanks to those nutritious oils in the germ. It should be purchased fresh, stored in a cool, dry place and ground in small quantities for immediate use.

CORN (MAIZE)

Corn* is the world's third most important cereal crop, after wheat and rice. Early American settlers, who relied on Indian corn for survival while the wheat industry was evolving, became very fond of it. That fondness survives today. This old and trusted grain can be ground to different textures and used in a huge collection of delicious recipes from around the world. Some American favorites include cornbread, polenta, muffins, corn-rye bread, Boston steamed brown bread, spoon bread, corn puffs, hush puppies, tortillas, tamales, tamale pie and Anadama bread. Corn can also be added to wheat products such as bread, pancakes, muffins, and a host of other baked goods. A really ambitious corn lover could even make hominy and grind it into grits.

Like wheat, many varieties of corn are grown, but some are better suited than others to particular products. The sweet corn we eat for dinner does not dry nor store well, so it is not commonly used for grinding. *Flint, dent* and *popcorn* are the types most commonly available at grain outlets. Flint varieties, which have a grittier texture, are better for standard cornmeal and the chunky texture of traditional polenta. Dent varieties make better flour for use in soup thickeners, tortillas, finely textured cornbread and tamales. Although popcorn can be used in a pinch, it is not the first choice for grinding because of

---

*In antiquity, the word "corn" referred to wheat, as it does today in England. In Scotland and Ireland, it refers to oats.

a somewhat grittier texture than other varieties and a slightly higher moisture content which keeps it from storing well. Some mill manufacturers discourage milling popcorn with their machines.

Corn comes in different colors: yellow, white, blue, and red. Nutritionally speaking, white corn lacks the concentration of carotene contained in yellow corn, but otherwise, the two are interchangeable. Blue and red corn are not widely available for purchase as grains.

Like other lipid-rich grains, corn must be consumed shortly after milling or stored in the refrigerator to avoid rancidity. And only home-ground corn is guaranteed to contain all the riches of the original grain: sweet, fresh cornmeal flavor, healthful bran, and a lush supply of Vitamin E, linoleic acid, phospholipids, carotene and phytosterols.

THE OATS STIGMA

Historically, oats had a recurring stigma of "class" because they were first and foremost animal feed, and secondly peasant fodder. Earliest man loved his animals and was proud to put on the same feedbag. But the Greeks had contempt for anyone who sat down with his horse to munch oats. And the Romans, who had lifted grinding and breadmaking to the level of art, considered the oat-eating Germans less civilized than their horses. This Roman snobbery passed into the Middle Ages. Then the Crusaders of the eleventh through the thirteenth centuries brought oats back from the Middle East to plant in the fields at home. This reintroduction was by no means an instant success. French and English knights refused to eat the same food their horses ate. Samuel Johnson's (1709-84) English dictionary defined oats as "food for men in Scotland, horses in England." The Scots replied "England is noted for the excellence of her horses; Scotland for the excellence of her men." Oats are still popular in Scotland, Ireland and Northern England, and in the "colony" of North America.

OATS

Oats never became king of grains because they did not domesticate well. If not carefully watched, they fell back to wild oat habits—tougher beard, looser husk and smaller grain. And they blew off in the wind, an irritating habit. But oats remained an important food source because they contain more protein and fat than other grains, plus lots of iron and B vitamins. A recent trainload of clinical studies linking significant health benefits to the soluble fiber in oat bran triggered a marketing frenzy to cram oats and oat bran into a vast assortment of supposedly more healthful packaged foods. But only home-rolled oats provide *all* the benefits attributed to this wonderful grain.

Unrefined oat groats are processed to remove the inedible hull, but the germ and bran are left intact. Steel-cut oats are unrefined oats that have been dried and rough-sliced, so they retain much of their original B-vitamin content. Rolled oats (or old-fashioned oats) are sliced, steamed, then rolled into flakes and dried, losing some nutrients in the process. Both quick oats and instant oats (which are further processed with heat to reduce cooking time) suffer nutritionally. Raw or cooked oats make a hearty and flavorful addition to yeasted breads. While they are not normally milled into flour, they can be.

Because the soluble fiber in oats is so beneficial, it would behoove the home miller to try every possible use for this nutrition warehouse. Fortunately, all basic cookbooks include lots of great oat recipes: oatmeal cookies, oatmeal bread, hot oatmeal, date-nut bars, fruit crisps with oatmeal and butter topping, etc. Oats can add extra nutrition to bread dough, muffins and other baked goods. (Some recipes are included in the chapter on quick breads and cakes.)

Many manufacturers offer stand-alone oat flakers/rollers and attachments to existing grain mills and other appliances. An inexpensive hand-operated oat roller can be a powerful opening salvo in the battle to increase soluble and insoluble fiber in diet. Kids love to roll the oats and they love to eat the oats. The significance of *that* shouldn't be missed.

BARLEY

Barley has been everywhere, and for a long time. Apparently, the sun-baked flat cakes of our Stone Age ancestors contained more barley than wheat. Both grains were grown by Egyptian farmers. It was mentioned in the Bible 32 times. Barley was popular with the Chinese of the Hsia Dynasty (around 1520 B.C.). And while English noblemen of the fifteenth century ate wheat bread, peasants choked down leaden loaves of barley and rye with ground beans, lentils or millet added to make them palatable. Barley never made good leavened bread, but it was a hardy crop in the face of insects, floods, frosts, and droughts.

Although barley's main American role is in soups and breakfast foods, in Eastern Europe and Russia a sweet, grayish flatbread made from barley remains a popular staple. This sweet, nutty grain is high in protein, niacin, folate, thiamin, calcium, magnesium and phosphorous. Barley substitutes well for rice and millet in recipes and can be rolled, like oats. Barley is commonly used as an animal food or in malt extracts for alcoholic beverages or sweeteners, but barley malt has long been added to dough to improve bread quality. Although it makes poor yeasted bread by itself, about 25 percent barley flour added to wheat bread provides variety.

Recent clinical research has catapulted barley to prominence as a health promoter because, like oats, half of its fiber is the soluble type, which has been linked to lowered blood cholesterol and protection against type 2 diabetes. Most barley available for

BARLEY'S BUM LUCK

Vital a role as it eventually played in Western history, bread wheat faced a long struggle with barley for the title "King of the Cereal Grains." Barley's high crop yields and ability to grow on poor soils sustained it until leavened wheat bread hit the billboards of history and mouth-to-mouth advertising beat barley back. Ultimately, barley went down a side road of history solely because it made lousy leavened bread.

purchase (outside the occasional health-food store or mail-order house) has been *pearled,* or processed repeatedly until the husk, germ and bran layers have been removed. As usual, nutrients are sacrificed in the process. If you want to mill barley into flour, buy *hull-less* barley, which has had the husk, but not the bran and germ, removed.

 ## BUCKWHEAT

Buckwheat is not a grass like wheat, but a fruit in the *Polygonaceae* family, which originated in Asia. It was introduced into Western Europe in about the sixteenth century and Dutch colonists planted it along the Hudson. The kernel inside the buckwheat shell is known as a groat. Buckwheat groats can be steamed, boiled or baked, or served as a cereal like oatmeal. When roasted, groats are called *kasha,* which is popular in Russia, the Balkans and some health-food delis. *Soba* are Asian buckwheat noodles. Fresh buckwheat seeds can be sprouted. Buckwheat pancakes have been a health-food staple in the United States for decades.

Since the outer hull of buckwheat is very hard and does not soften up in cooking, it must be removed during processing. Commercially milled buckwheat flours can be dark or light. The dark flour has some particles of finely milled hulls, but excess hull makes the flour bitter. With buckwheat's iron and other minerals and an impressive supply of B vitamins, vegans and wheat-sensitive people may find this an appealing dietary addition, particularly as soba or in pancakes.

 ## AMARANTH

The amaranth plant group,* which includes nutritious weeds like pigweed, originated in the same area of the Andean highlands as the common potato. Natives in the area still eat it toasted and popped, as

---

*For more information on amaranth, try the library (or an out-of-print book service) for the books, *Amaranth from the Past for the Future,* by John N. Cole (Rodale Press, Emmaus, PA, 1979), or *Amaranth—Modern Prospects for an Ancient Crop* (National Academy of Sciences, reprinted by Rodale Press, Inc., Emmaus, PA, 1985).

flour, or boiled as porridge. But its greatest use is in countries like India and Nepal, where it is combined with wheat to improve the protein content of a local flatbread called chapatis.

Today amaranth is experiencing a rebirth, primarily because of its good amino acid balance. According to devotees, if assigned a number on the protein perfection scale from 0 to 100, amaranth would measure 75 to 87, compared with corn at 44, wheat at about 60, soybean at 68 and milk at just over 72. Still, amaranth, like most grains, does not have a perfect balance of essential amino acids, so it is improved if combined with a food high in the amino acid pegs that fit into amaranth's nutritional holes. Its perfect companion is wheat. So very light eaters who need to boost their protein intake may find this a valuable addition to the pantry. Amaranth zealots (and there are plenty) even suggest planting amaranth in the garden, for the nutrition-packed leaves (which taste like spinach) as well as the small ivory-colored seeds. The tiny amaranth seeds can be milled into flour (although not in all mills) or rolled like oats and used in breads, rolls, muffins, soups, pancakes, crepes, dumplings, tortillas, and cookies, or added to high-protein fruit drinks.

 # BULGUR

Bulgur is an American version (developed in 1945) of a dish called *Arisah* in the Old Testament. Commercial millers developed it in an effort to make surplus American wheat palatable (and sale-

ARISAH

Boil a cup or more of whole wheat (soft white or soft red) until tender. Spread it in thin layers in the sun (or oven, presumably). Remove the outer bran layers by sprinkling with water and rubbing by hand. The old process was to then crack the grains by stone or with a crude mill. (If you have a coarse setting on your grinder, try that, or try putting small amounts in a blender.) To cook, steam in a colander over a pot of boiling water.

able) to cultures that preferred rice. It succeeded as a passable substitute for pilaf, couscous, and some rice products.

Modern bulgur is made in various ways. In general, cleaned white or red soft wheat is soaked for eight hours or until it reaches a moisture content of 45 percent. It is then steamed briefly under pressure then dried to a moisture content of about 10 percent. If it has bran, it may be removed, then the grain is lightly milled and sieved by size.

For those who want to try this at home, the inset provides the biblical process for *Arisah*. For purists who dislike the idea of removing bran, here is reassuring technical information: during cooking of the whole grain, some of the vitamins and other nutrients in the outer layers of the kernel move to the inner part of the grain, so removing bran (and using it elsewhere to retain the fiber) should not destroy the nutritive value of the *Arisah*.

 ## SORGHUM AND MILLET

Both millet and sorghum are staple cereals in parts of Africa, Asia, Central America and the Arab Middle East. In Africa, sorghum and millet are still pounded in a mortar to loosen the husks. The grain is then ground to the size of semolina and the husks are blown off. Flour and meal are prepared daily because hot climates encourage rancidity. Oatmeal-like dishes, semisolid dumplings, and couscous are some of the vast array of sorghum and millet products eaten around the world.

Millet has been important in food and brewing in Asia, Africa and Europe since prehistoric times and was probably around before the plow. The Chinese were cultivating it by 2800 B.C. Millet appears to have arrived in India 3,000 years ago, but was not cultivated in the United States until 1873. It has become a popular crop in any area with dry, hot conditions. While 75 percent of all millet is used for human food, its popularity in some areas has declined in this century. Still, about 400 million people in countries such as India, Africa, China and Russia depend on millet for survival. In America, Western Europe, Australia, Canada and Japan, it is used almost exclusively as animal feed, although it is widely available in health-food stores.

There are at least 12 distinct millet species (six of which make up most of the world's production). Finger millet has one of the highest calcium contents in known cereal grains and is also rich in iron, riboflavin, niacin and phosphorus. Most millets have protein levels comparable to wheat, barley and maize. They are adequate in all essential amino acids and richer in the amino acid lysine than rice, corn or oats. Combining it with any of these grains improves protein. Millet sold for human consumption in health-food stores has been hulled and may be added to wheat bread at one-quarter cup per loaf if uncooked or toasted without oil, or one cup per loaf if cooked in water. It can be popped, roasted, sprouted or malted, but is not usually ground into flour.

Sorghum is a tropical grass grown in cool areas where it is too dry for corn and other grains to survive. Immature sorghum grains can be roasted whole. White-seeded sorghum can be popped—it is more tender than corn, and has less hull to get caught between the teeth. Sorghum is widely used to make flatbreads like chapati. It can be mixed with wheat to make variety breads or with legumes or legume flours to increase nutritional value. White sorghum flour can be substituted for or mixed with corn in tortillas. Sorghum is deficient in lysine, tryptophan and the sulphur-containing amino acids. It should not be sprouted for human consumption, as the roots and sprouts are toxic.

QUINOA

Quinoa (pronounced *keenwa*) is a recent addition to America's grain smorgasbord. Dubbed "the mother grain" by ancient Incas in the Andes of South America, quinoa's popularity receded after the arrival of the Spanish but is experiencing a revival in traditional growing areas of Bolivia, Peru, Ecuador and Chile. A hardy plant that grows at altitudes up to 13,000 feet, quinoa is very high in protein and rich in fat. Its good protein balance (with ample supplies of the amino acids lysine, methionine, and cystine) and high iron, magnesium, phosphorus and calcium content, gave it an entrée to the United States health-food market. Quinoa's small seeds can be used as a substitute for brown rice, or to replace cracked wheat in recipes like tabouli or rice pilaf. It can be made into a pudding, ground into a flour for use in pasta, and, as one gluten-sufferer reported to me, even made into bread. Quinoa seeds have a coat of saponins when harvested. Most of this bitter substance is washed away before sale, but soaking the seeds for five minutes then rinsing until all foam disappears removes any remaining residue.

FLAXSEED

These small, shiny, dark-brown seeds did not count for much in the American diet until the 1980s, when the FDA permitted additions of from 10 to 12 percent in commercial breads. But flaxseed oil or the seeds themselves were considered food items by the Greeks, Romans, Egyptians, Russians, Poles and Hungarians, among others. Today, flaxseed enjoys great eminence as a health promoter due to its healthful omega-3 fatty acids, which have been linked to reduced cholesterol, hypertension and inflammatory and autoimmune disorders. Over 70 percent of flaxseed fats are polyunsaturated. But it is flaxseed's high percentage of omega-3 (about 60 percent) versus omega-6 fatty acids that has garnered attention. Although an equal balance of these fatty acids is seen as about right in diet, we consume far more omega-6 fats, which are dominant in vegetable oils. Eating up to two tablespoons of flaxseed a day can return these fatty acids to a healthful balance. Like other grains and seeds, flaxseed provides all of the health benefits attributed to both soluble and insoluble fibers.

The coarse outer shell of items like flaxseed must be penetrated before nutrients can be digested. One option is to mill flaxseed into a pleasant, nutty meal and add to bread, muffins or almost any baked good. Or, to make sure nutrients are protected from heat, sprinkle it raw on salads, fruits, vegetables or yogurt. Flaxseed is also a popular item for rolling or flaking, like oats. Because of the high fat content of seeds, milled or rolled flax should be consumed immediately or refrigerated for no longer than a week. This small seed can make a significant contribution to diet with a minimum of effort.

SUMMARY

The Internet is a remarkable source of information, recipes, and purchasing contacts for the grains mentioned in this section, and many, many more. With so many grains to choose from, even recalcitrants who simply cannot give up white bread can still get more nutrients and fiber into their diets by learning to enjoy alternatives like fresh oats, flaxseed, buckwheat, corn, amaranth and kasha. Remember, the more ways you find to eat whole grains, the healthier you will be. So whether you do it for health, for variety or for excitement, why not launch a bold new eating plan. Buy a spelt cookbook, an amaranth cookbook, or a cornmeal cookbook and say *au revoir!* to culinary boredom as you dash into the world of delicious new grains that a home mill opens up before you.

CHAPTER *10*

Stocking the Home Granary

Winter Storage

Imagine that you live in Beijing, China.
One crisp, fall morning you stumble out,
half-blinded by the coal smoke from the breakfast fire,
and bash into a mountain of cabbage.
You stumble back.
Was that this morning?!
Yes, the entire winter cabbage supply
dumped on the corner in the black of night.
Can you survive another winter of
kicking it under the table, in corners and hallways…
anywhere it won't be stolen…
anywhere the smell won't be fatal…?!
Then ask yourself:
What's the big deal about storing a little wheat?

Egyptian wheat harvests were estimated by measurers, recorded by scribes, then lugged by slaves up 15-foot ladders and dumped into cylindrical mud granaries. Throughout the year, grain was removed through a bottom opening that was scrupulously guarded from rodents. The Greeks hoarded their wheat like the gold in Fort Knox, doling it out as they deemed wise. The Anasazi Indians in the American southwest stored grain in bricked-up crevices in the sides of sheer cliffs, in mud-and-mortar rooms off their homes, or in underground granaries. Impressive as these storage programs were in their time, America's grain storage and transportation systems rival anything the world has ever seen. Colossal concrete and tin granaries dot the farmlands of this country and modern grain elevators make an ocean of wheat kernels flow virtually nonstop from millions of acres of growing fields to the far edges of virtually every continent.

You, too, will need a system for buying and storing grains and it will run more smoothly if you are prepared to buy the right wheat, in the right quantities, from the right sources and have a well-conceived plan for storing what you buy. To help with this plan, this chapter starts by explaining how to examine and judge grain—so you recognize the best and reject anything that falls short. Then, because space limitations determine how much grain can be ordered, you will learn how and where to store grains. After a brief review of various wheats and the products for which they are best suited, you will find a sample shopping list and hints for locating suppliers. After that, you will learn how to dispose of any stowaways who arrive in your bag of grain and how to evaluate your wheat's capacity for making bread. Finally, you will find technical information to help you decide whether or not to risk nutritional losses by "aging" your flour in order to improve bread performance. So, before we start crawling around the house looking for grain cubbyholes, let's learn how to examine grain for problems.

EXAMINING AND JUDGING GRAIN

The ability to intelligently examine grain for problems can save time, money and disappointment. When buying in small quantities from a local health food store or grain outlet, you can examine grain before purchase. This is not possible with specially ordered 25- or 50-pound bags. Fortunately, most bags will impart only the earthy aroma of high-quality grain. But it is possible to open a new bag of grain and find surprises, such as poor-quality grain, dirt, or even an explosion of winged creatures. Just in case, this section starts by telling you how to examine and identify wheat by visual characteristics, then moves on to things that shouldn't—but may—arrive in the bag.

Kernel Characteristics

Wheat is identified and graded largely by visual examination and home millers should definitely be able to distinguish one wheat from another just by looking at it. Then, if the contents of a poorly marked bag are not what was ordered, an exchange can be made. The ideal way to learn about wheat is to buy a small quantity of every type that can be located in local stores. Carefully label the samples with all the information provided by the supplier, then take them home for examination and comparison. It may be helpful to refer to the chapter on wheat to jog your memory about the characteristics of the various wheats you have purchased.

Put your samples in separate bowls or on undecorated plates. Label each sample so your observations are constantly linked with the type of wheat being studied. First, compare your samples with each other. Note that they may be different colors, usually reddish, whitish or yellowish. Note that some types are plump and some are slim. Some are opaque while others are more translucent when held up to a bright light. Now, go back to the chapter on wheat and study the characteristics associated with your samples. To test yourself, remove the labels and see if you can identify the different wheats by visual characteristics only. Which are the soft wheats, the hard wheats, the winter wheats, the spring wheats?

Next, study the individual kernels in just one sample. Ideally, all the kernels will be similar in color and size. Too many wrinkled or shriveled grains is not ideal. The best wheat will be free-flowing, healthy-looking and uniformly shaped.

Finally, mill some of each sample into meal and examine it under a magnifying glass. Notice that the meal consists of tiny chunks of endosperm and flecks of bran. Rub the various samples between your fingers. Notice that the hard wheats feel gritty and fall easily from your fingers. The soft wheats feel softer, oilier, and may stick to your fingers. Next, squeeze the samples in your hand, one by one. Can you differentiate the soft wheats from the hard wheats? (Soft wheats remain somewhat clumped after you open your hand; hard wheats act more like sand.) Based on what you have observed, can you anticipate which sample will make the best bread or best cakes and cookies?

Now that you know what your wheat should look like, let's consider things that might arrive in the bag with it.

Dirt

Large harvesters and millers have an elaborate process for cleaning wheat intended for human consumption, which ideally includes washing and drying. But not all wheat suppliers have the full range of cleaning equipment, so it is possible that you will one day receive a bag of wheat that is dirty. This means dirt in the hopper, dirt in the bottom of containers, and, worst of all, dirt in the bread or cake. Dirt can be an irritating problem or a horrible problem, depending on the quantity present. A small amount may go undetected. But if it destroys the flavor of your baked goods, call the vendor and tell him the wheat is dirty.

To test the cleanness of wheat, roll some around between your hands, then check for a gritty, dirty feeling. Or put a cup of grain on a white paper towel, close it up and shake it around. When opened, the paper towel should still be a fairly pristine white sheet, although there may be a small residue of straw-colored dust from the chaff, which is acceptable. Incidentally, moisture is an important variable in grain that is best measured with scientific instruments, so attempting to wash dirty wheat at home is not recommended. Although you will rarely know the moisture content of a bag of wheat, that information is available. As reference, for long-term storage, commercial wheats are dried to a moisture level of 14.6 percent or less.

Foreign Matter

Fortunately, most wheat is not only dirt-free, but has also been purged of foreign matter such as seeds, chaff, metal bits, pebbles, rodent feces and insect parts. On occasion, however, an inadequate cleaning job will have been done and contaminants will be encountered. Most fall in the dread category of black: rodent feces, tiny pebbles (which can damage some mills), errant seeds and insect parts. A few others fall in the nearly-as-alarming green-yellow-gray category: too much chaff or straw, cobweb necklaces, moth-like creatures, tiny snail-like rounds, or green seeds. Finding these colors in otherwise beautiful wheat can be disconcerting. But it is quite possible to utilize dry grain that contains contaminants, if a way can be found to pick or sift them out. Because most busy people will find this an irritating and time-consuming job, however, it is a worthwhile precaution to buy only small quantities of grain until a source has proven reliable.

Odors

You have the right to expect grain to arrive smelling fresh and pleasant, not moldy, mildewy or damp. If it was cleaned and stored properly, it will flow freely and have no clumps. Grain should also not smell rancid. Excessive temperatures can cause the large supply of lipids in grains like rye and brown rice to become rancid. Rancid grain is unhealthful and should not be eaten under any circumstances. If you are not sure you can identify the smell of rancidity, try buying a small bag of chopped nuts in the baking section of the grocery store. Open and sniff it. Chances are very good that these nut fragments will yield the typical odor that accompanies rancidity. Butter that has sat too long at room temperature will also bear a rancid odor.

If you buy directly from a wheat grower or feed store, be sure to ask for cleaned wheat, so you do not get chemically treated wheat intended for seed or uncleaned wheat intended for animal feed. Seed wheat will certainly have an alarming chemical odor that should not be ignored. It may also be pink. Also be cautious about wheat whose origin is unknown. It may be dirty, intended for animals, or chemically treated as seed.

 FINDING SQUIRREL HOLES

Between study sessions on the quality of wheat, friends or family members can be sent on a sort of scavenger hunt—for the surprisingly great number of places in a house or apartment where grains can be stored. In fact, large quantities of grain should probably not be ordered until storage containers and areas have been identified. Whether grain is stored in one large container or packed in smaller ones, the rules are the same: start with fresh, dry grain and pack it so moisture, rodents and bugs cannot get inside, then keep it as cool as possible. If you do use large storage containers in the garage or a separate building, you may want to keep smaller containers of grain near the grinder for easy and quick access.

The following are some possible storage areas, to get the scavenger hunt going.

Garages, Closets and Beds

If you have a garage, or other large storage area, 50 or 100 pounds of grain should not pose a storage problem. But remember that grain must be protected from moisture and excessive heat. This leaves out the water heater area, sunny windows, hot attics, near a wood stove or other heat source, or even a hot garage or garden shed. The worst place is a hot, humid area where mold or fungus can get a foothold. If you have hot summers, consider using small containers that can be kept in the garage most of the year, then moved to a cooler inside closet during hot months.

If storage space is limited, a bit of imagination will turn up un-used holes that can serve as grain bins. Some examples include inconvenient cupboards, closet shelves or corners, and an old favor-ite, the wasted space under beds. Armoires, hope chests, window seats, guest rooms or partially filled bookcases are other un-grain-like places that would suit grain perfectly.

Containers

Once storage spaces have been identified, decide what contain-ers to use. Grain can be stored in the shipping bag in a dry, cool place that is inaccessible to insects or rodents, but sealed containers offer the best protection in the long run.

Big metal or plastic garbage cans (preferably with tight lids, wheels and handles) are good options for those with a garage and lots of wheat to store. These containers are relatively inexpensive, hold from 50 to 150 pounds of grain, and can be moved easily. To keep critters and moisture out, line the can with a double thickness of large plastic gar-bage bag. Fill the doubled bags with grain and close with a rubber band or anything that keeps moisture out. Protect from rodents by closing the lid tightly. Then, be sure the can remains accessible, not buried under boxes or hidden behind the lawnmower. As suggested earlier, keeping small containers of grain near the grinder saves time.

Small plastic buckets with lids are handy as they can be stacked on top of each other, moved easily, and are easy to dip grain from. But be aware that grain is very heavy. If you have difficulty lifting or mov-ing heavy containers, stick to the smaller one- or two-gallon sizes. Light-weight containers with handles are also excellent choices be-cause they are easy to lift and pour from. Very clean, very dry plastic milk jugs fall in this category, but may be difficult to fill without a funnel of the right size. Containers with secure lids reduce spilling. Large plastic bags tear easily under the heavy load of grain, but can be used if the grain is double-bagged, protected from rodents, and moved infrequently. Also, dip, don't pour, the grain from these bags. Tracking down kernels is time-consuming.

THE SHOPPING LIST

Once your grain storage limitations are established, you are ready to prepare a shopping list. Even the most basic cooks will want one or more breadmaking wheats plus a wheat for cakes and cookies and probably some corn. These grains can be integrated into any modern kitchen, without more complex appliances than a flour mill and bread machine. Eventually, culinary adventurers and gluten sufferers will supplement this basic list with other grains. Let's look again at the wheat options from which you can choose for your initial wheat order.

Grains for Breadmaking

Any miller's shopping list must begin with a good supply of high-protein wheat for making bread. The following brief review of commonly used breadmaking wheats (covered in more detail in the chapter on wheat), plus rye and durum, will help you select the right wheat for the breadmaking process you use.

Hard red spring is a hard, vitreous, high-protein wheat that will be the first choice for people who like tall, light-textured loaves of bread. The highest, least crumbly loaves can be made from hard red spring with 15 percent or more protein. This wheat is the ideal choice for bread machine baking or for standard loaves produced by four-hour hand-kneading methods. Hard red spring can also be added to weaker wheats to improve the latter's baking performance.

Hard red winter is also a hard, vitreous, high-protein wheat. As a winter wheat, it generally contains slightly less protein than spring wheat but is preferred by many bread makers for its stronger wheat flavor. Hard red winter makes adequate loaves of light bread and is probably the first choice for those who bake European-style hearth loaves or wheat and rye breads, both of which are appealing for reasons other than height or lightness. Protein content remains important in any breadmaking wheat, so hard red winter with 14 to 14.5 percent protein will perform best in the bread machine or in standard manual recipes.

Hard white spring is a hard, vitreous, high-protein wheat with a flavor that may be too mild for some yet preferred by others who are genuinely fond of white bread. Hard white spring containing 15 percent or more protein makes high, good-textured standard or bread-machine loaves. It can be combined with other wheats to mellow the flavor of strong-flavored wheats or improve baking performance of weaker wheats.

Rye contains relatively little breadmaking protein, but is an important bread grain for European-style breads. Careful processing can produce excellent 100 percent rye bread, but special recipes and expert handling are required. Rye is commonly used as a flavor addition to wheat bread and as the basis for sourdough starters. One-half cup of rye contributes a distinctive flavor to any wheat loaf without much loss of volume. Bakers who regularly include a high percentage of rye in their loaves should start with 25 pounds. If only small quantities are added for flavoring, five pounds should be sufficient for the initial order.

Durum is a very hard, vitreous, high-protein wheat, grown primarily for pasta and noodles. It produces better flavor and quality in homemade pasta than other wheats. Some varieties contain sufficient glutenins to make excellent yeasted bread. These high-protein breadmaking varieties can be added to weaker wheats to improve texture and performance. Durum contributes interesting flavor to bread and a distinctive amber color that is noticeable in both bread and pasta. Unless durum is sold specifically as a breadmaking wheat, order only small quantities until it is clear that it *is* amber durum and that it has good breadmaking qualities.

Wheat for Sweet Treats

If you intend to bake cakes, cookies, or other desserts, or to add this flavor-booster to bread, you will need a supply of soft wheat. Select from the following two options.

Soft White is a soft, mealy, low-protein wheat that is ideal for non-bread products that require little gluten. Soft white adds a distinctive and wonderful flavor to muffins, quick breads, cookies and cakes. This wheat is a staple in any baker's pantry. Knowing the protein content is far less important with soft white than with breadmaking wheat because small amounts of a stronger wheat can be added when making baked goods that benefit from more gluten, such as pie crust or muffins.

Soft Red is a medium-gluten soft wheat. It is not widely available through distributors outside its growing areas, but is commonly used by white flour bakers for cakes and other products that don't rely on yeast for leavening. If it is encountered or can be tracked down, soft red is certainly worth trying as an alternative to soft white.

Corn and Other Grains

Corn is a grain with so many uses that it should be included in the pantry of any home miller. Although corn has a high lipid content, it does not carry the same high risk for rancidity as rye berries until it has been ground. If not consumed shortly after milling, cornmeal or corn flour should be refrigerated or frozen. *Flint* varieties are better for standard cornmeal and the chunky texture of traditional polenta. *Dent* varieties make better flour for tortillas, finely textured cornbread and tamales. Corn is readily available but not usually identified by variety, so it is necessary to specify variety when ordering. Try small quantities until you become familiar with the performance of different varieties of corn, then order a 25-pound bag, if you use it regularly.

Gourmet bakers and people allergic to gluten may want to order a supply of other grains. The chapter entitled *More Grist For Your Mill* should assist in these individual decisions. Because the quest for high protein content is not an issue with these grains, shipping price is probably the primary consideration when selecting sources.

 # PREPARING THE ORDER

At this point, you have a pretty good idea which grains you will use. But what's a ballpark quantity for the first order? Since two big advantages of home milling are never having to run to the store for a loaf of bread and being prepared for emergencies, most people with space will probably want to stock up. Exactly how much you buy will depend on the number in the household, the combination of wheats used for bread and how many loaves will be made. Each loaf of bread requires roughly a pound of grain. Two hearty bread eaters can do with a loaf every other day. A small family will need at least a loaf a day. Grains are usually sold in 25- and 60-pound bags with smaller quantities available from health food stores and mail-order houses.

Those who just want a good loaf of bread every day or two and an occasional batch of pancakes or loaf of banana bread can get by for at least six months with a 60-pound bag of hard breadmaking wheat and 10 pounds of soft white or red wheat. Those who devour bread, then use leftovers in everything from stuffing to bread pudding, can begin with 60 pounds of hard wheat and 25 of soft but will be ordering more within a few months.

The following is a sample shopping list. Cross off items you do not need and change quantities to suit the size and appetite of your family (and friends and neighbors).

A BASIC GRAIN ORDER

bread wheat	60 lbs of hard red spring, hard red winter, or hard white spring
dessert wheat	10 lbs of soft white or soft red
durum	25 lbs (if used)
corn	10 lbs (if used)
rye	25 lbs (if used regularly)
	5 lbs (if used occasionally)
beans	5 lbs of garbanzo or soy (if used)

 # THE SUPPLY LINE

Once you have your shopping list ready, the next job is to actually buy grain. Remember, the objective is to find a reliable source that has handled the grain carefully, protecting it from moisture, insects and excessive heat. Buy in small quantities, if possible, until the source proves reliable. Check your grain carefully. It should have dry, pleasant-smelling kernels of uniform size and color. There really should not be anything black in there. But if there is, give the vendor a chance to replace the bag (at his expense). A *second* bag of contaminated wheat, however, indicates that the source has inadequate cleaning equipment and should be removed from your list of suppliers. The chapter entitled *Finding Time to Grind* includes information on wheat prices.

Which source you use for grain will depend in large part upon where you live. Here are some possibilities.

Back to the Farm

If you live near or vacation in a wheat-growing area, you're in luck. Many medium-sized towns in wheat-growing areas have consumer grain outlets that sell fresh, inexpensive 25- or 60-pound bags of cleaned wheat. Some of these outlets ship individual bags of wheat, but shipping costs will probably exceed the cost of the wheat (which can still be relatively inexpensive).

The Health Food Store

If you live in or near a city with a health food store or co-op that sells bulk grains, you are in luck. In fact, this may be as good an option as buying from the farm itself because it allows you to test grains before purchasing in large quantities and provides access to grains from other wheat-growing areas. Also, health food stores that offer products in bulk are the best source for specialty grains. When buying breadmaking wheat, test the store's wheat until you find one that makes good bread, then place a bulk order. But be cautious when you order. Product ordering books provided by distributors usually contain limited information. Make sure the wheat listed is actually the wheat you tested. If protein content is not known, ask the clerk to call the distributor, or place the call yourself. If the distributor does not know the protein content, this should raise a red flag in your mind. If your health food store cannot locate a source for high-protein wheat, refer them to the sources listed in the Appendix, or order from one of these sources yourself.

Local Groups

Many of the same groups that kept home flour mill manufacturers in business while the rest of us were eating white bread also kept wheat supply lines open. A good, inexpensive supply of grain can sometimes be located at state or county fairs or through local nutrition-oriented groups such as co-ops, buying clubs, Seventh Day Adventists, Mormons, Amish, or Mennonites, to name a few.

Mail-Order Catalogs

Although mail-order houses abound and may, in the end, be the only source for small quantities of hard-to-locate grains, they are truly a last resort because shipping charges are very high. In many cases, the grain prices are also high, ranging from expensive to astronomical. (But always check for the exception.) Another drawback to ordering from catalogs is that a wheat's protein content is rarely given nor is it known by those who take telephone orders. Most of the suppliers of high-protein wheat listed in the Appendix are exceptions to these rules. Some mail-order sources are also included in the Appendix for locating specialty grains, which might otherwise be difficult to track down.

The Internet

Buying at the end of the extensive network that gets grain from the farm to you can be frightfully expensive and frustrating because so little information about the grain survives the trip. Cheaper and more reliable sources probably exist closer to the growing area of a desired grain. The Internet can help you find them. So, start by discovering where the grain is grown. This requires a quick Internet search for subjects like *whole grain sources, soft white wheat, wheat farms*, that sort of thing. For example, if you searched for *durum wheat suppliers*, you would quickly learn that 70 to 80 percent of durum is grown in South Dakota, with smaller amounts coming from Arizona, Montana and California. That gets you in the local area. Then if you happened to live in California, you might try *California durum suppliers*.

Although it is easy to confuse quantity with quality when it comes to the Internet, if you carefully consider the source, much can be gained from even the briefest foray. The Internet is an indispensable tool for people without access to a co-op or other source of high quality grains. It is easy to get lost in this infinitely branching labyrinth, but all is made worthwhile when you locate an inexpensive (or possibly the *only*) source for a special grain that you hoped, but never really expected, to find.

BOOTING OUT UNWELCOME GUESTS

As discussed earlier in this chapter, bulk grains usually arrive free-flowing and fragrant, but they may also be dirty, stinky, or even have unwelcome guests. Let's now discuss stowaways and what you can do about them.

The bran and germ fractions that are removed during white flour processing contain four to five times more minute traces of herbicides, fungicides, insecticides and rodenticides than are present in white flour. For this reason, many health-conscious home millers prefer to buy organic grains despite the huge jump in price. But this may present problems, too. For example, even if the grain looks clean when it arrives, you may later open a bucket of stored wheat and find it moving. Or you may find grains dangling from cobweb necklaces, or winged creatures may fly in your face. Although unpleasant, these visitors are not dangerous, but you do not need to put up with their company, either. Here are some solutions, just in case you encounter (or suspect) critters in your grain.

Gas 'em

Putting dry ice in with grain is a common home remedy for weevils (and eggs) or other living things, but it also adds moisture to a bucket of grain, which may be undesirable in a damp, warm climate. Here is how to do it, in case you have the right climate. Half-fill a plastic bucket with wheat and add a quarter pound of dry ice. Fill the rest of the bucket with wheat and set the lid on top (without sealing it) for six hours. Then put the lid on tightly and leave it for seven to ten days. This is a good precaution if you plan to store organic grains for some time, since creatures can be invisible but hatch later.

Freeze 'em

The best solution to an infestation—if feasible—is to put the grain in moisture-proof plastic bags and store them in the freezer for two weeks. This kills both insects and larvae. If freezer space is limited, the job can be done in several batches. In fact, if you use organic grains, this may be a valuable preventive treatment even if you detect no movement or black specks. The presence of cobweb necklaces with grain hanging from them (you'll recognize them...) indicates an infestation that has not yet hatched. Remove the necklaces and throw them away. Dispose of any winged creatures that have hatched by sifting or picking them out individually. Then bag the grain and freeze it. If you have caught the problem early enough, you may not have to throw the grain away.

Sift 'em Out

Frass is the technical term for insect parts in grain, which are more repugnant than harmful. If their presence is not excessive, you may prefer to sift them out rather than discard the grain. Finding an appropriate screen is not a snap. One option (which also works to sift out bran) is to make a square wooden frame and staple nylon window screen on the bottom. Anything with holes smaller than the grains will allow the parts to pass through while the kernels stay in the box. If there are too many black specks in the grain and you are not in the middle of a food disaster, you may choose to replace the grain, perhaps from a different source.

Pick 'em Out

If your guests are small in number, large in size, and dead, it may be practical to spread the grain out on a large tray and manually remove them. This might prove an engrossing activity for seven-year-old boys.

 ## DEALING WITH PROBLEM WHEAT

The ultimate proof of quality for many people will be how spectacular the loaf is that steams out of the oven. Unfortunately, there is always the possibility that your new wheat will not knead up beyond a sticky mess, or produce anything but dense or crumbly loaves. Before you return or toss it, here are some ways to salvage it. First, buy some high-protein hard red spring wheat (from a new source, probably). Bake a loaf or two. If the bread is satisfactory, mix this wheat with the weak wheat, half and half. You can also prod a weak wheat to improved performance by using a longer fermentation process or adding one or more of the dough conditioners mentioned in the breadmaking chapter of this book. If you are really desperate, replace a cup of wholemeal with a cup of white bread flour.

TRACKING INVENTORY

Even after you have learned to identify grains by sight, you should label all containers with type of grain, protein content, purchase date, price and supplier name. This tracks the speed at which you are using all grains, makes reordering easier, and documents the reliability of sources. Labeling may seem unnecessary, but it is amazing what can be forgotten in six busy months.

AGING FLOUR

Aging flour is, at best, a tangential issue for home millers, but this information is included for very serious bread makers who might wish to try it. In the white flour baking industry, "aging" flour improves the action of gluten during fermentation, resulting in larger loaves with more finely textured crumb. The value of aging flour is so accepted by the baking industry that chemical improvers are added to white flour to get the aging done more quickly. Because aging is contrary to everything we know about the loss of nutrients and encouragement of rancidity in whole-grain flour, here are some technical excerpts from a basic textbook*, so very serious cooks can determine whether the benefits outweigh the costs.

Here's what happens technically when flour is aged.

"The breadmaking quality of freshly milled flour tends to improve during storage...of 1-2 months. The improvement occurs more rapidly if the flour is exposed to the action of the air. During such aerated storage, fat acidity increases at first, owing to lipolytic activity, and later decreases, by lipoxidase action; products of the oxidation of fatty acids appear; the proportion of linoleic and linolenic acids in the lipids falls; and disulphide bonds...decrease in number."

Of further interest, the authors of the same textbook say:

"Stored at 62°F, the shelf-life of...wholemeal (100% extraction rate) is closely related to the moisture content and temperature...For wholemeal

---

*Kent's Technology of Cereals, 4th ed., by N. L. Kent and A.D. Evers (Pergamon, Oxford, 1994).

*stored under the most favorable conditions, a shelf life of 3 months may be expected, or of 12 months if the product has been entoleted."**

A final quote from page 68:

"In wheat, lipase activities in the embryo and aleurone layers are 10-20-fold that of the endosperm...The storage lives of bran, germ and wholemeal flour are considerably less than that of white flour for this reason."**

Some people will feel nothing justifies allowing flour to sit around for a month or two, while others may be curious whether aging really does make a difference in the quality of bread. Fortunately, each home miller can make this decision for himself or herself.

 ## A FINAL WORD

How much grain to buy and where to store it are very individual decisions. Historically, city dwellers with ready access to markets have tended to maintain a smaller food supply than country folk, many of whom still preserve fruits, vegetables and even meats. This means that in the event of a natural disaster or interruption in transportation or power systems, many urban dwellers remain quite vulnerable. But even if you feel secure with a small inventory, remember that wheat quality varies from one year to the next. If a new bag of wheat makes better bread than any prior wheat, stock up. Since wheat keeps for years under proper conditions, there won't be any regrets unless you have to move it, it washes away in a flood or mice somehow get in (and if they can, they will). Then, as long as you keep your grain dry, have a way of grinding it and can build a fire, you and your family can eat your way through any disaster. (It might not hurt to have a sack of beans and a case of tuna on hand, either.)

---

*Entoleted means that any bugs have been beaten to death in a high-impact machine called an entoler.

**The embryo is the germ and the aleurone layer is a large-celled bran layer next to the endosperm.

CHAPTER *11*

The Staff of Life

Jennie D. Chalmers homesteaded
in Steel County, North Dakota, over a century ago.
During fall harvests, she rose at 3:00 a.m.
to bake bread and biscuits for a thrashing crew of 25,
to whom she served three full meals each day.
When her nephew, D.L. Pepper, was 12, she told him:
"The ladies in North Dakota liked making bread
because it made their hands so clean"

      Whether bread develops in a bread machine or under the doting flutter of a bread zealot, whether it is baked in a brick oven, Dutch oven, wood stove, bread machine or multitiered, steam-spritzed, stainless steel commercial oven, the same basic chemical activities take place, even if they are not observed or understood by the bread maker. So...the more you know about the chemistry of breadmaking, the more control you have over the appearance, fragrance and flavor of the end product. Even bread-machine bakers need at least a rudimentary understanding of what's going on when wholemeal, water, yeast, sugar and fat are mixed together and allowed to ferment. This chapter peeks into the bread laboratory, at the two separate-but-equal areas in which the success or failure of your loaf lie: the ingredients and the breadmaking process.

      Bookstore shelves are sinking under the load of attractive, informative books on the many different ways to make bread. This book, on the other hand, is about home milling, so it provides just enough breadmaking information to help home millers get some delicious, healthful bread on the table with a minimum of instruction. Its primary focus is on chemical activities that take place during all breadmaking processes and on ingredients as they interact with wholemeal during any process. This information can be very instructive regarding the differences between wholemeal and white-flour baking.

The underlying assumption is that you will start with the highest protein wheat and use either a bread machine or a standard four-hour, knead-rise-proof manual process. The end product, which you should be able to produce with a minimum of fiddling, will be tall and appealingly brown, with a texture that holds together with sandwich fixings between the slices. This bread has a delicious old-fashioned bread flavor that will please a majority of the people in this country. But even gourmands itching to get to heartier specialty loaves can learn a lot by perfecting this lighter American version before they move on to more complicated shapes, ingredients and processes.

After you have boned up on ingredients and process, we'll head into the area of judging a good loaf of wholemeal bread. Here it is important to understand that a light, fluffy, mild-flavored loaf is no better nor worse than a solid, rye-flavored dome. It is baking performance, not the shape or flavor, that we'll learn to judge. *Did we do a good job with the ingredients selected,* not *Did we create Wonder Bread out of wholemeal.* Then, just in case the first loaf isn't perfect, you will find some troubleshooting hints.

Once armed with basic information about ingredients and process and a vague idea what the loaf should look, feel and smell like, you will be ready, and no doubt eager, to tackle the simple recipes for bread and other dishes in the next chapter.

 ## BREAD INGREDIENTS

The basic ingredients in bread couldn't be simpler: flour, water, yeast, sweetener, salt and fat. Technically, only flour and water are necessary. The yeast will show up on its own and the other ingredients merely enhance the bread in some way. Simple as these ingredients are, though, there remain tricky areas that can result in a lump instead of a loaf or a honeycombed texture that crumbles easily.

Many problems associated with wholemeal bread can be traced to wheat with insufficient breadmaking gluten. Other problems result from wholemeal's extra components (compared with white flour) that may run like hooligans through the breadmaking laboratory if the baker is not able to handle them. Most problems can be solved by tinkering with ingredients, which is why it is so important to know something about ingredients and how they act in breadmaking. We'll start with the largest, most important and potentially most troublesome ingredient in bread, the flour.

WHERE'S THE RESEARCH?

There is a prodigious body of research on white flour and products made from it. Unfortunately, most wholemeal research in the last century has been of the trial-and-error type, conducted out of necessity by health-conscious wives and mothers or stalwarts in small specialty bakeries. Few have published in scientific journals or otherwise preserved their wholemeal knowledge for posterity. To complicate matters, grains have changed so much in just 50 years that wholemeal advice and recipes from 100 years ago may not apply absolutely to our grains. So, in lieu of lessons from a small village baker in rural France, we must rely on anecdotal information from wholemeal cookbooks and whatever we can extrapolate from the volumes of scientific research done exclusively on white flour.

Flour

In the past, if a particular wheat component aggravated bakers, millers found a way to neutralize it in white flour. Then they standardized the solution so that one bag of flour performed exactly like the next bag and the next and the next. Home-ground wholemeal, *au contraire*, flutters into the flour catcher with all the angelic and devilish characteristics that Mother Nature programmed into the original kernel and then the soil, fertilizer, temperature and moisture exacerbated. The good news is that once you tinker with the water-flour ratio to produce a good loaf, the rest of the bag will usually perform well—in other words, you have standardized your recipe. The bad news is that you may need to standardize again with the next bag of grain.

The single most important flour factor affecting the volume and texture of wholemeal bread is the protein content of the wheat. Any baker who likes high, well-textured loaves of wholemeal bread must buy the strongest bread wheat and add some simple ingredients to compensate for the presence of bran and germ. (See the chapter entitled *Grist for Your Mill* for details.) Bakers who want a heartier bread, a variety bread, a sourdough bread, or composite-flour bread, can benefit from combining some of the highest-protein wheat with the other grains they select. In any case, all wholemeal bread bakers must take the bran and germ into consideration.

Bran. Those large bran flecks that are so good for the colon also have sharp edges that can tear gluten, thus reducing its rising strength. The more finely the meal is milled, the less influence the bran has on gluten and the higher the loaf will be. To use large bran flecks and still get the highest, fluffiest loaves, here are some options:(1) Add other ingredients such as an egg or powdered or fresh dairy products, which improve the volume and crumb of the loaf, or (2) use a long, slow fermentation period (for example, a sponge, which allows part of the recipe's flour and water to ferment overnight), which softens the bran.

Germ. The germ makes up two to three percent of the wheat kernel. Research shows that adding more than three percent wheat germ to white bread weakens the dough. This is thought to be caused by an agent in the germ called glutathione that alters the gluten protein, thereby weakening the dough and ultimately contributing to a more open grain and lower loaf volume. Thanks to Mother Nature, wheat milled at home contains a maximum of three percent germ, so this should pose no problem for wholemeal bakers using high-protein wheats unless additional wheat germ is added. As a precaution, substituting milk for some of the recipe's liquid lessens the damage from germ. A small amount of ascorbic acid in the dough can prevent, and even repair, damage. Since heat inactivates the glutathione in toasted wheat germ, a small amount of the toasted type can be added without effect (although it seems redundant to add wheat germ to wholemeal).

Water

The second most important ingredient affecting bread quality is moisture. The moisture content of grain can change at many stages, from grain harvest to oven baking. Thus, the home baker may experience a few failed loaves while tinkering with the flour-water ratio. Bread made in a damp coastal area will require less added water than bread made in the desert. Following are some other moisture factors that could come into play.

Moisture and Damaged Starch. A certain amount of starch must be damaged in the milling process for flour to make dough of the right consistency. Damaged starch is valuable because it increases the capacity of the flour to absorb water, and makes sugar available to the yeast. Damaged starch also extends the storage life of bread.

Harder wheats sustain more damage in grinding than softer wheats, so they absorb more water. (Severe overgrinding results in excessive water absorption, which reduces bread volume.) Breads made using shorter fermentation periods demand greater water absorption and thus benefit from the higher levels of damaged starch produced by fine grinding. Bran absorbs water more slowly than starch does, so additions of extra water during the early kneading stages, should be made very slowly.

Moisture in Flour. Once grain has been ground, it must be stored in an airtight container or it can gain or lose moisture. Even meticulous measuring and a practiced recipe can yield inconsistent loaf quality if the meal has not been protected from moisture gains or losses.

Yeast

Yeast is a microscopic plant. At the right temperature, it converts sugar into carbon dioxide, ethyl alcohol and other byproducts. If there is enough well-developed gluten in the bread dough, the bread rises when these gasses push against the gluten walls. (Adding more yeast will not compensate for weak gluten structure; the bread will rise faster but not higher.) Yeast-generated gasses also contribute to the flavor of bread.

Although yeast is in the air and will install itself in bread dough if allowed to do so, this time-consuming and unpredictable approach is rarely used today. Instead, virtually all yeast is commercially produced. Yeast is cheap, plentiful, easy to use and very predictable, as long as it has been stored properly (in a cool, dry place) and the expiration date has not passed. Large bags of vacuum-packed yeast are significantly cheaper than small packets or jars. Infrequent bakers can store small amounts for easy access at room temperature while the bulk is kept in an airtight container in the refrigerator or freezer. Products such as nutritional yeast will not make bread rise.

If loaves from a faithful recipe suddenly become squat and dense, check the vigor of the yeast. Fill a measuring cup half-full of warm water (usually 90 to 100 degrees, or manufacturer's recommended temperature). Dissolve a few drops of honey or a teaspoon of any sugar in the water. Add a teaspoon of yeast. If there is no foam on top within 15 minutes, buy new yeast.

DEVILS & HEIRLOOMS

Yeast has a history nearly as long as leavened bread. Bakers once cut a cross in the top of bread to keep the devil (who they thought was inside making the bread rise) from escaping into the surroundings. In 1688 the Faculty of Medicine of Paris pronounced yeast dangerous to human health. Scientists squabbled about how yeast worked until Louis Pasteur settled it in 1857 by siding with those who believed it was a living organism.

In traditional French breadmaking, yeasts and lactic bacteria were transferred from grain to flour during milling, and ancestral techniques were used to select the flour with the right yeast. During long-fermentation processes, these treasured yeasts and lactic bacteria infused the bread with a native tang.

Specially selected, mass-produced microbial strains of yeast are the most common leavening agent in American breadmaking. There are, however, alternatives to yeast. Sourdoughs kept bread going for millennia, many passing like family heirlooms from mother to daughter. Some pioneer varieties of sourdough starter reportedly bubbled in pots near the stove and every conceivable leftover made its way into them. They became so ripe they occasionally oozed out over the tops like gooey green monsters.

Shortening

Shortening is the fat and oil used in dough and batter. Although not strictly necessary, some shortening is usually added to bread to improve flavor, lubricate the internal structure of dough for greater expansion during proofing and baking, and to make it keep longer. Shortening also tenderizes bread by shortening the gluten strands. The lipid-rich germ in wholemeal contributes to this shortening effect, so shortening should not be overused or the gluten strands may be shortened too much, making the bread crumbly and reduced in volume. Care should be taken that rancid shortening not be used, as it is unhealthful and can spoil the flavor of the bread. Individual shortenings act in specific ways in cakes and cookies and are not necessarily interchangeable. But bread makers have more latitude. For example, shortenings such as butter and oil can be combined to take advantage of different contributions made by each.

Vegetable oils are the most commonly used shortening for bread because they are relatively inexpensive. Unfortunately, most have been refined, deodorized and bleached. Some have been further processed to assure liquidity and some have been partially hydrogenated, a process that creates trans fatty acids, which are detrimental to health.

Olive and peanut oils are more expensive but have greater conditioning effect on the bread for reasons related to their higher melting point.

Soy lecithin may be preferred by bakers who want a very healthful type of shortening, although too much can alter flavor noticeably.

Lard, which is made from the fatty tissue of hogs, was traditionally preferred for bread because of a desirable trace of pork flavoring, but modern processing produces a much blander product. Still, lard continues to be used in commercial baking because of its superior shortening qualities.

Butter has adequate shortening value but is more often used in bread for its uniquely desirable flavor. Butter is more expensive than oil, but cost can be reduced by using butter for only part of the shortening. Butter is graded principally by flavor (with the highest grade, AA, having the least flavor, and C having the most). Buying lower grades of butter can provide more butter flavor at lower cost, unless the butter is graded lower because it has a *bad* flavor. Butter is best in bread if used soft and worked into the dough near the end of the kneading period. If butter is used infrequently, freeze it to prevent rancidity.

Coconut Oil/Butter is a healthful vegan substitute for vegetable shortening, margarine or any other hydrogenated or partially-hydrogenated oil, particularly if is unrefined and processed without heat. It is referred to as both an oil and a butter because it is solid up to 76 degrees then it starts to turn into a liquid. This product adds a sweet and pleasant flavor to baked goods. To substitute for one cup of shortening, use either three-quarters of a cup of coconut oil or a combination of one-half cup dairy butter and less than one-half cup coconut oil.

Sweeteners

Although sweetening is not necessary in bread, Americans are familiar with the flavor and like it. Besides adding flavor, sweeteners give bread a more tender crumb and finer texture, improve keeping qualities by retaining moisture, contribute to a pleasant browning of the crust, and provide food for the yeast. Yeast does not actually require added sugar, as it can eat converted dough starch, but, like most of us, it heads for sugar first. Any sweetener can overstimulate yeast (as demonstrated by an open, holey texture in the center, possibly denser around the edges or caved in on top). Excess sugar problems can be solved by reducing sugar or yeast or (to a point) increasing salt, which inhibits yeast activity.

If using a tablespoon or less per loaf, sweeteners are interchangeable. Beyond that, individual characteristics will begin to be noticed in the bread. Here are some common sweeteners that can replace white and brown sugars.

Molasses has been favored historically by wholemeal bakers for its flavor and iron content. Since it is rarely made in big iron pots anymore, it is questionable how much of an iron boost it provides or, for that matter, how healthful it is, since sulphur is used in the process. Today, commercial bakers use it primarily to evoke a sense of wholemeal heartiness.

Molasses is a byproduct of refined white sugar. The darker the color of molasses, the less sugar it contains and the stronger its flavor. The flavor of even one tablespoon of the lighter-flavored variety is noticeable in a loaf. According to one old source, molasses is ideal for long-fermentation wholemeal breads because it provides food for the yeast later in the fermentation process. This may be true because molasses contains more than one type of sugar or it may no longer be true because of changes in processing.

Honey flavors and colors vary wildly from one jar to the next but a tablespoon of pleasantly mild honey can be a wonderful flavor addition. Like other sweeteners, it causes moisture to be retained in bread. Honey is approximately 17 percent water, which in small quantities should not affect a recipe. But if solid fats are also replaced by oils, or liquids are otherwise increased, you may need to consider the net moisture gain. Many people consider honey a healthful alternative to white sugar but the honey on most grocery store shelves costs far too much for a product that is (after processing) little more than simple sugar. Raw, unblended honey has more than 80 organic compounds that are nutritionally beneficial but can also act like renegades in bread. Problems rarely occur with short fermentation times such as bread machines employ but may occur in long-fermentation breads.

Maple Syrup. The expense of this mild-flavored natural sweetener may make it impractical for anything but speciality breads. Additionally, it must be refrigerated or the taste can become very bad. Maple-flavored syrups sold for pancakes and waffles contain only about three percent real maple syrup, so there is no nutritional advantage to their use.

Malt Supplements. French and Italian breads contain little or no sweetening. Enzymes in the flour convert some starch particles to dextrin and malt sugar (maltose), which the yeast then eats. Bakers in the early nineteenth century added malt to stimulate yeast, increase starch conversion, add a sweet flavor, and improve moistness. Some modern wholemeal recipes call for malt supplements, but varying potency in commercial products makes them problematic in baking. There are two types of malt syrup (or extract), as follows.

- *Diastatic* malt contains enzymes that convert starch to maltose (sugar) for the yeast to eat. Small amounts can be valuable in very short fermentation breads. Excessive malt can, however, cause too much starch to be broken down, resulting in gummy bread. Because of unpredictable potency in commercial diastatic malts, problems can materialize in long-fermentation breads. Some bakers recommend against using them at all.

- *Non-diastatic* malt has undergone heat processing that destroys the enzymes that convert starch to maltose, but it can still be used as a source of sugar or flavor and also contributes to keeping qualities.

Salt

Salt plays several important roles in the breadmaking drama: it adds a familiar flavor; improves crumb color; controls fermentation by acting on the yeast to reduce gas production; and toughens the gluten to produce a less sticky dough. By controlling yeast, salt increases processing time. Conversely, adding too little salt will allow yeast to run wild, producing a gassy, sour dough and loaves with open, poorly textured crumb. Troubleshooting an unsatisfactory loaf of bread may involve experimenting with a better balance between sweetener and salt, since one stimulates and the other inhibits yeast activity.

Dough Improvers

Dough improvers (also known as enhancers or conditioners) are very important to wholemeal bakers. They can mitigate the impact of bran and germ, improve loaf height and texture, and affect many other areas of breadmaking. In fact, when everything else has been tried (water-flour adjustments, tinkering with the sugar-salt-yeast ratios) and the crumb still scatters or sandwiches fall apart, one or more dough conditioners must be considered.

MAKING MALT FLOUR

To make malt flour, sprout wheat kernels until fully developed, then dry thoroughly and grind into a flour using a home mill (at temperatures below 120 degrees to avoid inactivating the enzymes). Although barley is used for most malts, wheat produces a malt that causes only moderate enzyme activity, which is probably best for home bakers. Use sparingly: a scant ¼ teaspoon per loaf.

SOME ADVICE

In centuries past, when bakeries were sweatshops, supposedly the only salt added to the dough was in the sweat that dripped from the workers' brows. So, if you add salt and knead by hand, wear a headband...

Commercial dough conditioners provide a timesaving option for harried home bakers. Although expensive and not at all necessary when using high-protein wheats, these premixed products are convenient and long-lasting. Most contain familiar ingredients like whey, soy lecithin, citric acid, dry yeast, sea salt and ascorbic acid, but none of the chemicals used in commercial breadmaking. One tablespoon of a premixed dough conditioner can visibly improve texture in a wholemeal loaf made from medium-strength wheat. These products are available from some health-food stores and some mail-order houses. (See list of sources in Appendix B.)

The best dough conditioners are household items that have been used for centuries, items like milk, potatoes, eggs, mashed cooked beans, and bean flours. Conditioners that must be purchased, such as whey and powdered milk, are convenient but can increase the cost of bread. Most of the following improvers or conditioners don't even require a trip to the store.

Eggs can be a valuable addition to wholemeal bread. They help improve loaf height and texture. The high lecithin content in egg yolk makes the crumb tender and later reduces the starch retrogradation that causes crumb staling. In terms of nutrition, the complete amino acid balance in eggs improves the amino acid balance in wheat, the yolk provides a nutritious source of fat, iron and vitamins, and the white contains valuable protein. Eggs also mute wholemeal flavor somewhat, which may be desirable when wheat overpowers the flavor of other ingredients. One large egg weighs 1.68 ounces and is 73 percent water. For each egg added to bread, the water should be reduced by one-quarter cup (or 60 ml).

Dairy products have been popular additions to bread for 6,000 years. Like eggs, dairy products improve amino acid balance, thus raising the protein quality of bread to that of meat. One milk protein, casein, strengthens gluten so bread can rise higher, but two other proteins that are destroyed by scalding can inhibit rise. Tenderness, keeping qualities, and improved flavor are other benefits that accrue from adding products like milk, buttermilk, yogurt or nonfat dried milk.

Milk makes bread crust browner (so baking time or oven heat must be reduced) and causes bread slices to toast more quickly. Dairy's muting effect on wheat flavor may please recent converts from white bread, and allows other flavors to reign. (Hard cheese is a high-calorie alternative that requires large quantities to affect flavor much.) Replace no more than one-third of the moisture in a recipe with milk. Be sure to scale then cool milk before adding to bread. It is generally unsafe to use dairy products or eggs in long-fermentation breads or with the delayed timer feature on bread machines because of risks posed by bacteria.

Potatoes have been historically popular as dough conditioners in bread and, in times of shortage, to extend wheat flour. In 1883 America, potatoes were a common addition to home bread sponges. By 1911, when considerable breadmaking had moved to commercial bakeries, fresh potatoes had been replaced by other materials, such as potato flour and malt extracts. Home-ground wholemeal does benefit from the addition of potato water or cooked, mashed potatoes (but not highly processed dehydrated or flaked potato products). Improvements from potato additions include a lighter loaf that is moist and chewy. Potatoes do well in combination with dairy products and produce a good hearth loaf. Be sure to peel, cut out dark spots and wash potatoes thoroughly to ensure against a relatively rare bacterial contamination called Rope (*Bacillus mesentericus*), which can make the inside of the loaf virtually disappear.

Bean flours. Centuries of bakers have used beans or bean flours in bread. Soy flour is a currently popular addition to bread because it is nutritious and because it contains enzymes that bleach flour and condition dough so that it rises higher. Only small amounts (a tablespoon or two per loaf) should be used, however, or the taste may become noticeable and the bread heavier. Garbanzo bean flour contributes less nutrition than soybeans but is equal in conditioning power, milder in flavor and not as rich in fats.

Ascorbic acid is yet another dough conditioner that strengthens gluten. It is inexpensive, stores well and the addition of only one-quarter teaspoon per loaf causes improvement.

Commercial Gluten. Many wholemeal bread recipes call for added gluten. But commercial gluten is a very expensive, super-refined product that imparts a cardboard flavor to bread and throws off the amino acid balance. Unless labeled "vital," commercial gluten may provide little improvement to bread because excessive drying heat has denatured the gluten, thus reducing its ability to absorb water. If you feel your wheat needs help, try adding one-quarter to one-half cup of white *bread* flour instead of gluten. Even this small amount can boost the performance of a recalcitrant wheat without gluten's negative effects on nutrition and flavor. If you absolutely must use commercial gluten, at least improve the amino acid balance by adding an equal amount of flour from a source high in the amino acid, lysine, such as soy, rye, or triticale.

 # THE BREADMAKING PROCESS

There is no single process for making bread. In fact, the moment the first loaf of yeasted bread was cheered out of an Egyptian fire, everyone in the village probably hustled home to find his own way to do it. Then and ever after, many brilliant variations have been developed to accomplish the same fundamental thing: to initiate and sustain the chemical reactions that produce bread. This means that with the right grain and a grinder, almost any method will produce a wholesome, nutritious, delicious product. And, even if the grain is not ideal, a process has probably been found to work around its personality.

Whether bread is made quickly, as modern commercial bakers do, or very slowly, certain basic processes must occur. First, the ingredients are mixed into a dough that is kneaded by hand or machine until the gluten is properly developed. The dough is then subjected to one or more fermentation periods for further development. It is then shaped, allowed to rise and, finally, baked. If this is all done by a bread machine, it is easy to lose sight of the fact that there are probably as many variations on this basic chain of events as there are trees in the forest. Breadmaking can be as simple or complex as the baker wishes!

Let's look more closely at what actually happens chemically during each stage of the breadmaking process. The more a home baker knows about the basic process, the better are his chances of crawling out of any wholemeal pits into which he stumbles.

Mixing

When proper proportions of flour, water, salt, fat and sweetener are thoroughly mixed together, these components start a long chain of chemical changes that produce the unique product known as yeasted bread.

Kneading

During kneading, the insoluble proteins (glutenins and gliadins) in flour combine with water. They uncoil, separate, then rejoin into long strands that form a strong network known as gluten. When properly developed, this gluten network has a unique capacity to stretch like elastic and to be shaped and reshaped into loaves that can retain their form for long periods. If kneading is continued too long, the network begins to break apart again.

A second, and vital, function of kneading is to aerate, or incorporate air bubbles into the dough. Although yeast produces gasses during fermentation that penetrate these bubbles, it cannot produce the bubbles itself.

Inadequately kneaded dough is frequently a problem in wholemeal breadmaking. Kneading time can vary greatly with grain and method used (hand, bread machine, dough hook, food processor, intense-kneading machinery). Without aid, it can take years to learn to recognize a perfectly kneaded dough. The professional baker's test outlined in the inset is a far better guide than any kneading time given in a recipe or instruction book. Using this test on dough that has been kneaded in a bread machine can be instructive about the "feel" of a well developed dough.

KNEADED DOUGH TEST

When your bread machine (or arms) tells you kneading is done, wet your fingers and gently and slowly stretch some of the dough out into a thin sheet. If the gluten is properly developed, it can be stretched quite thin without tearing. If it tears, more kneading is needed (or there is not enough gluten in the meal for proper development). Flecks of bran can be seen against the lighter background of dough. A good high-protein wheat will produce a firm dough that stretches quite thin.

Fermentation

With proper temperatures and sufficient food, yeast brings about many changes in the dough. Most importantly, enzymes in the yeast break down various sugars into alcohol and carbon dioxide. This carbon dioxide permeates and inflates the gas cells that were incorporated during kneading. These inflated gas bubbles press against the strong gluten structure created during kneading and, unable to escape, force the dough to expand. The fermentation period may be interrupted one or more times for a brief kneading. Among other things, kneading aerates the dough, moves yeast to new feeding areas and breaks down carbon dioxide bubbles into smaller sacs. After each brief kneading, the dough is set in a warm place to rise.

As these and other chemical reactions take place, the dough develops, losing stickiness and becoming more rubbery. There is an optimum point in this process, beyond which the dough begins to disintegrate and bread quality suffers. Strong flours can hold this optimum point for some time; weak flours cannot. This optimum point can be judged by gently poking a finger about one-quarter inch into the side of the dough. If the dough springs back and the dent disappears, the dough needs more time; if the dent fills in slowly, the dough is ready.

Proofing

The final rise before baking (which is still technically part of the fermentation process) is called the *proof*, and is most important to the final appearance of the loaf. If the dough is underproofed, it will not be as high and airy as it should be. If the dough is overproofed, ethyl alcohol (a byproduct of the yeast, which helps create the aroma of fresh-baking bread) kills the yeast and the bread will probably be grayish and taste less than wonderful.

Baking

When the dough has reached an optimum point, baking heat is needed to arrest dough development. Chemical activity in the dough continues in the oven, however. When the protein structure of dough is subjected to enough heat (beginning at about 165 degrees), it coagulates. Too much heat causes early coagulation which causes poor volume and perhaps a split crust; too little heat may cause the proteins to collapse while they are waiting. Chemical changes in the starches and sugars in the crust (including conversion of sugar to caramel) cause oven browning. Added egg, sugar and dairy products increase the browning effect. Wholemeal bread may take longer to bake than white bread. A properly baked loaf will produce a hollow sound when tapped on the bottom.

 ## HOW TO JUDGE BREAD

Ideally, after ten minutes or so of baking, but never sooner, you will peek into the oven and the loaf will have g-r-o-w-n. This "oven spring" is the reward for getting everything right—the precise ratio of flour and water; gluten kneaded to an optimum point; ideal temperature and nourishment for yeast; a perfectly proofed loaf popped into a precisely heated oven. The obstacle in this road to heaven is the recurring need for informed judgments as to the development of the dough. Without expert advice, there can be a gap between the first loaf and the first oven spring. But as long as one sticks with high-protein wheat, uses a minimum of added ingredients, and consults a good wholemeal bread book, the process of wholemeal breadmaking (even by hand) can be mastered in a relatively short time.

But how will you know when you have mastered breadmaking? In 1913, statistics showed that half the bread consumed in America was baked at home (most from roller-milled white flour but with somewhat less processing than today's). Even then the Department of Household Science at the University of Illinois lamented that the average housewife was woefully ignorant about which flours to use and how to judge a good loaf of bread. Could we possibly know more than they did? Maybe, but it seems worthwhile to run through some characteristics that are attributed to an ideal loaf—in other words, how should a good loaf of bread look, feel and smell?

Shape and Appearance

The ideal loaf will arch nicely above the pan (or bread machine bucket) into a pleasant, symmetrical shape. It will have no lumps or craters on top. It will not have drooped down over the rim, nor torn as it rose. Ideal hearth loaves will also have a full arch, not be lopsided, and not have potholes on top.

Crust

On a superior loaf, the crust will be thin, crackly and not overly chewy. The top, sides and bottom will be an even golden brown, with no pockmarks and no dimples. (Crust is one job on which a bread machine sometimes falls down, a minor failing considering its overall contribution to home breadmaking.) The top crust should feel firm when pressed lightly, with no cavernous air pocket just under the surface.

Crumb

The crumb is the inside of the loaf, everything, in fact, but the crust. It should look and feel light. A gentle press of the finger should leave no indentation. The texture should be tight and even, with no large holes and no dense areas at the sides or bottom. The gas cavities should have thin cell walls that are small, oblong and evenly distributed. The crumb should be moist, not doughy, and gentle rubbing across the bread surface should yield only a moderate amount of crumbs.

Aroma and Flavor

Aroma and flavor are virtually inseparable. Take a fresh piece of bread and literally wrap it around your nose and mouth. The bread should smell pleasantly fresh, like the flour as it was milled. There should be no "off" flavors from rancid fat, dirty flour, too much of an added ingredient or excessive proofing. Bread without salt tastes noticeably bland. In truly good bread, the crust will taste every bit as good as the crumb.

The preceding standards are helpful in evaluating the technical success of virtually any loaf of yeast bread. But technical standards should not be confused with personal preferences when it comes to loaf height, shape, density and flavor. In fact, a lofty, light loaf that mimics white bread may have entirely too much fluff for someone accustomed to heartier breads. But the hearty loaf should still meet the above standards. For example, a loaf of rye and wheat bread may be half the height and tighter in texture than a loaf made from 100 percent wheat, but if properly developed, it will not be open in the center and dense around the edges. It will have no large caverns from improper shaping, no dimples in the crust, and no gummy texture. And it certainly will have no yeasty smell from sitting too long during the critical final proof.

Just in case your loaf does fall short of ideal, however, here is some troubleshooting help.

BREADMAKING THROUGH HISTORY

In ancient Egypt, a peasant's daily wage was three breads and two jugs of beer; the wealthy toted up their worth in "number of breads;" and in bad times, the lower classes ate almost nothing else. In Rome, knowing the "color of one's bread" was knowing one's place in society. And if you didn't know, you'd find out as a dinner guest: the lowlier your place, the darker your bread. Bakers were respected citizens, with guilds (unions) and special rights guaranteed by the Roman state. Many elected officials including the second mayor of Pompeii were bakers. Perhaps that's why murdering a baker earned three times the punishment meted out for murdering an "ordinary" man.

The baker's life swirled into the drain along with the Roman Empire. The conquering "barbarians" from the North were nomads, not farmers, so by the early Middle Ages the Roman baker had lost all his government perks. He sweated 14- to 18-hour days by a hot oven, although no one else was permitted to work at night. He lived in the bakery, slept little, ate less, breathed flour dust. He got baker's eczema or baker's knee or baker's lung.

Like the miller, he stole what he could, by hiding a small family member beneath a table to reach up through a hole and snitch bits from the bread dough that customers brought for baking. Or the baker puffed up scanty bread with yeast. He was blamed for things he did and many he did not do. Rules and regulations abounded. In Hamburg after 1375 A.D., weighers and inspectors could immediately seize any bad-tasting or underweight bread and levy a fine. After several incidents, the baker was turned over to the people, who suspended him in a huge basket called the "baker's gallows" and ridiculed him. The English limited the baker's profit to 13 percent and draped a loaf around his neck if it was too light. True, he might bribe officials to ignore lighter loaves, but when famines spurred food riots, the mobs killed the baker on the way to the miller.

After a few more centuries of famine, war, and toppled rulers, things started improving. Good weather and soil revitalization ideas hit simultaneously. Then, thanks to the Industrial Revolution, agricultural and milling implements began to wipe out food shortages. People became richer and healthier, and the baker found himself back on top.

So the beeper or oven timer goes off, the entire family gathers around, you pull the loaf out, and...well, you're *ecstatic!* or *disheartened.* Fortunately, unless you have a total lump, it will be edible and minor corrections will probably solve the problem. If a high-protein wheat has been used, the dough has been kneaded to the point where it can be pulled and stretched thin without tearing, and the yeast is fresh, the problem probably lies with the ingredients. Before anything else, double-check the recipe. Make sure tablespoons have not been confused with teaspoons. Make sure you have measured meticulously. Try the more accurate option of weighing flour instead of measuring in cups.

After everything has been double-checked, use the troubleshooting guide that accompanies your bread machine, or the one in your wholemeal bread book. They will probably lead you quickly to the problem. But just in case you followed the basic wholemeal bread recipe at the beginning of the next chapter and it failed on the first attempt, and you are home alone and desperate, here are some troubleshooting tips to help get an ideal loaf as quickly as possible.

- If the loaf is squat, or dense inside, first test the yeast, as described earlier in this chapter. If the yeast is okay, repeat the original recipe exactly but increase liquids by one tablespoon (15 ml). If things seem to be improving, repeat the original recipe exactly, but increase liquids by two tablespoons (30 ml). If the problem persists, repeat the original recipe exactly but this time try increasing yeast by one-quarter teaspoon or sweetener by one-half tablespoon.

- If the loaf top looks like a mushroom or has caved in, or the texture is holey or crumbles badly, repeat the original recipe exactly but reduce the liquids by one tablespoon (15 ml). If things seem to be improving, repeat the original recipe but reduce liquids by two tablespoons (30 ml). If the problem persists after three tries, repeat the original recipe exactly but this time try reducing yeast by one-quarter teaspoon or reducing sweetener by one-half tablespoon.

- If things appear to be improving, keep incrementally increasing or decrecreasing the same ingredient in each new loaf. But make only one change per loaf. If the loaf fails to show improvement after experimenting with several ingredients, chances are good that the grain contains insufficient protein to make the highest, best-textured loaves of bread. (To test your wheat, replace one cup of wholemeal with one cup of white bread flour in the original recipe. If this produces a good loaf, inadequate breadmaking proteins in the wheat is your problem.)

 ## WHY BREAD STALES

Fresh, home-baked bread (white or wholemeal) is at its best for one day, edible for two, and can still be toasted on the third day. If left to air-day, it remains delicious *for months* in stuffing, bread pudding, or any other recipe for "day-old bread." This progressive degredation in quality is the result of a process called *staling.* Technically, staling starts the moment a baked product steams out of the oven. But this is not a simple process of drying out, as most people think. Bread stales in two ways, one way in the crust and another in the crumb.

The crust of bread starts out crisp and dry. Then, as moisture moves from the loaf's interior, the crust becomes increasingly soggy and tough. Humidity can exacerbate this effect since the crust also absorbs moisture from the air. Wrapping the bread in plastic is exactly the wrong solution to this problem, because the moisture gathering in the crust from the loaf interior cannot evaporate. When wrapped tightly, the crust becomes soggy and flavor deteriorates within hours.

The second kind of staling is internal, in the crumb of the bread. This staling is not strictly a matter of moisture loss but of "retrogradation," a slow change in starch molecules from amorphous to crystalline form, which causes them to bind less water. The bread interior stales just below the crust in the first 24 hours; thus the traditional slashing of prices for day-old bread. Some natural preservatives that extend loaf life include milk powder, sugar or malt supplements, small amounts of soy flour or additional fat.

Of course, bread does eventually dry out, but this is a separate issue from staling. Be aware that bread may seem dry if too little water has been added to the dough, the surface has been allowed to dry during fermentation, or dough has been overproofed or overbaked.

STORING BREAD

In the old world, houses had wooden or metal bread boxes. Some attractive (and very practical) wooden replicas with roll-up doors have begun to appear in stores. But they do require space. For those with no counter space to spare, the solution is to slice a piece from one end of the loaf, place the loaf, cut-side down, on a paper towel and store it in a cupboard or on a kitchen counter. The outside stays crisp (which makes good bread crumbs), while the inside stays soft and moist for a couple of days. Bread should never be stored in plastic bags or airtight plastic containers. These solutions do keep the bread soft, but they quickly destroy flavor and provide an incubator for mold, which will make the bread inedible within a short time, anyway. Bread should never be stored in the refrigerator, either, because the temperature maximizes staling.

Bread can be frozen for future use, particularly if frozen as dough that has been shaped and is ready for final proofing. Already-baked bread can be frozen, but it should be completely cool and wrapped in something airtight. Real culinary geniuses slice the bread before freezing so pieces can be taken out as needed, since it takes a chainsaw to slice frozen bread. Besides, frozen bread stales very quickly after thawing. An even better option is to bake often—half-loaves if necessary—and use leftover bread in croutons, bread pudding, French toast, au gratin topping and the many, other delicious recipes that our bread-eating ancestors devised for day-old bread.

GOING ON FROM HERE

At one time, commercial and home bakers used cake flour for cakes, pastry flour for pie crust and bread flour for bread. Many had strong preferences for a particular miller's flour, such as Gold Medal, and much advertising money was devoted to brand loyalty. Eventually, "all-purpose" flour became popular with consumers. The convenience of using just one flour persuaded home bakers to overlook the mediocre results of a single-use compromise and brand loyalty largely disappeared. Inevitably, the ability to use different flours for different baked goods also disappeared. Today, the mediocre flavor and abysmal nutrition of white flour are driving people back to wholemeal; this also brings them back to the use of different flours for different baked goods.

The rest of this book contains recipes, but it also offers opportunities for new millers to explore the use of different wheats in bread. Rather extensive information is provided in the chapter on desserts for those who want to explore the somewhat more complex subject of combining wheats for desserts. While some people will consider wheat-mixing fun and challenging, inexperienced, harried cooks baking with bread machines can make delicious bread with just one bag of high-protein bread wheat and wonderful desserts with just a small bag of soft white wheat.

So, let's start enhancing your health and well-being, as well as that of your family and loved ones, by making some fresh wholemeal bread.

CHAPTER *12*

Simple Wholemeal Recipes

Six or seven thousand years ago,
an Egyptian—probably fooling around
with home brew—stumbled onto bread.
Now, we have six or seven thousand
bread recipes to fool around with.

This book is about home flour milling and does not pretend to be a book about breadmaking. But some simple recipes are provided to help new bakers get a good loaf of wholemeal bread out of the bread machine as quickly as possible. If you regularly make white bread by hand, you will have no difficulty switching to wholemeal, although kneading may take a bit more muscle. If you are new to breadmaking altogether and do not intend to use a bread machine, you will need help. Buy a wholemeal bread book. I recommend again what I consider to be the textbook of whole-grain breadmaking, the revised version of *Laurel's Kitchen Bread Book*, by Laurel Robertson et al (Random House, NY, 2003).

Because wholemeal is different from white flour, and because bread machines are persnickety about precise measuring, this chapter begins with some measuring tips. Then, following a brief introduction to the subject of mixing wheats, you will find some simple bread recipes. Because wheat is just one of the grains that can be ground in a flour mill and bread is just one way to use wheat, recipes are also included for other delicious daily fiber hits like waffles, pancakes, and pizza. And, of course, there are suggestions for that leftover bread. Finally, for a peek at the baking universe opening up to the new home miller, there are even a couple of recipes for corn (and one that includes rye in the next chapter).

 ## MEASURING TIPS

The optimum method for measuring recipe ingredients is to weigh *everything*–liquids, flours, fats, spices. Unfortunately, home recipes customarily specify measurements in volume (e.g., cups, tablespoons, teaspoons) rather than weight. The cup system leaves room for error and can create a beginner's minefield. This minefield is less treacherous when making bread by hand because the baker can add water or flour along the way, if he judges that the dough needs it. But a bread machine, which cannot adjust for even small variations in quantities, requires very careful measuring.

First, be aware that measuring errors compound. A tablespoon too little of water and a tablespoon too much of flour can make a big difference to a bread machine. Second, adjustments made to perfect a loaf should be recorded on the recipe so you will know what changes you made and how the bread felt about it.

Let's begin with some hints for measuring liquids then move on to measuring wholemeal.

Measuring Liquids

The most accurate device for measuring liquids is a tall, slim cylinder bearing both cup and metric markings, like the one you may have used in a high school chemistry class. The next-best option is a glass measuring cup with marks on one side for cups and marks on the other side for milliliters (ml). Being able to

LIQUID VOLUME CONVERSIONS

1 tsp.	5 ml
1 tbsp.	15 ml
1 fl oz.	30 ml
1/4 cup	60 ml
1/3 cup	80 ml
3/8 cup	90 ml
1/2 cup	120 ml
5/8 cup	150 ml
7/8 cup	210 ml
1 cup	240 ml

compare two systems makes it easy to convert odd measurements in a recipe like seven-eighths of a cup to the easier equivalent of 210 milliliters. It is important to have the measuring device at eye level, even if this requires stooping down.

Measuring Wholemeal

Flour comes out of a mill with air in it, but if it is stored in a cannister that is raised and plopped back down, it compacts. For this reason, a cup of freshly milled wholemeal can weigh *less* than a cup of meal from a cannister. In addition, measuring in cups is time consuming. At the very least, flour from the cannister can be sifted or fluffed with a wire whisk before measuring. But a small digital kitchen scale that measures in grams offers a much quicker way to measure dry ingredients. To standardize your recipe, set the scale on the counter and adjust the indicator to zero. Fill measuring cups with the amount of flour specified in the recipe, leveling each cup with the edge of a knife. Gently empty the ingredients into the scale's container then record the weight on the recipe, preferably in grams. If the recipe does not work out (after all, the author of the recipe may not have used a scale...), increase or decrease (by weight) flour until the recipe does work. Once you know the correct weight, the flour can be weighed quickly forever after.

The recipes in this book have been developed using the weight of the meal. Since the metric system and our standard cup-and-spoon system do not translate directly, amounts have been rounded off to realistic numbers.

 MIXING WHEATS

Once the basic wholemeal loaf has been perfected, home bakers can try mixing different wheats and other grains for flavor and effect. A few of the recipes in this section specify a particular type of wheat, or more than one wheat. Use these hints as a guide to the wonderful world of mixing flours, where serious bakers are limited only by their imagination and sense of adventure.

One simple mixing trick can be helpful in converting staunch white-bread lovers to the flavor or wholemeal (like children who resist anything new or anything that must be chewed). Although the flavor of hard white spring wheat is generally too mild for true wholemeal bread lovers, a bread made from two-thirds hard white spring and one-third hard red spring may be quite acceptable to white-bread addicts.

 ## ABOUT THE RECIPES

The bread recipes that follow make one loaf but can be doubled. They can be kneaded by hand, by dough hook, in a high speed dough mixer or assembled in a one-and-a-half- or two-pound bread machine bucket. Wheat can be ground as finely or coarsely as desired, but large bran flecks may interfere with the rising action of the gluten and produce a slightly less lofty loaf. Any hard wheat can be used for wholemeal bread, but hard spring wheat with a protein content of 15 percent or higher produces the highest loaves.

Most busy people quickly work a few good recipes into their routine and save culinary experimentation for weekends and holidays. So, the sooner you perfect your quick-and-easy recipes, the sooner you will be getting your daily boost of nutrition and fiber—effortlessly!

Basic (Delicious! Nutritious!) Wholemeal Bread

This basic wholemeal bread recipe, which makes one 1-1/2 pound loaf of bread, provides a standard for experimenting with the performance of various wheats. Once you have mastered the recipe using high-protein hard red spring wheat, here are other mixtures to try:

Option 1. Three-quarters hard red spring and one-quarter soft white
Option 2. One-third each: hard red spring, hard white spring, and durum
Option 3. Half hard spring and half hard red winter
Option 4. One-half cup of rye and the rest hard red winter

1/4 c. (60 ml) warm water
1½ tsp. yeast
1 large egg, beaten
1 c. (240 ml) warm water
2 tbsp. brown sugar or honey
2 tbsp. oil
3½ c. (450 g) wholemeal
2 tbsp. garbanzo bean flour
1/4 tsp. ascorbic acid
1 tsp. salt
1/3 c. non-instant nonfat powdered milk

Bread Machine Instructions: Assemble ingredients in bread machine bucket according to manufacturer's instructions. (If you are using rye, add it partway through the kneading process to prevent overworking.)

To Mix by Hand: Stir yeast slowly into ¼ cup of warm water and set aside. Place egg in a two-cup glass or plastic measuring cup and fill with warm (not hot) water to the 1¼ cup (300 ml) line. Beat well with a small wire whisk or fork. Add sweetener and oil and stir or whisk until sweetener has dissolved.

Kneading. Set aside about ½ cup of the flour for dusting. Combine in a large bowl the remaining wholemeal, bean flour, ascorbic acid, salt, and powdered milk. Mix well. Make a well in the center of the dry ingredients and pour the yeast and egg mixtures in. Stir the liquids slowly, drawing in more and more flour, until all the flour has been incorporated into the dough. Turn the dough out onto a floured surface and knead. Add kneading flour to keep dough from sticking to hands and board, but be cautious because bran absorbs water very slowly. Kneading should take 15 to 25 minutes, but could take longer if kneading lacks vigor. Do not give up until dough can be carefully stretched thin with wet fingers without tearing. It should be smooth and shiny.

Rising. When properly kneaded, dough should be placed in a large bowl with lid (no oil is necessary) and allowed to rise in a warm place (80 to 90 degrees) until doubled (1½ to 2 hours). (The best place I have found for this job is a microwave with the light on.) To test, press a finger gently in the side of the dough. If the finger dent springs back, it needs more rising time. If it sighs and shrinks back, it has gone too long—watch more closely during the next rising period. If the dent fills in slowly, it is ready. When properly risen, dough may be punched down and returned to the covered bowl for an additional rising (45 minutes to 1 hour) or prepared immediately for the final rising or *proof*, as follows.

Final Proof. On a lightly floured surface, flatten the dough to remove air pockets. Shape into a round hearth loaf or fold and press into a standard loaf shape. Place in a buttered or oiled ovenproof pan. If the bowl used for rising is large enough, set the filled bread pan on the inside of the lid and place the inverted bowl over it. Find a warm place for the bowl (or pan) and let it rise until doubled (25 to 45 minutes). Monitor carefully during final proof. Loaf should double, but definitely not sigh when a finger is pressed gently in the side. If there is a little spring left in the dough, it will spring up in the oven—a very exciting event!

Baking. Bake in a preheated 400-degree oven for 10 minutes then reduce heat to 350 degrees and bake for another 25 minutes, or until nicely browned. Empty the loaf from the pan and tap it lightly on the bottom. If tapping produces a hollow sound and the bread bottom feels firm, the bread is done. Otherwise, put it back in the pan and bake for another five minutes, or until tapping on the bottom produces a satisfying thump.

Sunflower Seed "White" Bread

This intricately flavored bread is a bit rich because of the extra fat contributed by the seeds and nuts. The hard white wheat plays down the wholemeal a bit and the butter and seeds add complexity to the flavor. It is a perfect transition loaf for those who remain skeptical about whole-grain breads. And *everybody* likes it. Use all hard red spring or half hard red and half hard white. If you do not have powdered milk, replace one-quarter to one-third of the warm water with scalded, then cooled, milk. Unless time makes it impossible, be sure to add the seeds near the very end of kneading to reduce tearing of the gluten strands in the dough.

3½ c. (450 grams) wholemeal
2 tbsp. garbanzo bean flour
1/4 tsp. ascorbic acid
1½ tsp. salt
1/3 c. non-instant nonfat powdered milk
1/4 c. (60 ml) warm water
1½ tsp. yeast
1 large egg, beaten
1 c. (240 ml) warm water
2 tbsp. brown sugar
1 tbsp. oil
1 tbsp. soft butter
1/4 c. chopped sunflower seeds
1 tbsp. (fresh!) poppy seeds
1 tbsp. millet or amaranth seeds

Bread Machine Instructions: Assemble ingredients in bread machine bucket according to manufacturer's instructions. Add butter and seeds just before the end of the bread machine's kneading cycle.

To Mix by Hand: In a large bowl, combine flours, ascorbic acid, salt, and powdered milk. Mix well and set aside.

Stir yeast slowly into ¼ cup warm water and set aside. Place egg in two-cup glass or plastic measuring cup and fill to the 1¼ cup (300 ml) line with warm (not hot) water. (One large egg equals about ¼ cup or 60 ml of water.) Mix well with a small wire whisk or fork. Add brown sugar and oil.

Make a well in the dry ingredients and pour the yeast and egg mixtures in it. Stir slowly until the dry ingredients have been incorporated into the liquids. Turn the dough out onto a floured surface and knead until smooth, shiny and supple (15 to 25 minutes, depending on kneading vigor). Properly kneaded dough should not tear when carefully stretched thin with wet fingers. Near the end of kneading, slather the butter and seeds on the kneading surface and gently but thoroughly knead into the dough.

Continue, using the rising and baking instructions provided in the preceding Basic Wholemeal Bread recipe.

"Featherpuff" Bread

This recipe, which was adapted from *The Laurel's Kitchen Bread Book* (Robertson, Flinders & Godfrey, *Random House*, rev. 2003), makes one light and lovely loaf. It can be made in a 1½ or 2-pound bread machine bucket, kneaded by hand and baked in a standard loaf pan, or used in the cinnamon roll recipe that follows. When making by hand, it is best to allow only one rise before the final proof. Hard red or white spring wheats are best for this bread.

3/4 c. (180 ml) cottage cheese
1 egg, slightly beaten
2 tbsp. honey, dissolved in
1/4 c. (60 ml) water
1/4 c. (60 ml) warm water
1 tsp. yeast
2½ c. (375 gr) wholemeal
2 tbsp. garbanzo bean flour
1/4 c. non-instant powdered milk
1/4 tsp. ascorbic acid
3/4 tsp. salt
1 tbsp. soft butter

Bread Machine Instructions: First, prepare the cottage cheese and egg mixture as if making bread by hand (see below), then assemble ingredients in the bread machine bucket per manufacturer's instructions. (To save time, the butter may be replaced with oil and included with other ingredients.)

To Mix by Hand: Heat cottage cheese to tepid in stainless steel pan, then add egg. Dissolve honey in ¼ cup water and add to cottage cheese mixture. In a glass measuring cup, slowly sprinkle yeast in remaining ¼ cup warm water and stir until dissolved.

Continue, using the instructions provided in the Basic Wholemeal Bread recipe, above, and reserving the butter to slather on the board and work into dough when kneading is nearly complete.

Sinful Cinnamon Rolls

Although any dough can be made into cinnamon rolls, Featherpuff bread (above) makes particularly tender rolls. For an extra-rich version start with a sugar/nut layer in the bottom of the pan. After removing rolls from the oven, invert the pan and dump the rolls upside-down on a plate. The rich sauce will then be on top. (Nuts and raisins are optional.)

1/2 c. brown sugar
1/4 c. butter
1 tbsp. light corn syrup
1/2 to 1 c. pecans
1 loaf of Featherpuff dough (preceding recipe)
1/4 to 1/2 c. melted butter
1/2 to 1 c. brown sugar
2 tsp. or more cinnamon
1/2 c. finely chopped nuts
1/2 c. finely chopped raisins

Instructions: (*To reduce calories, omit this first layer.*) Put brown sugar, butter and corn syrup in a small saucepan over medium-low heat and stir until dissolved. Pour this in the bottom of a greased 9" x 13" pan. Sprinkle pecans over this mixture and set aside.

If you do not use the sugar layer above, butter the pan and set aside. Preheat oven to 350 degrees. Referring to the preceding recipe, prepare dough up to final proof stage, then punch it down. Shape dough into a ball and place it on a floured surface. Sprinkle with flour and use a floured rolling pin to shape it into a large rectangle. Use a pastry brush to spread melted butter over the surface of the rolled-out dough, (leaving the edges clean so they can be pinched together to close the roll). Sprinkle brown sugar evenly over dough. Sprinkle cinnamon to taste and chopped nuts and raisins, if used.

Starting at the edge closest to you, carefully roll the dough into a long cylinder, pinching the ends closed as you roll. If you have included raisins and nuts, roll very carefully so they do not punch holes in the dough. When the dough is in the shape of a long cylinder, pinch the final edge and the rolled dough together to close. Using a *very* sharp flour-dusted knife (serrated works well), slice the cylinder into individual cinnamon rolls. (Note: The best way to get them even is to slice the cylinder in half. Then slice one of the halves into halves. Keep cutting pieces in half until you have the right number of cinnamon rolls for your pan with space between them.) Lay the slices flat in the pan. Allow to rise in a warm place until a finger poked in the edge of one roll leaves a slight indentation or the dough returns to shape very slowly. Bake in a 350-degree oven until nicely browned (about 25 to 30 minutes, probably). The rolls in the center of the pan may take longer to bake than those near the outer edge, so check regularly after 20 minutes. When rolls are done, dump the pan upside down on a serving platter and serve hot.

Pizza Dough

Homemade pizza needn't be as fatty as they serve it down at the parlor. In fact, this dough tastes so good that all it needs is some tomato sauce (below) and a teensy-weensy bit of Parmesan and mozzarella. (Good Parmesan cheese can be kept in the refrigerator for months wrapped only in waxed paper. The harder it gets, the better it is. A few tablespoons of the grated fluff provide extravagant flavor for minimal calories.)

The flavor of hard white wheat most closely resembles the mild-flavored crust we're familiar with. Use spring wheat for thin crust (to minimize sauce soaking into crust and making it soggy); use winter wheat for thick crust (to minimize dough shrinkage and make finished crust chewy). Makes one 12-inch pizza crust.

2/3 c. (160 ml) warm water
1½ tsp. yeast
1½ c. (190 gr) hard white wholemeal
1/2 c. (60 gr) soft white wholemeal
1 tsp. salt
3 tbsp. olive oil
flour for kneading
1/2 tsp. Italian seasoning
1/2 c. freshly grated Parmesan cheese (optional)
Instructions: Dissolve yeast in warm water; set aside until it bubbles up.

In a bowl, mix salt and flours together. Make a well in the middle and pour in the yeast mixture and oil. Use fingers to form a soft dough. Turn out on a lightly floured surface and knead the dough five minutes. Shape dough into a ball and allow it to rest for ten minutes under a damp towel. When time is up, continue kneading the dough until it is shiny and smooth (10 to 20 minutes more). Near the end of kneading, add Italian seasoning and Parmesan cheese to the dough, if desired. Dough should be soft and supple and stretch thin without tearing. Allow the dough to rise in a warm place until doubled (1 to 2 hours). Punch dough down. Roll out on a lightly floured surface into a 12-inch circle. Place in a pizza pan that has been dusted with coarse cornmeal or greased with olive oil. Pinch up the edges of the dough so sauce will not drip off. Spread pizza sauce (below) on dough, cover and let rise in a warm place for 30 minutes or until nicely puffed up. After about 20 minutes of rising time, but before dough is ready for baking, preheat oven to 400 to 425 degrees. Just before placing pizza in oven, add any cheese or other toppings desired. Bake for 20 to 30 minutes or until crust has browned and sauce is bubbly.

Pizza Sauce: Saute 1/2 chopped onion and two or more minced garlic cloves in one tablespoon of olive oil. Add one 14-ounce can of tomato sauce and one teaspoon of Italian seasoning (or more to taste). Boil down to a thick sauce. Spread on pizza dough before final rise.

Toppings: Start by spreading sauce on the pizza crust, then add 1/2 to one cup each of grated mozzarella and Parmesan cheese. Optional additions: sliced onions, feta cheese, ripe olives, mushrooms, tomatoes, green peppers, pineapple, precooked hamburger, sausage, ham, pepperoni or anything else in the refrigerator.

World Class Pancakes

Mill 2½ cups hard red winter or other hard wheat. If your bread flour is usually finely ground, this may be an opportunity for your colon to get some coarse bran. It all cooks up into beautiful pancakes. Soft white wheat is an alternative with an almost cake-like flavor that some will find particularly delicious. Small amounts of cornmeal or other grains can replace some of the wheat for variation. Buckwheat pancakes are classic, but the flavor may be too strong for some. Makes pancakes for four but recipe can be cut in half for two people. Be sure to start with all ingredients at room temperature for even cooking.

2½ c. (325 g) wholemeal
1 tsp. baking powder
1/2 tsp. baking soda
1 tbsp. brown sugar
1 tsp. salt
2 eggs
2 to 3 c. buttermilk
2 tbsp. of oil

Instructions: Combine flour, baking powder, soda, sugar and salt and mix thoroughly.

Combine eggs and 1½ cups of room-temperature buttermilk. Add to dry ingredients. Add additional buttermilk (½ cup at a time, up to a total of three cups) until batter has reached the consistency of thick mud. Add oil. (Hints: Thick batter is better than thin, which makes gummy pancakes. Batter will thicken while waiting to be cooked, as the bran absorbs moisture. Do not stir the batter any more than necessary.)

Heat a large, non-stick pan, griddle or iron skillet to medium-hot. Oiling the pan should not be necessary, but pancakes might stick if the pan is too hot. Spoon batter into pan in dollar-sized pancakes or larger. Spread the batter with the back of the spoon if necessary to achieve a round shape. Fresh or frozen (but thawed) blueberries or raspberries or banana slices can be dropped on the uncooked side of the pancake. When bubbles appear on the surface but have not burst, turn the pancake over. It should immediately begin puffing up—to about one-half inch—if proper liquid-flour ratio and cooking temperature have been achieved.

Serve with maple syrup, low-sugar preserves, or apple or peach butter. And trust me here...cold wholemeal pancakes are a *delectable* snack anytime with absolutely nothing on them!

Fantastic Sunday Waffles

These particularly healthful and delicious waffles take a little time (15 minutes to mix up and one hour for yeast batter to rise) but are definitely worth it. Make a double batch on a leisurely Sunday morning, bake them, then freeze any that are left. On busy mornings, frozen squares or halves can be popped in the toaster for a crisp, delicious, healthful breakfast. Try hard red spring wheat one time and soft white another. Each has its own wonderful flavor. Recipe makes about four large waffles. (For children, who need more fat than adults, top with softened butter rather than sweet toppings.)

1 tbsp. dry yeast
1½ c. warm water (360 ml)
1 tbsp. honey
1 tbsp. molasses
2 egg yolks
4 tbsp. soy or other bean flour
4 tbsp. non-instant milk powder
1/4 c. (30 g) cornmeal
1/2 tsp. salt
1½ c. (190 gr) wholemeal
1/4 c. chopped sunflower seeds
3 tbsp. sesame seeds
1/2 tsp. cinnamon
2 tbsp. oil or melted butter
1 tsp. vanilla extract
2 egg whites

Instructions: Dissolve yeast in warm water. Add honey, molasses and egg yolks. In a large bowl, mix dry ingredients together then add the yeast and honey mixture. Add oil and vanilla. Cover bowl with a towel or lid and let this mixture rise one hour (if possible) in a warm place. When ready for next step, stir down waffle mixture. In separate bowl, beat egg whites until stiff, then fold them carefully but thoroughly into batter. Bake in waffle iron per manufacturer's instructions. To store, wrap cooled waffles in plastic bags and freeze.

Cornmeal Muffins

Recipes for cornbread abound—featuring every fat from bacon drippings to lard to corn oil—and embellished with a trainload of ingredients from green chilies to corn kernels to cheddar cheese. Cornmeal should be finely milled to prevent grittiness or coarse meal can be softened by soaking in the buttermilk for half an hour. This basic recipe makes six deliciously corn-flavored muffins. It may be doubled for 12 muffins or cornbread baked in an 8" x 8" x 2" pan. Start with all ingredients at room temperature to ensure even cooking.

1 ½ c. (180 gr) cornmeal
1/2 tsp. salt
1/4 tsp. baking soda
1/2 tsp. baking powder
2 pinches of pepper
1 tbsp. brown sugar or honey
1 large egg, beaten
1 c. (240 ml) buttermilk
1 tbsp. melted butter or oil

Instructions: Preheat oven to 425 degrees and grease pans for six muffins. Thoroughly mix together cornmeal, salt, soda, baking powder and pepper. In a separate bowl, combine sugar, beaten egg, buttermilk, butter or oil. Make a well in the dry ingredients and pour in buttermilk mixture. Stir only enough to moisten dry ingredients. Batter should be quite thick. If it seems runny, add another tablespoon or more of cornmeal. Fill muffin tins two-thirds full. Bake for 20 to 25 minutes or until muffins have peaked and center is firm to a gentle touch.

Polenta

Polenta is an Italian favorite that is first cooked in a pan on top of the stove, then served soft (as cornmeal mush) or firm (cut into squares), with the firm squares often fried in butter. Both soft and firm polenta serve as the base for a great variety of dishes featuring tasty items like tomatoes, eggplant, cheeses and spinach and also used in Mexican-style dishes. Because polenta can be boiled, then left to thicken in a flat pan for up to 24 hours, it can be prepared in advance then used in a quick meal when time is short—a tamale pie or eggplant casserole, for example. For in-depth information and recipes, try *Polenta*, by Brigit Legere Binns (Chronicle Books, San Francisco, 1996).

Commercial polenta consists of uniform chunks of corn, called semolina, which are a little larger than farina, a consistency most home mills cannot reproduce. Fortunately, cornmeal from very fine to quite chunky can be used with good results. The finer the meal, the less time the polenta will take for the initial stove-top cooking and the greater the risk of overcooking because of the large amount of exposed starch. Do not stir the polenta too much or cook it too long or the starch will taste overcooked. Very fine meal may take no more than three minutes. Do not omit the salt unless absolutely necessary, as it slows the development of the starch. The following basic polenta dish is a Mexican version that serves four to six as a side dish.

1/2 c. white onion, chopped
1 tsp. cooking oil
3 c. boiling chicken or vegetable stock or milk (or any combination)
1½ c. (200 gr) cornmeal
1/2 tsp. salt
4-oz. can diced green chilies
1 tsp. chili powder

Instructions: In a two-quart, heavy-bottomed sauce pan, saute onion in oil. Add salt and liquids. Bring to a boil. Reduce heat and add cornmeal *very* slowly, while stirring constantly with a wire whisk. Keeping polenta at a very slow boil, switch to a wooden spatula and stir every minute or so to keep it from sticking. It will make lots of steam-exhausting plop-plop noises. Cook until polenta is very thick and pulls away from sides of pan. This can take anywhere from three minutes to 25 minutes, depending on coarseness of meal, but mine takes about five. Do not overstir or polenta will taste starchy.

Meanwhile, butter an 8" x 8" x 2" pan or something similar. When polenta is very thick, remove from heat and quickly mix in diced chilis and chili powder. Pour the polenta into the buttered pan. Using a wet spatula or wet fingers, pat the polenta about an inch thick. Cover with aluminum foil or towel and allow polenta to sit for 24 hours in refrigerator or one hour at room temperature. (Actually, many hours at room temperature or in the refrigerator seem to do no damage, particularly with coarse meal, which may appreciate the softening time.)

Before using the polenta in a recipe, bring it to room temperature. To use, either cut polenta into squares and brown in a skillet, using a small amount of butter or olive oil, or bake in a preheated 350-degree oven until warm (up to 25 minutes). Cut into squares and serve hot with salsa. (Polenta may also be reheated in a microwave.)

Italian Version: Omit chopped chilies and chili power. Use instead ½ to 1 tsp. Italian seasoning, a 4-oz. can of drained ripe olives, and ¼ to ½ c. of grated Parmesan cheese.

Kitchen Sink Versions: Try adding any of your favorite foods to polenta after stove-top cooking and before spreading it in the pan: sun-dried tomatoes, cooked, chopped spinach and feta cheese, pesto, etc.

Hearty, Healthy French Toast

This recipe makes three or four pieces of French toast, enough for two people. Bread can be a couple of days old, but not like a brick.

2 eggs
2 tbsp. milk or cream
Dash of cinnamon
Dash of salt and pepper
2 drops vanilla extract (opt.)
1 tbsp. or more oil
3 or 4 slices day-old bread

Instructions: Using a fork, beat eggs, spices and cream together in a flat bowl. Pour as much oil as the diet permits (but at least one tablespoon) in a non-stick frying pan. Quickly dip three large or four small slices of bread into egg mixture and fry until golden brown. Set fried toast on paper towels to soak up excess fat. Serve with powdered sugar, maple syrup, marmalade or other topping, or reduce calories by serving with fruit butter (below) or applesauce.

Fruit butter:
2 c. tart cooking apples, chopped (or other fruit)
1/4 tsp. cinnamon
1 tbsp. apple cider vinegar
2 tbsp. sweetener
1/4 c. raisins

Combine ingredients in a small saucepan and cook over medium heat until very soft (20 to 30 minutes, depending on the fruit). Puree in blender, if a smooth consistency is desired. Serve warm on pancakes, French toast or waffles. Can be made in advance and stored in refrigerator or freezer, then reheated before serving.

SOME USES FOR DAY-OLD BREAD

Bread is best right after baking and only loses its good flavor if it is put in a plastic bag. If allowed to air dry, it becomes crisp and *still* tastes good months later. So if you find your bread piling up, don't toss it. Here are some delicious and healthful ways to use dry leftover bread.

 ## Italian Bread Crumbs

Allow leftover wholemeal bread to dry completely in open air. Grate or use blender to create one cup or more crisp, dry bread crumbs.

Add to taste: Italian seasoning, garlic powder, pepper, freshly grated Parmesan cheese. This mixture can be stored in an airtight plastic bag in the refrigerator for a week or longer in the freezer. Sprinkle as desired on any item that benefits from *au gratin* topping—chicken pieces, baked potato casserole, zucchini, tomatoes, or spinach, for example—and bake until brown.

 ## Old-fashioned Bread & Tomatoes

Cut fresh or stale wholemeal bread into squares. Sprinkle Italian seasoning (or oregano, basil and rosemary) on fresh or canned tomatoes and heat. Pour over bread pieces for a delicious and healthful snack or side dish. Grated Parmesan cheese is a tasty addition that adds few calories.

Italians make a bread salad, using day-old bread, tomatoes, basil and any other ingredients they have on hand (olives, sliced onions or cheese, for example).

 ## Old-fashioned Bread & Milk

Fresh or stale wholemeal bread can be cut into squares, put in a bowl and covered with warm or cold milk, for a classic bedtime snack. Some people add cinnamon. Bread and milk provides excellent protein for few calories and is particularly valuable for people who have difficulty falling asleep or are awakened by hunger. Served warm, this dish has also been a favorite of mothers trying to get something nutritious into sick children. Fruit, brown sugar, nuts or raisins may be added if calories permit.

Bread Stuffing
for Turkey, Chicken or Pork Chops

This recipe provides enough stuffing for a small turkey or four pork chops or it can be baked in a buttered casserole dish with two chicken breasts on top. Sunflower seed bread is particularly good in stuffing. For a vegan version, use vegetable oil and replace egg and liquids with soy milk or vegetable broth and, of course, forget the meat.

1/4 c. butter or oil
1 white onion
4 stalks celery, chopped
2 cloves garlic, chopped
1 tbsp. or more sage
1 tbsp. or more poultry seasoning
1 tsp. salt
1/2 tsp. pepper
4-6 c. dry bread cubes
1 egg
1/2 c. milk or chicken stock

Instructions: Preheat oven to 325 degrees. Chop onion, celery and garlic and saute in butter until the onions are translucent. Add seasonings and cook one minute longer.

Put bread cubes in large bowl, add sauteed onion mixture and stir together. Add the egg and as much milk or stock as needed to wet the bread cubes. Stir with a spoon, then squish the mixture with your fingers, adding more liquid, if necessary, to get a moist (but not wet) texture that holds together. Taste and add more salt, pepper, sage or poultry seasoning until you are satisfied with the full flavor.

For fowl: Stuff and truss bird (see any basic cookbook) and place it on a rack in a baking pan. Bake until a meat thermometer inserted between the thigh and body registers done (about 25 minutes per pound).

For four pork chops: Preheat oven to 350 degrees. Place four 12-inch pieces of string in a tic-tac-toe grid (#) on a bread board or other flat surface. Salt and pepper both sides of a pork chop. Lay it in the center of the string grid. Pile one to two inches of stuffing on the pork chop. Place another pork chop on the stuffing. Repeat twice, ending with a pork chop. Draw the strings up to the top of the pork-chop-and-stuffing pile and tie them. Press the stuffing back between the pork chops if it falls out. Carefully turn the tied-up pork chops on their side and place them on a rack in a pan. Bake for about an hour or until pork chops and edges of stuffing are brown and crispy.

For stuffing alone: Oil or butter a baking dish, fill with stuffing, cover and bake at 350 degrees for approximately 25 minutes or until brown.

CHAPTER 13

Quick Breads, Muffins, Cakes & Other Sweet Treats

When all else fails,
let them eat cake.

White flour barely had one toe tapping on the stage before wild applause drove wholemeal into the wings. The first reason for the excitement was the egalitarian nature of white flour: for the first time, the lightest, whitest, loveliest baked goods became plentiful for all classes of people. But in the long term, because of its solidly predictable performance, white flour's greatest audience was the large-scale, automated processing and baking industries. Today, white flour beguiles home bakers far less than it once did but it remains a staple for desserts because nobody has shown them a practical alternative. In truth, home-milled wholemeal makes more delicious and far more healthful sweet treats than white flour.

Desserts provide an untapped opportunity to work whole grains into the diet. Of course, claims that wholemeal desserts have incredible flavor will strike some as an exaggeration. That's because people who wisely encourage us to switch to wholemeal foods usually insist on using other more healthful ingredients as well, like black strap molasses, unrefined sugar, carob powder, soy this and soy that. Unfortunately, their nutritional intelligence far exceeds their ability to persuade people that no lips should ever touch a refined carbohydrate. Time has shown that while consciousness can be raised about what people should eat, they won't eat it unless *they* think it tastes good.

So, those people who have the self-discipline to do the nutritionally intelligent thing no matter *what* may be horrified by the ingredients in some of the recipes that follow. That's why the first four recipes–for zucchini bread, banana bread, Boston brown bread and bread pudding–are lower in fats and sugars than subsequent recipes. They are also quick, easy and so delicious that you do not *need* to move on to the higher-calorie recipes that follow. But in my experience, a limited repertoire can lead to sneaking out for double-fudge brownie ice cream, or worse. My compromise is to periodically bake something irresistibly decadent then hide most of it in the freezer, wrapped in individual pieces. One piece a day and only after meals are my rules; others may be more restrictive. Nearly every recipe in this chapter can be cut, wrapped, stored and then doled out perspicaciously. And remember that when bad carbohydrates like sugar are consumed with fiber (and in conjunction with a full meal), they cause far less of a blood sugar surge than they would if eaten alone or with white flour.

Fortunately, wholemeal performs exceptionally well in, and adds distinctive flavor to, quick breads like banana, zucchini, pumpkin, gingerbread, muffins, and other baked goods that sit on the lighter side of the fat and sugar scales. Baking finely textured cakes with large amounts of sugar and fat (called "high ratio" desserts), on the other hand, requires a bit more familiarity with wholemeal. For that reason, these cakes should not be among the wholemeal baker's first projects. After some successes with the quick breads, however, you may want to try the Delmonico Cake at the end of the chapter because it is, thanks to the soft white wholemeal, buttermilk and coconut, one of the most delicious cakes that ever existed. Once you have succeeded with this high-ratio cake, and assuming calories permit, you can confidently tackle similar cakes that have been formulated for white flour.

Since home millers do need a little background to start baking sweet things from their freshly milled meal, this chapter provides guidance for selecting the right wheat for a specific baking project and some hints for using wholemeal in place of white flour.

THE RIGHT WHEAT

In a twist back to the old days, home millers must now begin their baking project by deciding which wheat to mill. The following technical information need not be mastered in order to make basic desserts. It should be read for general background and is presented primarily for wholemeal bakers who dream of becoming culinary artists.

As a general rule, soft winter wheats are best for desserts because they have the opposite characteristics of a good bread wheat—good extensibility and very low elasticity. When baking desserts, which usually contain high levels of sugar and fat, the structure and stability depend on (1) as little starch damage as possible during milling, (2) uniformly swollen starch granules and (3) as little a-amylase (enzyme) activity as possible, because it can cause stickiness in these products. Soft wheats with less than 10 percent protein exhibit these characteristics. Since there are only minor technical differences between the baking performance of soft red and soft white wheats, wholemeal bakers can use them interchangeably.

MIXING WHEATS

As presented earlier in this book, commercial white flour bakers use two major types of flour–cake and pastry–each milled from a different wheat. *Cake Flour* is a highly refined, ultra silky white flour that produces a very fine cake structure. Delicate baked goods like high-sugar cakes benefit from the very weak gluten structure of this flour, which prevents toughening. Commercial cake flour is milled from soft red winter wheat. *Pastry Flour* is a standard white flour with slightly increased protein content. It is used in products that require more gluten to hold them together. Examples are pie crust and puff pastry, which contain lots of fat and need to be stretched or rolled. Pastry flour is milled from soft white winter wheat.

Commercial white flour bakers are actually not limited to the above two flours. Since millers can virtually dismantle wheats and combine their various parts into a flour that meets specific baking needs, some very knowledgeable (large-scale) bakers actually design their own flours, which the miller then assembles. It is ironic that at the point in history at which this art of mixing flours is on the decline in the American commercial baking industry, very serious home millers may well choose to become proficient in it. Here are the protein quantities of wheats that white flour bakers prefer for individual dessert products:

High-sugar cakes	Very weak soft
Heavier cakes	Medium soft
Muffins	Medium soft
Drop Cookies	Medium soft
Pie crusts	Strong soft or medium hard
Cinnamon rolls	75 percent strong hard; 25 percent medium soft
Croissants	80 percent strong hard; 20 percent very weak soft

Note that the range of protein in soft wheats is 8 to 11 percent. Thus a very weak soft wheat would be at the bottom of that range, around 8 percent. A medium soft wheat would be in the middle, say 9 to 9.5 percent. And a strong soft wheat would fall near the higher end of the range, at 10 to 11 percent. If you are among the very enthusiastic home millers who wish to design their own flours for specific baked goods, start by reviewing the chapter on wheat, including the all-important information about protein content.

The average home miller who is not interested in becoming an expert in wholemeal baking may not pay too much attention to the above list. Fortunately, they can simply (and successfully) buy whatever soft white wheat is available and use it for all their sweet products. If muffins or carrot cakes seem to crumble too much, the protein content may be too low, in which case a third of the soft white can be replaced with whatever wheat is being used for bread. The gluten present can also be developed by beating the batter. To make pastry, which requires even more gluten strength, about half the soft white can be replaced with finely milled hard winter or a third with hard spring wheat, although flavor changes will be noticed.

Finally, it is important to remember that because of the presence of bran and other components in wholemeal, home milling cannot duplicate the silky texture of cakes baked from white flour. Still, quite good texture can be achieved by grinding meal as finely as possible. If your mill cannot produce a very fine meal, sift out some bran to use in muffins or granola. Fortunately, whether milled finely or coarsely, wholemeal enhances the flavor of anything in which it is used.

 ## WHOLEMEAL ECCENTRICITIES

Most wholemeal bakers will probably be quite content to bake products that are well-suited to wholemeal like quick breads, muffins and cookies. There's nothing too tricky about this, particularly when using recipes specifically formulated for wholemeal. But when adapting a white flour recipe, adjustments may be necessary to compensate for the extra components. Here is what to watch for.

- The fat may need to be reduced slightly to compensate for the oil in the germ.

- When replacing one cup of white flour (pure endosperm) with one cup of wholemeal (which contains only about 83 percent endosperm, plus 14 percent bran and 2 to 3 percent germ), liquids may need to be reduced or the quantity of wholemeal increased slightly.

- Desserts generally require very fine, uniformly sized particles, so wholemeal intended for these products should always be milled as finely as possible. Because desserts have no long fermentation period during which bran can soften, coarse meal can also add a gritty texture to the baked good, which some people object to.

Now, let's get started with some easy recipes that work with wholemeal.

Some Simple Recipes

Following are some recipes to get started with. Use soft wheat unless other wheat is called for. If possible, weigh meal rather than measuring with cups.

Easy Bread Machine Banana Bread

If your bread machine has a cake or quick bread program, use it to make this bread.

1/3 c. vegetable oil	1½ c. (180 gr) wholemeal
1/2 c. sugar	1 tsp. baking powder
2 large eggs, beaten lightly	1/2 tsp. baking soda
1/4 c. sour cream, buttermilk	1/2 tsp. salt
or yogurt	1/2 c. ripe, mashed banana
1 tsp. vanilla	1/3 c. chopped nuts

Bread Machine Instructions: Measure ingredients into bread machine pan according to manufacturer's directions. Or put in liquid ingredients first and dry ingredients last. Select the cake or quick bread option on your bread machine.

If your bread machine mixes for awhile then emits a beeping sound to tell you to add final ingredients, reserve the banana and nuts to add after the beep. If your bread machine has no provision for adding nuts after partial mixing, include the banana and nuts with the other ingredients.

To Mix By Hand: This recipe can also be baked in a small loaf pan. Just assemble the liquid ingredients in one container and the dry ingredients in another, then combine them in a mixer bowl and beat for two minutes. Bake in a buttered loaf pan at 350 degrees for 30 to 40 minutes (or until a toothpick inserted in the center comes out clean.)

Zucchini or Carrot Bread

Grated zucchini or carrots work well in this easy and delightful low-fat, low-sugar treat.

1/4 c. vegetable oil
1/2 c. sugar
2 large eggs, beaten lightly
1½ c. (180 gr) wholemeal
1/4 tsp. baking powder
1/2 tsp. baking soda
1/2 tsp. salt
1 c. grated zucchini or carrots
1/2 c. chopped nuts

Bread Machine Instructions: Measure ingredients into bread machine pan according to manufacturer's directions. If your bread machine has no provision for adding nuts after partial mixing, add the zucchini (or carrots) and nuts with the other ingredients now. Select the cake or quick bread option on your bread machine.

If your bread machine mixes for awhile then emits a beeping sound to tell you to add final ingredients, start the machine, then add the grated vegetable and nuts after the beep.

To Mix By Hand: If you choose not to use a bread machine, this recipe can be prepared for baking in a small loaf pan. Just mix up the liquid ingredients and the dry ingredients in two separate bowls then combine them in a mixer bowl and beat for two minutes. Bake in an oiled or buttered loaf pan at 350 degrees for 30 to 40 minutes (or until a toothpick inserted in the center comes out clean.)

Boston (Steamed) Brown Bread

Many recipes can be found for this hearty pioneer bread that is steamed in aluminum cans on top of the stove. The preparation time for this cross between bread and cake is offset by its advantages: a triple fiber hit that keeps for two-to-three weeks in the refrigerator or longer in the freezer, wrapped in aluminum foil. Eat it fresh or allow the flavors to meld for a week in the refrigerator. This is a perfect high-fiber, high-nutrient snack with milk or tea, but it is also great with (lite) cream cheese, peanut butter or jam. And don't judge it too quickly. It is much *better* after aging and it really does *grow* on you.

1 c. (130 gr) yellow cornmeal
1 c. (120 gr) rye meal
1 c. (120 gr) soft white wholemeal
2 tsp. soda
1 tsp. salt
2 c. (480 ml) buttermilk
1/2 c. (120 ml) molasses
1 c. chopped raisins

Instructions: Wash and remove labels from four 15-oz aluminum cans. Oil or butter the insides of the cans. Set a cake rack in the bottom of a pot on the stove. In a separate pan or tea kettle, boil two to three quarts of water.

Place the cornmeal, rye and wholemeal in a bowl. Stir in soda and salt and mix thoroughly with a spoon. Combine liquid ingredients and add to dry ingredients. Add chopped raisins. Fill oiled cans one-half to two-thirds full with batter. Fold pieces of aluminum foil into 5" x 5" squares that fit over the top of each can. Rub the center of the foil with oil so the bread won't stick to it if it rises that high, then cover each can with a piece of foil. Tie a piece of string tightly around the can to secure the foil during steaming.

Place the cans on the cake rack inside the pot. Carefully pour enough boiling water in the pot to reach half-way up the sides of the cans. Cover the pot and simmer for 1½ to 2 hours (check at 1½ hours). To check, remove the aluminum foil from one can and press lightly on the center of the bread. It should have a nicely domed shape and feel firm to the touch. If necessary, replace cover and continue simmering. When done, remove foil and allow to rest for an hour before removing from cans. When cool, wrap in foil and store in refrigerator or freezer.

Old-fashioned Bread Pudding with Apples

Recipes for bread pudding can be found in any traditional cookbook and many new ones, as well. That's because it is a luscious way to use leftover bread. The drier the bread cubes are, the more important it is to let the pudding sit for 20 minutes after adding the milk. If the cubes are pretty soft, the pudding could be baked immediately after assembly. Happily, the pudding texture of this dish can fool kids into eating more bran, which will clear up any constipation problems. A small dish of bread pudding, warmed lightly and served with a little warm milk, is a night-time snack that will make *anyone* sleep like a baby.

This recipe serves four to six people.

2 eggs, slightly beaten
2 c. (480 ml) milk
1 tsp. vanilla
1½ tsp. cinnamon
1 c. grated apple, or more
4 c. old wholemeal bread cubes
1/2 c. brown sugar (optional)
1/2 c. raisins or dried currants
1/2 c. chopped nuts
1 tbsp. butter (optional)

Instructions: Butter a two-quart baking dish and set aside. Combine eggs, milk and vanilla; add cinnamon and salt. Fill the buttered baking dish with *several layers of ingredients* in the following order: bread cubes, grated apple, brown sugar (if used), cinnamon, raisins and nuts. Pour liquid ingredients over the top. Dot with butter, if desired. Cover with a lid or aluminum foil and allow to sit for 20 minutes.

Meanwhile, preheat oven to 350 degrees. When ready to bake, set a larger, shallow pan in the oven and pour into it one-half inch of hot water. Uncover the baking dish and set it in the pan containing water. This keeps the bottom from burning. Bake until firm (about 45 minutes) or until a knife inserted between the center and outer edge of the bread pudding comes out clean and the top is crisp and brown. Serve warm with milk, nonfat yogurt and honey or frozen yogurt. Also excellent cold or rewarmed.

Multifiber Oat Bars

These delicious bars contain soluble and insoluble fibers from several sources—wholemeal, rolled oats, nuts *and* raisins.

1 c. (2 sticks) butter, softened
1 c. firmly packed brown sugar
1/2 c. granulated sugar
2 eggs
1 tsp. vanilla
1½ c. (180 gr) wholemeal
1 tsp. baking soda
1/2 tsp. salt
1 tsp. cinnamon
3 c. rolled oats (not instant)
1/2 c. chopped nuts
1/2 c. raisins

Instructions: Preheat oven to 350 degrees. In mixer bowl, beat butter and sugar until creamy. Add eggs and vanilla and beat one minute.

Combine flour, soda, cinnamon and salt. Add to butter-sugar batter and beat for one minute. By hand, stir rolled oats, nuts and raisins into the butter-flour mixture. Use spatula or fingers to pat dough into a 9" x 13" baking pan. Bake for 30 to 35 minutes or until brown. Cut into squares before totally cool. If storing, cool bars, wrap them individually in plastic wrap, and freeze.

Multifiber Apple-Oat Cookies

These cookies provide a great source of both soluble and insoluble fibers but have slightly less fat and sugar than the preceding oat bars. And they need not be eaten all at once. Keep them frozen for months!

3/4 c. butter, softened
1 c. brown sugar
1 egg, beaten
1 tsp. vanilla
1 c. (120 gr) soft wheat
1/2 c. (65 gr) hard wheat
1 tsp. baking powder
1/2 tsp. salt
1 tsp. cinnamon
1 c. diced unpared apple
1½ c. rolled oats
1/2 c. chopped nuts
1/2 c. raisins

Instructions: Preheat oven to 350 degrees. In the bowl of an electric mixer, cream butter and sugar until smooth. Add egg and beat one minute. Add vanilla. Mix flours and spices thoroughly, then add to mixer bowl and beat for one minute. By hand, stir apple, oats, nuts and raisins into the flour-butter mixture. Drop by tablespoon onto ungreased cookie sheet. Bake about 20 minutes or until brown and the center springs back when pressed lightly with a finger. Cool on a cake rack, wrap and freeze or store in a sealed plastic bag in a *cool* place for a week or more.

Gingerbread

This gingerbread has a lovely texture and a lighter flavor than it would have if a heavier molasses were used. Despite all the sweeteners, it also contains important nutritional components, thanks to the molasses and large amount of wholemeal. It is delicious plain but the flavor can be mellowed by adding low-fat yogurt topping (see below), frozen yogurt, vanilla ice cream, butter or fresh peaches or berries. Or cut cooled cake in squares, wrap in plastic and freeze.

1/2 c. butter
1/2 c. sugar
1 egg
3 c. (360 gr) wholemeal
1½ tsp. soda
1 tsp. cinnamon
1 tsp. ginger
1/2 tsp. salt
1/2 c. (120 ml) light molasses
1/2 c. (120 ml) honey
1 c. (240 ml) hot water

Instructions: Preheat oven to 350 degrees and grease an 8" x 8" x 2" pan. Melt the butter in a heavy saucepan and let cool. In a mixer, beat the cooled butter and sugar together until creamy. Add the egg and beat for one minute.

In a separate bowl, stir the flour, soda and spices together until thoroughly mixed, then set aside. In a two-cup (or larger) measuring cup, pour ½ cup molasses, then ½ cup honey, then 1 cup hot water. Stir to dissolve the honey and molasses. Add the flour and water mixtures alternately to the butter mixture, stirring the batter thoroughly after each addition. Pour batter into greased pan and bake for one hour or until the center springs back when pressed gently. Cool slightly before cutting into squares.

Low-fat topping: Stir together one cup nonfat yogurt, one to three tablespoons honey, juice from half a lemon and a few drops of vanilla. The stirring required to dissolve the honey can be shortened by letting the mixture sit for half an hour in the refrigerator.

Carrot Cake

This cake is rich and full of calories but it is a *scrumptious* source of soluble and insoluble fibers plus beta carotene. It is particularly delicious (and even more fattening) when garnished with the traditional cream cheese icing shown below. So cut it in pieces, and wrap them in plastic wrap for freezing. For an instant dessert on busy days, thaw at room temperature for half an hour. Proper mixing is important for this cake.

1 c. butter or oil	1½ tsp. baking powder
2 c. sugar	1 tsp. salt
4 eggs	2 c. grated raw carrots
2 c. (240 gr) wholemeal	1 8-oz. can crushed pineapple
1 tsp. cinnamon	1 c. chopped nuts
1/2 tsp. baking soda	1/2 c. raisins

Instructions: Preheat oven to 350 degrees and grease a 9" x 13" baking pan. Cream butter and sugar in the bowl of a mixer, add eggs one by one and then continue beating until thoroughly creamy.

Mix flour and spices together then add to the creamed butter mixture in the mixer bowl. Beat for one minute longer. Batter should be fairly thick. If it seems too thin, add up to ¼ cup more flour.

By hand, stir carrots, nuts and raisins into batter, pour into greased pan, and bake in preheated oven for 40 to 50 minutes or until top is browned and the cake springs back after a light touch in the center. Cool the cake, frost if desired, then cut it into squares. Wrap in plastic wrap and freeze if not eaten within a couple of days.

Cream Cheese Frosting: Cream one softened 8-oz. block of cream cheese. Add powdered sugar to taste (up to three-quarters of a box) but frosting tastes best when the cream cheese flavor is not overwhelmed by sugar. Add a few drops of vanilla. Ice the cooled cake and sprinkle chopped nuts on top. For a very special decoration, find a tiny carrot or two with the greens still attached and arrange them on top.

 ## *Magnificent Muffins*

These truly magnificent muffins will please *everyone*.

1½ c. (190 g) *hard white* or *red* wheat	1/2 c. chopped nuts
	1/4 c. coconut
1½ c. (180 g) *soft white* wheat	1/2 c. raisins
1/2 c. (45 g) rolled oats	3 eggs
1¼ c. brown sugar, packed	1 c. oil
2 tsp. soda	1 tsp. vanilla
2 tsp. cinnamon	2½ (½ lb.) grated carrots
1/4 tsp. salt	1½ (½ lb.) grated apples

Instructions: Preheat oven to 400 degrees and grease pans for 12 to 15 muffins. (Also grease rims, as tins will be filled to overflowing.) Combine flours and oats. Add sugar, soda, cinnamon, salt, nuts, coconut and raisins. Mix thoroughly.

In mixer bowl, beat eggs, oil and vanilla together until creamy and smooth. By hand, add grated carrots and apples and stir until well coated.

Combine dry ingredients with wet ingredients and mix lightly. Batter will be *very* thick. Mound batter in muffin tins. (Slight overfilling is very important to final result.) Bake in preheated oven for 35 minutes or until the center of the muffin feels firm when touched gently with a finger. Allow muffins to cool five minutes before removing from tins and take care that the tops don't pull off. Serve immediately or keep in an open container for a day. May be wrapped individually in plastic wrap and frozen.

Delmonico Cake

This cake is *very* special, loved by anyone who tries it. But the soft white wholemeal needs to be milled very finely or some bran must be sifted out and used elsewhere. If you, your guests or your family insist on a finely grained cake, which is hard to achieve with wholemeal because of the bran, you *may* choose to replace one-half cup of wholemeal with all-purpose white flour.

1 stick butter
1/2 c. vegetable shortening
or slightly less coconut butter
2 c. sugar
5 egg yolks
1 tsp. vanilla
2 c. (240 gr) soft white wholemeal
1 tsp. baking soda
1 c. buttermilk
1 c. shredded coconut
1 c. chopped pecans or walnuts
5 egg whites

Instructions: Butter and flour a 9" x 13" baking dish or pan (or two 9" rounds). Line with waxed paper. Preheat oven to 350 degrees (325 degrees for glass pans).

In an electric mixer bowl, thoroughly cream butter and shortening or coconut butter. Gradually add sugar and beat until light and fluffy. Continue beating while adding egg yolks one at a time

Sift flour and soda three times. Stirring by hand, alternately add dry ingredients and buttermilk to batter, beginning and ending with dry ingredients. Stir in coconut and three-quarters of the nuts.

Beat egg whites until stiff. Stir a heaping tablespoon into batter and stir vigorously by hand until blended. Carefully fold in remaining egg whites. Pour batter into the baking dish or pans. Bake in preheated oven for one hour, or until center of cake springs back when touched lightly. Cool completely. If baked in a 9" x 13" dish, leave in pan and frost with Cream Cheese Frosting from preceding Carrot Cake recipe. Sprinkle remaining nuts on top. If baked in two pans, remove layers from pans. Place one layer on a plate and frost it. Place the second layer on top of the first one and frost the entire cake. A coating of coconut and nuts adds beauty and flavor to this layer cake.

CHAPTER 14

A Final Word

One of New York's biggest ecological
challenges at the beginning of the twentieth century
was what to do with all the manure
deposited on the streets
by the primary mode of transportation.
Then people embraced the horseless carriage
and vaporized the problem.
Today, technology is poised to deliver us from the
greatest nutritional threat of the twenty-first century—
a lack of insoluble fiber in our diets.
But have we embraced the flour mill and bread machine?
So far, we are tolerating the manure.

The loss of vitamins, minerals, enzymes and fiber from white flour would not, by itself, lead to the crumbling of Western Civilization. Unfortunately, the following cultural and dietary factors have exacerbated these nutritional losses:

- a trend toward less physical activity and reduced need for calories;

- a food system that decreases nutrients and increases fats and sugars;

- a bias against foods that require preparation time;

- an obsession with reducing diets that lack fiber and nutrition; and

- a growing tendency to replace traditional meals with snack foods.

The nutritional losses from our consumption of processed foods, combined with changes in our eating and exercise habits, have produced a kind of post-industrial undernourishment in this country. For differing reasons, this affliction strikes the rich as well as the poor, the thin as well as the fat, the young as well as the old. Unlike traditional malnutrition, we are not collapsing in the streets from lack of food. In fact, we may be living longer than our ancestors because of medical science and adequate dietary protein. Unfortunately, we are enjoying it less because of the food selections we make.

Setting modern medicine aside and pretending everything else is equal, in order to be as healthy as the pioneers, we would have to get the same quantity and quality of nutrients while eating only half the calories they did. This is a tricky proposition. Particularly when daily time constraints make it difficult to resist the plethora of processed products that tempt us.

This does not mean that we are unaware of the deficiencies in our diet. Health and nutrition groups have successfully alerted us to the need to eat more fruits, vegetables and whole grains. Unfortunately the bright light they cast on our need for more insoluble fiber failed to enlighten us about how to do it. In the end, many consumers who wanted to improve their diets simply threw up their hands in defeat and went back to familiar, easy-to-prepare foods with far less nutrition than is available to us, or low-carbohydrate diets that are deficient in vital plant nutrients.

This problem is so crucial that it deserves restating: *People want to eat more whole grains. But they have not found a simple, delicious way to do it.* Fortunately, *you* now know that bread machines and an exceptional collection of home flour mills make milling and baking a totally practical home operation. Delicious, nutritious bread can be a daily joy for everyone, whether harried or relaxed, married or single, rich or poor. You also know that setting up a home milling operation is less about finding time or money than about finding the determination to do it. It's about deciding to restore nineteenth century goodness to twenty-first century bread without taking on the drudgery that drove the job out of the home in the first place. And it's about deciding that although there is precious little we can do about damage caused by environmental factors, we *can* infuse our bodies with all the health-building nutrients available from whole, natural foods like grains. And those who do decide to mill and make bread for loved ones, friends and selves will also be warming their souls with the fragrance and flavor of freshly baked bread, which nurtured Western Civilization through at least 6,000 years of history.

Who could *possibly* claim they can't spare ten minutes to do *that*?

APPENDIX A

Grain Mill Sources

The following listings include a full range of available grain mills and oat rollers but are by no means exhaustive. More mills pop up on the U.S. market from time to time and others not listed are available in other countries. (See websites below). Local health food stores, kitchen specialty stores, mail-order catalogs and the Internet offer other opportunities for tracking down mills. Names and addresses of manufacturers have been provided when available because they sometimes sell directly to customers, occasionally are the only source for the mill, and may be the last recourse if a mill breaks down. Distributors may also be listed. If manufacturer and distributor do not sell directly to consumers, they should be able to provide names of dealers. Dealers, who sell directly to consumers, can best be located via the Internet and may be contacted for price comparisons, which may vary from one source to the next—sometimes significantly. Manufacturers rarely undersell dealers, but Internet merchants often undersell everyone.

Here are other things to bear in mind during your search:

- Any merchant presents his mill(s) in the best light possible. Use the questionnaire at the end of Chapter 7 to compare features and quality.

- Information provided in this Appendix or printed in manufacturer or dealer literature should be double-checked to make sure it remains current.

- Shipping costs should be considered part of the purchase price when comparing mills.

- For use in comparing motor strength: 1HP = 745.7 watts.

- "Convertible" (from electric to manual and vice versa) sometimes means separate purchase of required parts (such as motor, pulley, etc.) which can be expensive and may require mechanical ability. Inquire.

- Nearly everyone claims that their mills generate low milling temperatures. The question is, *How low?* And remember that heat generated by a manual mill can increase significantly if the mill is motorized. Scrutinize.

- Ask what recourse you have if the mill requires service or replacement. If the dealer or distributor knows little about the mill, cannot provide technical information or is not helpful, consider whether he will be there to help in the event of trouble. Internet merchants who offer very low prices should be queried about procedures for service or replacement of mills, particularly if the machine is of foreign origin.

- Most importantly, scrutinize warranties before purchase, if possible. Pay particular attention to terms and shipping or extra charges if mill must be returned or repaired.

Proliferation of grain mills and oat rollers on the Internet in just the last five years attests to a strong market for these wonder appliances. As a buyer, you benefit from competition. So if you're not on the Internet, get on it, or cultivate a friend who is. It is the best way to locate, learn about and compare home grain mills. For that reason this section begins with a list of websites in several countries that carry an extensive collection of mills. Postal addresses and phone numbers are also provided because many of these sellers also offer mail-order catalogs. Flitting through these general websites will be an eye-opening introduction to the vastness of the grain mill market.

Lehman's
One Lehman Circle, P. O. Box 321
Kidron, OH 44636
US and Canada (888) 438-5346
Fax: (888) 780-4975
International: (330) 857-5757
Fax: (330) 857-5785
http://www.lehmans.com

Nutrition Lifestyles
2636 Shaw Road
Gilmer, TX 75645
(888) 227-5395; (903) 797-6736
http://www.nutritionlifestyles.com

Pleasant Hill Grain
1604 N. Hwy 14
Aurora, NE 68818
(800) 321-1073
http://www.pleasanthillgrain.com

Albion Enterprises
5577 Skylane Blvd 5A
Santa Rosa, CA 95403
Inside California: (800) 247-1475
Outside California: (800) 248-1475
(707)528-1473; Fax: (707)528-0608
http://www.albionjuicer.com

Bears In The Woods Products
P. O. Box 2884
Covina, CA 91722-8884
(626) 339-5060; Fax: (626) 339-4864
http://www.bearsinthewoods.net

Miracle Exclusives, Inc.
205 Park Avenue
Hicksville, NY 11801
(800) 645-6360
(516) 933-4766; Fax: (516) 933-4760
http://www.miracleexclusives.com

Be Smart
4 Hillcrest Ave
York 6026 6LD, Great Britain
0787 6766470
http://www.grain-mills.co-uk

Bio Supply, Ltd.
6-310 Goldstream Ave.
Victoria, B.C V9B 2W3, Canada
(888) 225-3322; Fax (250) 478-3057
From outside the U.S. and Canada:
(250) 478-3244
http://www.biosupply.com

IMPACT-STYLE MILLS

NOTE: Three manufacturers in Utah produce all of these mills. The older-style square versions in this category (Kitchen Mill, Magic Mill series and Ultramill) have been around for years and are similar in design, price and features. They remain on the market because of their low prices. Only the Kitchen Mill is reviewed here, as representative of this group. Two newer mills in this category, the Grain Master Whisper Mill and the newest, the NutriMill, sell at higher prices because of additional features. They all mill flour very finely, and lots of it, but they do not crack grains and temperatures should be carefully monitored.

Kitchen Mill—Under $170 to $199

Medium-sized electric; 1¾HP motor, 25,000RPM—impact teeth—not convertible to manual; 8 pounds. Made in USA. Compact; clean; no-dust flour cannister; mills all dry grains, corn, and soybeans, but not seeds or nuts. Widely available on the Internet; long track record; 100,000 mills sold; lifetime warranty on milling mechanism; five years on chamber & pan.

K-Tec USA (Manufacturer)
1206 South 1680 West
Orem, UT 84058
(800) 748-5400, (801) 222-0888
http://www.k-tecusa.com

Grain Master Whisper Mill—about $200 to $250

Medium-sized electric; 1¾HP motor, 28,000RPM—impact teeth—not convertible to manual; available as 110V 50 cycle, 220V 50/60 cycle (international specs) or 240V 50 cycle; 15 pounds. Made in USA. Mills all dry grains, corn and beans, but not seeds or nuts; highest quality; compact; clean; filtered; no-dust flour cannister and noise reduction features; lifetime warranty; widely available in stores and on the Internet.

Creative Technology (Manufacturer)
(Sells only through distributors)
1959 S. 4130 West, Suite F
Salt Lake City, UT 84104
(801) 977-8226

Health for You (Distributor)
P.O. Box 715
Almont, MI 48003-0715
Sales: (888) 219-6191
Service: (815) 344-2127
http://www.healthforyou.com

For international purchases:
http://www.grainmaster.com
http://www.grainmills.com/au

NutriMill—about $200 to $250
Medium-sized electric; 1¾HP, variable speed 21,000 to 27,000RPM—impact teeth—not convertible to manual; 110V 50 cycle;15 pounds. Made in USA. Mills all dry grains, popcorn and most beans, but not seeds or nuts; compact; clean; filtered; no-dust flour cannister; grain flow and texture control; lifetime warranty; widely available on the Internet. (Manufacturer also makes and sells the older-style Ultra Mill in various colors.)

Kitchen Specialties (Manufacturer/Distributor)
3767 South, 150 East
Salt Lake City, UT 84115
(800) 692-6724, (801) 261-3222 Fax: (801) 261-3235
http://www.boschmixers.com

Miracle ME 821—under $40

Small power mill, 130W—stainless steel burrs—not convertible to manual. Imported from Poland; grinds coffee and good for cracking small amounts of small grains but not valuable for flour; must press on button continuously; small top feeder; limited life.

Miracle Exclusives, Inc. (Manufacturer/Distributor)
205 Park Avenue
Hicksville, NY 11801
(800) 645-6360
(516) 933-4766; Fax: (516) 933-4760
http://www.miracleexclusives.com

NOTE: Similar to the potentially confusing situation involving American impact mills described above, certain look-alike burr mills from Germany are offered by different manufacturers. The first group includes moderately priced mills with a white motor base produced by Jupiter. They accommodate multiple attachments, including a grain mill. Various mills (Jupiter, Miracle Exclusives, the Family Grain Mill and possibly others) are in this group. These mills all have the same basic motor and stainless steel or composite stone milling mechanisms, and they accommodate each other's attachments. The Family Grain Mill has been described in detail below because it is the easiest to locate in the U.S. and because it is very reliable and convertible to manual use. (The other mills may be more readily available in Germany, Canada, and other countries.)

Family Grain Mill—$189 to $250

Small electric with Jupiter 150W motor and white plastic housing; gears reduce speed from 7,000RPM to 130RPM—hardened steel cone burrs—imported from Germany; convertible to manual. Grinds small dry grains but corn and beans need pre-cracking before milling; never overheats flour; flour texture adequate but not superfine; offers many attachments including oat flaker, grater that handles nuts, and meat grinder that also makes peanut butter. Mill mechanism and attachments useable with separate manual base that starts at $85; with adapter, attachments fit Bosch mixers; with adapter, Schnitzer stone grinding attachment fits this mill. Lifetime warranty for manufacturer defects. Exceedingly versatile, widely available, very popular.

Cris Enterprise (Distributor)
46 Old Sunbeam Dr.
South Daytona Beach, FL 32119
(386) 763-2177, Fax: (386) 322-2297
http://www.grainmill.com
(Website has extensive dealer list by state.)

NOTE: A second group of similiar-looking burr mills from different manufacturers involves high quality (and attractive) imports from Germany. They include the Schnitzer, Hawo's (which is no longer widely available in the U.S.), Fidibus and Wolfgang. To complicate things, though, a group of related mills sold in Europe under the brand name KoMo are a collaboration of the two brains (Wolfgang Mock and Ralf Pigge) who created the Hawo's, Fidibus and Wolfgang mills. (Oh, and the Fidibus and Wolfgang are the same mill marketed under separate imprints in the U.S.) A large collection of these and other mills can be viewed on the British *Be Smart* website at http://www.grain-mills.co.uk.

Fidibus—$250 to $350 (also sold as Wolfgang–$250 to $400)
Medium-sized electric with industrial motor: Fidibus Classic at ½HP, 360W (3.5 oz flour/min) and Fidibus 21 at 260W (3 oz flour/min)—composite stone burrs of corundum and ceramic—not convertible to manual. Imported from Germany; both grind all dry grains, beans, corn; quiet at 72 decibels; industrial motor; solid beechwood casing; stunning good looks; highest quality; three-year warranty.

Wolfgang Mock GmbH (Manufacturer)
Habitzheimer Strasse 14
D-Germany 64853 Otzberg-Lengfeld
06162-960351; Fax: 06162-960353
http://www.wolfgangmock.de
(Website in German; KoMo mills also shown.)

Best Mills (Distributor, Fidibus)
P.O. Box 775
East Olympia, WA 98540-0775
(360)-456-6072 Fax: (360) 459-8324
http://www.bestmills.com

Albion Enterprises (Distributor, Wolfgang)
5577 Skylane Blvd 5A
Santa Rosa, CA 95403
(707)528-1473; Fax: (707)528-0608
Inside California: (800) 247-1475
Outside California: (800) 248-1475
http://www.albionjuicer.com

Schnitzer—$350 to $700+

Several electric: the Pico (replaces Clou) at 250W (100g/min fine); Grano at 600W (200g/min. fine); and Vario (grain mill and flaker in one) at 360W (110g/min. fine)—composite stone burrs of corundum in ceramic—all mills are for grains and corn; not convertible to manual. Imported from Germany; highest quality; stunning good looks; industrial motor; solid beechwood case on all; two-year warranty; widely available on Internet.

Schnitzer GmbH & Co. KG (Manufacturer)
Marlenerstrasse 9
77656 Offenburg / Germany
0781/504-7500 Fax: 0781/504-7509
http://www.schnitzer-bio.de (in German)

Widely available in U.S.
(See Multiple-Mill listings at
beginning of Appendix for
Bears In The Woods and others.)

Schnitzer Mills (Australia)
420 Freemantle Road
Bathurst NSW 2795 Australia
Phone: 02 6336 9100 Fax: 02 6336 9111
http://www.schnitzer.com.au
In Canada: http://www.biosupply.com

Mill-Rite—under $400

Medium-sized electric, 1/4HP motor, 40RPM, 60Hz, 115 V—composite stone and/or metal burrs—convertible to manual. Made in USA. Still not beautiful but a reliable workhorse; heavy-duty motor features gear reduction to less than 40RPM, so flour remains cool (115 degrees or less) and quieter than many; exclusive feature disengages motor, so mill works easily manually. Mills all dry grains, corn, beans, etc. Built to last; in business 30 years; excellent combination of features; fine machine; warranty on parts and workmanship ten years, forever on labor if used per manufacturer's instructions.

Retsel Corporation (Manufacturer)
P.O. Box 37, 1567 East Highway 30
McCammon, ID 83250
(208) 254-3737
http://www.retsel.com

Australian Retsel Distributor
P.O. Box 712
Dandenong, Victoria, 3175 Australia
03-9795-2725; Fax: 03-9713-2622
http://www.retsel.com.au

Hawo Mills/KoMo—$400 to $500

Medium-sized electric, ½HP—composite stone burrs—not convertible to manual. Imported from Germany but no longer widely available in the U.S. Many models available in Europe under the brand KoMo. Stunning good looks; modern beechwood case; several square and round models; highest quality industrial motor "suspended" inside case for reduced noise; grinds dry grains only; five-year warranty.

Hawo's Kornmühlen GmbH (Manufacturer)
Ober-Eschbacher Str. 37
D-61352 Bad Homburg, Germany
49 (0) 61 72 / 401 20-0
Fax: 49 (0) 61 72 / 401 20-19
http://www.hawos.de

In Ireland: http://www.fruithillfarm.com
In the U.K http://www.grain-mill.co-uk

Golden Grain Grinder—about $420

Large electric, ¾HP, 5-inch diameter burrs—composite stone with stainless steel inserts—convertible to manual. Made in USA. Unique early-American style wood cabinet; enclosed stainless steel flour drawer; separate flywheel available for hand use on newer models; grinds all dry grains, beans, corn, seeds; "self-cleaning" burrs; sturdy workhorse; excellent combination of features; long track record; five-year warranty; widely available on Internet.

Kuest Enterprises (Manufacturer/Sales)
311 Main Street, Box 110
Filer, ID 83328
(208) 326-4084 Fax: (208) 326-6604

Samap Stone Mill—$650+

Large (F-100, 1HP) or medium (F-50, 1/2HP) electric with industrial motor—composite natural stone burrs of Naxos-Basalt—not convertible to manual. Imported from France; very fast but has cooling turbine to prevent overheating of flour and prolong life of machine; filtered; dust-free flour catcher; not pretty but highest quality; long track record; five-year warranty; F-50 (which is not widely available in the U.S.) grinds everything but corn, garbanzo or oily seeds like flax at 15 to 30 lbs/hr; F-100 grinds all dry grains, beans, corn, millet at 25 to 50 lbs/hr.

Miracle Exclusives, Inc. (Distributor)
205 Park Avenue
Hicksville, NY 11801
(800) 645-6360
(516) 933-4766; Fax: (516) 933-4760
http://www.miracleexclusives.com

In New Zealand: http://www.goldenfields.co.nz
In Australia: http://www.saltoftheearth.com.au
Sold as Elasser in UK: http://www.grain-mills.co.uk

Bell Power Gristmill, No. 60—$300 to $400

Large power mill; 350RPM to 500RPM—5½-inch diameter iron/steel alloy burrs—convertible to manual. Price is for mill only, which requires separate 1 to 2HP motor (also available as "turnkey" package). Made in USA. Heavy-duty, high output; cast iron housing with red enamel finish; suitable for household or small farm use; handle for conversion; grinds everything; separate burrs included for extra-fine grinding. Manufacturer in business 140 years; also sells hand mills, corn sheller and larger mills.

C. S. Bell Co. (Manufacturer)
170 W. Davis Street, P. O. Box 291
Tiffin, Ohio 44883
(419) 448-0791 Fax: (419) 448-1203
http://www.csbellco.com

 ## SOLID STONE BURR MILLS

Meadows Mill—$1300 to $13,000

Large electric with 1HP motor, 1800RPM—8-inch solid Balfour pink granite burrs—not convertible to manual. Made in USA. Cast iron and stainless steel body; full grinding versatility except oily items like soybeans; high volumes at cool temperatures; manufacturer also makes full range of commercial-sized stone burr mills, with optional sifting screen; highest quality; 100-year track record.

Meadows Mill Company (Manufacturer/Sales)
1352 West D Street, Box 1288
North Wilkesboro, North Carolina 28659
(800) 626-2282; (336) 838-2282
http://www.meadowsmills.com

New River Mills—$2,250 to $10,500

Large electric, 400RPM—8-inch solid native granite stones—not convertible to manual. Made in USA. Modern, patented design features; all stainless steel construction meets commercial bakery certification standards; cooling fan; offers full line of mills from home-use to commercial sizes. Highest quality; high volumes at cool temperatures.

New River Mills (Manufacturer/Sales)
11459 US Hwy 221
Scottsville, NC 28672
(336) 982-2323
http//www.newrivermills.com

 ## *MANUAL BURR MILLS*

Corona—$40 to $70
Small manual ("El Molino")—interchangeable metal or composite stone burrs—cast iron, tin plated; not recommended for conversion to power. Classic imported from Colombia with fully adjustable steel milling heads to grind or crack grains, beans, corn, seeds, nuts, or coffee; still widely available; high-volume sales throughout world because of price; most popular now on home brewing websites. This and similarly styled mills have long track record, but work is required and up to three passes needed for fine flour. Styled like old-fashioned meat grinder.

Corona, Landers y Cia S.A. (Manufactured in Colombia)
http://www.americanfamilynetwork.com; 800-668-8181
http://www.homebrewadventures.com

Back to Basics—about $80
Small manual—nested-cone style stainless steel burrs—not convertible to electric. Made in USA. Small, inexpensive option for non-electric use; grinds most small, dry grains; work required but much easier than many; attractive style; adequate flour texture but not fine; widely available in health food stores and on the Internet; good back-up to electric mill; long track record; mounts on table top. (Manufacturer catalog also offers manual appliances such as dough mixer.)

Back to Basics Products, Inc. (Manufacturer)
11660 South State Street
Draper, UT 84020
(800) 688-1989; (801) 571-7349
http://www.backtobasicsproducts.com

Family Grain Mill—$85 to $150

Small manual—hardened steel cone burrs—convertible to electric using separately purchased base containing Jupiter motor. Imported from Germany. Sleek; white; large hopper; clever design for clamping to counter or table top; grinds small dry grains; flour texture adequate but not superfine; easier to operate than many small manual mills; great inexpensive backup for electric version; five-year warranty. Manufacturer offers other attachments, including oat roller, that fit both motor and hand bases. Five-year limited warranty.

(See Family Grain Mill listing under electric mills)

Uni-Ark—under $100; Little-Ark—about $150

Two small manual, Little Ark and Uni-Ark—composite stone or metal burrs—convertible to electric. Made in USA. Little Ark has large hopper and flywheel for easier operation; Uni-Ark has standard handle and hopper. Inexpensive options for non-electric use; clamps to table; requires work; hard grains, corn, beans may need more than one grinding for fine texture.

(See Retsel Corporation listing under electric mills)

The Farina by Korn Kraft—about $150

Small manual grinder, 4 lbs, 15 inches high—composite stone burrs—not convertible to electric. Made in Germany with solid wood housing; high quality; requires mounting; five-year warranty.

(See electric mills listing under Fidibus for Best Mills.)

Schnitzer Manual Stone Mill—$150 to $300+

Several manual grinders: Ligno Petit, Ligno Manual, CH (also sold as ME-1112), all for small, dry grains; Country for all sizes of grain (small to corn)—composite stone burrs—not convertible to electric. Imported from Germany. All high quality; three smaller mills for dry grains only; handle on top; Country grinds millet to corn but oily items must be mixed with dry; enclosed container; clamps to table or counter top; also makes attachment for Bosch mixers that works with Jupiter bases using adapter.

(See Schnitzer listing under electric mills.)

Bell Hand Gristmill, No. 2—under $200

Medium-sized manual—5½-inch cone-shaped iron/steel alloy burrs—not convertible to electric. Made in USA. Heavy-duty; red enameled cast iron housing; large counter-balanced handle makes milling easier; good for household quantities; for all grains, seeds, corn, beans. Company and mill have long track record.

(See Bell Power gristmill listing under electric mills.)

Samap 220 Manual Stone Mill—under $250

Medium-sized manual—composite natural stone burrs —not convertible to electric. Imported from France. Grinds small, dry grains; styled like old-fashioned quern with horizontal burrs and handle on top that turns horizontally; small hopper; loved by school children; definitely a conversation piece, but work required and somewhat awkward to use.

(See Miracle Exclusives listing at beginning of Appendix or electric mills.)

GrainMaker™ Grain Mill—Under $300

Large Manual—steel alloy burrs—convertible to electric. Made in USA. Attractive, white, clamps or bolts down; included flywheel and padded power bar reduce milling work and time; pulley included for use with motor or bicycle; grinds all dry items. Limited lifetime warranty except on burrs.

Wild West Machine (Manufacturer and Sales)
3921 Red Ranch Road, Unit D
Stevensville, MT 59870
(406) 777-7096; Fax: (406) 777-7001
http://www.grainmaker.com

Country Living Grain Mill—under $400

Large manual—carbon steel burrs—convertible to electric. Made in USA. Very attractive, white; work required but large flywheel and optional bar extender reduce grinding effort significantly; mills all dry items; needs accessory auger for large items. Highest quality; 25-year track record; 20-year warranty, one-year on burrs. (Note: $75 replacement cost for burrs but mine lasted 15 years). Widely available in catalogs and on the Internet.

Country Living Productions, Inc. (Manufacturer)
14727 56th Avenue, NW
Stanwood, WA 98292
(360) 652-0671 Fax: (360) 654-9287

Diamant (D-525)—under $600
Large manual—5¼ inch iron burrs—convertible to power with
v-belt pulley. Imported from Denmark. Highest quality; large flywheel
significantly reduces energy and milling time; grinds all dry or wet
items, including nuts and nut butters, with standard auger; standard,
extra fine and extra coarse burrs provide versatility; pioneer style in
green and gold; easiest to operate of all manual mills; *truly* the Cadillac
of manual mills since 1920; one-year warranty.

ABC Hansen A/S (Manufacturer)
Kirkegade 1, P.O. Box 73
DK-8900, Randers, Denmark
4586426488; Fax:4586413622

In-tec Equipment Company (U.S. Distributor)
(Also sells mill; responds to written inquiries only.)
Box 60123, D.V. Station
Dayton, Ohio 45406
(937) 276-4077
http://www.members.aol.com/righterwmx

Lehman's (dealer)
One Lehman Circle, P. O. Box 321
Kidron, OH 44636
US and Canada: (888) 438-5346; Fax: (888) 780-4975
International: (330) 857-5757; Fax:(330) 857-5785
http://www.lehmans.com

MILL ATTACHMENTS

NOTE: A great many milling attachments are available for existing appliances, some from the manufacturer and others as after-market add-ons. Following are a few, but searching the Internet may reveal others.

Grain Mill (G-90) Attachment to Champion Juicer—$75 range
Attachment to large electric juicer (1750RPM)—stainless steel burrs—not convertible to manual. Inexpensive option for those who own juicer; grinds dry grains plus soybeans and corn. Widely available at health food stores and on Internet.

Plastaket Manufacturing Inc. (Manufacturer)
6220 East Highway 12 (Victor Road)
Lodi, CA 95240
(209) 369-2154
http://www.championjuicer.com

Grain Mill Attachment to KitchenAid Mixer—$100 to $150
Attachment to large mixer—stainless steel burrs—not convertible to manual. Inexpensive, high-quality option for those who own 325W or larger KitchenAid mixers; always grind at highest speed to avoid lugging motor. Grinds all dry grains; household quantities generate low temperatures; good versatility but corn and beans bounce in hopper if not pre-cracked; widely available in stores or mail order from manufacturer.

KitchenAid (Manufacturer)
(800) 422-1230 (orders or brochures)
http://www.kitchenaid.com

Family Grain Mill Attachment to Bosch Mixers
(See Family Grain Mill listing under electric burr mills.)

Grain Mill Attachments for Bosch, Moulinex, Jupiter, Stiebel-Eltron, Zyliss, and Kenwood Kitchen Machines
(See Bio Suppply listing at start of Appendix.)

Lehman's
(See listing at start of this Appendix)

New River Mills
(See listing at end of electric mill)

In-Tec Equipment Company
(See listing under Diamant manual mills)

Miracle Exclusives, Inc.
(See listing at start of this Appendix.)

Kuest Enterprises
(See listing for Golden Grain Grinder under electric mills.)

Albion Enterprises
(See listing for Fidibus/Wolfgang under electric mills.)

Meadows Mill Company
(See listing at end of electric mills.)

C. S. Bell Co.
(See Bell Power grist mill listing under electric mills.)

Vivas (Austrian mills)
#2 Nejinskaya str. 69
Odessa 65045 Ukraine
tel +380 48 715331
tel/fax: +380 482 267284
http://www.vivas.hypermart.net

Roller Mills

NOTE: Small roller mills exist for two types of buyers: those who want to discretely crack grains for home brewing and the much larger market of people who want to roll oats and other small grains into flakes so the digestive system has access to the nutrients. The following list of oat rollers/flakers gives a flavor of what is available; most are from Germany where flaking grains at home has been popular much longer than in the U.S.

These mills are relatively simple to operate, whether manual or electric, and are available in a wide range of styles. The simple objective is to pass grain between two hard surfaces to flatten it, and texturing of at least one roller is necessary to keep the grain moving. An adjustment to vary thickness may be provided. Mills must be clamped down or attached to an existing appliance. Roller mechanisms vary and may be made from steel or composite stone. Styles may include (1) two textured rollers, (2) one textured roller and a stationary curved metal surface, (3) two textured wheels nestled together and (4) possibly others. Heat buildup does not seem to be a problem as oats are soft and a single pass through the mechanism generates little friction. Harder grains require some soaking so that they flatten instead of cracking into chunks. All of these appliances seem to do a fine job of rolling oats, although some produce a clean, flat flake and others tear the oat a little, producing more flour. All render the grain accessible to digestion and make delicious oatmeal, cookies and other oat products. Higher prices may reflect convenience features, size or quality.

There is also a surprising variety of roller mills available (particularly on the Internet) for cracking grains for home brew. These may be manual or electric or convertible one way or the other. Some can be operated with an electric drill. Many are handmade by home-brewing zealots who were unhappy with the job done by other options (the most common of which, over the years, has been the Corona mill from Colombia listed under manual mills). Two options for home brewers are provided at the end of the listing, but more are available from other home brew sites on the Internet.

OAT ROLLERS (FLAKERS)

Family Grain Mill Oat Roller Attachment—about $75
Small, white import from Germany with metal rollers; for use with motorized Jupiter base or with inexpensive hand base; easy either way; good for all small grains; large hopper; reliable low-cost option. Similar flaker attachment exists under Jupiter brand at about $100.
(See Family Grain Mill listing under electric mills.)

Marga Oat Roller—about $85
Small hand-cranked mill with small hopper and small catcher. Long track record; good for small quantities only. Widely available. (Similar to Marcato ME171, with stainless steel rollers and adjustment for flake thickness, which theoretically also mills flour.)
(For Marga: See listing at beginning of Appendix for Nutrition Lifestyles.)
(For Marcato: See listing at beginning of Appendix for Miracle Exclusives.)

The Flocino Flaker—$90
Small hand-cranked flaker; stainless steel milling wheels; 10 inches high, 3.5 lbs; adjusts for flake thickness; plastic body attached to wood base; stable; easy to use; large hopper; mounting hardware included; three-year warranty. Manufactured by Wolfgang Mock.
(See electric mills listing under Fidibus for Best Mills.)

Eschenfelder Flaker—$175 to $900
Handy wall-mounted oat flaker with wooden hopper ($210) and table-mounted version ($175 with metal hopper or $200 with wooden hopper) both with stainless steel rollers; infinite adjustment; good for all small, dry grains, including oily seeds; beech wood case.
(See Bio Supply listing at beginning of this Appendix.)

Schnitzer Manual Stone Flaker (Campo or ME1154)—$200+
Manual import from Germany; steel or composite stone rollers; 10 lbs, 14 inches high; adjusts for flake thickness; mills all small, dry grains plus soybeans. Schnitzer also sells attachment with stone rollers that works with Jupiter, Bosch mixer, and Family Grain Mill (adapter required).
(See Schnitzer listing under electric or manual mills.)

Schnitzer Vario Electric Mill and Flaker—$770+

Electric import from Germany combines flaker (stainless steel rollers) and grain mill (composite stone burrs); attractive wood housing; versatile; highest quality. Rollers accommodate all small, dry grains. (See Schnitzer listing under electric or manual mills.)

 ## ROLLER MILLS FOR HOME BREWERS

The Valley Mill—$150

Small manual roller mill—8-inch stainless steel, nickel-plated, ball-bearing mounted steel rollers—convertible to electric. Cracks grain to make mash for beer or bulgur.

Valley Brewing Equipment (Manufacturer/Sales)
1310 Surrey Avenue
Ottawa, Ontario, Canada K1V 6S9
(613) 733-5241
http://www.web.ca/~valley/valleymill.html

Crank and Stein–$90 to $220

Six sturdy roller-mill packages, pre-assembled or in parts; designed to be drill driven at 150RPM to 250RPM; two or three 5-inch or 4-inch long gnurled steel rollers with variable gap adjustments and one hand-cranked with 1-inch rollers at $50. Cracks grain for mash for beer; money-back guarantee.

Crank and Stein (Manufacturer/sales)
Fred Francis
1568 Milford Creek Lane
Marietta, GA 30008
http://www.crankandstein.com

APPENDIX B

Other
Sources

Local sources for bulk grains may be listed in the yellow pages—under health food stores, co-ops, or natural foods stores. But if you are having difficulty tracking down hard red (or white) spring wheat containing 15 percent or more protein for breadmaking, try one of the sources on the next page. They've been in business long enough to be dependable. Several ship in household quantities anywhere in the U.S. and Canada. Most offer catalogs. All offer other grain products, as well. Shipping costs are not included in the price of the grain and can grow substantially as distances increase, so pick the one closest to you or use one of their local distributors if possible. And reaffirm the protein content with each order.

Also included in this section are mail-order sources for other grains, for dough conditioners, and for some wholemeal bread books.

Wheat-Montana Farms
(Purchase directly or locate dealers for
high-protein wheat and other grains.)
10788 Highway 287
Three Forks, MT 59752
(800) 535-2798
(406) 285-3614
http://www.wheatmontana.com

Montana Milling
(Organic and conventional grains; high-protein wheat; amber
    durum; soft and hard white;
QAI certified organic and KOAOA certified Kosher Parve; min.
    order 25 lbs but can locate distributors by website or phone.)
2123 Vaughn Road
Great Falls, MT 59404
(800) 548-8554
http://www.montanamilling.com

Bob's Red Mill
(Sells wheat and many other grains direct, but catalog also
    includes list of dealers.)
5209 S. E. International Way
Milwaukie, OR 97222
(800)553-2258 Fax: (503) 653-1339
http://www.bobsredmill.com

Lehman's Hardware
(If you can't locate the grains on their website or in their
    wonderful catalog, call and ask, as they do sell grains.)
One Lehman Circle, P. O. Box 321
Kidron, OH 44636
US and Canada: (888) 438-5346; Fax: (888) 780-4975
International: (330) 857-5757; Fax:(330) 857-5785
http://www.lehmans.com

Sources for Other Grains

The following are general mail-order catalogs or websites that offer whole grains or specialty items that may be difficult to locate through other sources. An Internet search will yield many, many more.

Discount natural foods
(Organic specialty grains)
146 Londonderry Turnpike #10
Hooksett, NH 03106
(888) 392-9237 Fax: (603) 232-1356
http://www.discountnaturalfoods.com

Arrowhead Mills
(Use website or call to find a store near you
stocking Arrowhead products.)
The Hain Celestial Group
734 Franklin Ave, #444
Garden City, NY 11530
(800) 434-4246

Jaffe Bros.
(Organic grains, beans, nuts and dried fruits)
28560 Lilac Road
Valley Center, CA 92082
(760) 749-1133; Fax: (760) 749-1282

The Birkett Mills
(Buckwheat only)
163 Main Street
Penn Yan, NY 14527
(315) 536-7434; Fax: (315) 536-6740

Mathes Farms
(Organic grains, yellow dent corn)
1680 2000 Road
Barlett, KS 76332
Phone & Fax: (316) 226-3550
http://www.mathesfarms.com

Mosher Products
(Organic grains and other products)
Mosher Products
P.O. Box 5367
Cheyenne, WY 82003-5367
(307) 632-1492
http://www.wheatandgrain.com

For a list of Canadian Health Food Stores:
http://www.cwinds.com/topages/hfood.htm

For a list of U.S. food cooperatives,
natural food stores and health food stores:
http://www.organicconsumers.org/foodcoops.htm

PRE-MIXED DOUGH CONDITIONERS

K-Tec USA (Manufacturer)
1206 South 1680 West
Orem, UT 84058
(800) 748-5400, (801) 222-0888
http://www.k-tecusa.com

Nutrition Lifestyles
http://www.texramp.com

Global Gourmet
Lora Brody's Bread Dough Enhancer
http://www.globalgourmet.com/food/special/brody/dough.html

NutriTech
12 Fawn Drive
New Waverly, TX 77358
(936) 438-8829
http://www.nutritech.org/bread_making.htm

This book provides only a hit-and-run overview of breadmaking. It cannot replace a good wholemeal bread book. But beware. Any author who knows as much as you now do about wholemeal would not include large amounts of white flour in his or her recipes. Books that call for added gluten should be scrutinized closely, but not rejected offhandedly. Although commercial gluten is in some views an undesirable product, many authors include it for consumers who don't know how to (or for some reason cannot) buy high-protein wheats or those who like the flavor of winter wheat but want to boost performance for the bread machine. If performance is lacking, though, another option is to replace one-third to one-half cup of wholemeal with white bread flour which, at this quantity level, boosts performance without destroying bread flavor or nutrition.

The Laurel's Kitchen Bread Book by Laurel Robertson with Carol Flinders & Bronwen Godfrey (Random House, NY, rev. 2003). No wholemeal baker can be truly successful without this unique classic on whole-grain breadmaking. It is detailed, exhaustively researched and provides information on baking with whole grains that cannot be found elsewhere. The revised edition includes an invaluable section on baking with bread machines.

Whole Wheat Breadmaking: Secrets of the Masters Made Easy by Diana Ballard (Cedar Fort, 1993) is a relatively inexpensive and informative book published in Utah, where they know and use wholemeal and home mills. Recipe quantities given for both bread machines and manual preparation.

Beginning Breadmaking, a video by Shelly Vernon, is available at http:www.nutritionlifestyles.com.

Creative Cooking with Grains & Pasta, by Sheryl & Mel London (Rodale Press, Emmaus, PA, 1982) has some wonderful whole-grain recipes that aren't included in most cookbooks. This out-of-print book on (mostly) whole-grain foods is worth tracking down from an out-of-print book service. Includes bread recipes, but is not a basic breadmaking book.

The New Book of Whole Grains, by Marlene A. Bumgarner (St. Martin's Griffin, 1997) includes recipes for many unusual grains, which may be helpful for culinary adventurers and those who are allergic to gluten. Also not a basic breadmaking book.

Cooking & Baking with Freshly Ground Grains by Christine Downs can be purchased from Cris Enterprise, 46 Old Sunbeam Dr., South Daytona Beach, FL 32119; (386) 763-2177, Fax: (386) 322-2297; http://www.grainmill.com. Also not a basic breadmaking book.

ORDER FORM

YES, I want ___ copy[ies] of *Flour Power: A guide to modern home grain milling,* by Marleeta F. Basey, (ISBN 0970540116) at $24.95.

My check or money order payable to Jermar Press
for $_____ is enclosed.

Name _____

Organization/Company (if applicable) _____

Address_____

City/State/Zip_____

Phone/email (optional) _____

Please return to:

JERMAR
⋇ PRESS

Jermar Press
1790 NW Grandview Dr.
Albany, OR 97321-9695

Made in the USA
San Bernardino, CA
02 December 2016